Teacher Education, Learning Innovation and Accountability

Series Editor

Claire Wyatt-Smith, Institute for Learning Sciences and Teacher Education, Australian Catholic University, Brisbane, QLD, Australia

This book series offers research-informed discussion and analysis of teacher preparation, certification and continuing professional learning and the related practice and policy drivers for change and reform. The series fosters and disseminates research about teaching as a profession of choice while offering a unique link to the realities of pre-service experience in workforce preparation. It takes account of research on teacher formation that opens up issues not routinely connected: what teachers need to know and be able to do, and who they are, namely the person of the teacher and their capabilities in contributing to students' personal development and wellbeing. This goal provides a current, practical and international view of the future of initial teacher education programs.

Christopher DeLuca · Jill Willis · Bronwen Cowie ·
Christine Harrison · Andrew Coombs

Learning to Assess

Cultivating Assessment Capacity in Teacher Education

Christopher DeLuca 🆔
Queen's University
Kingston, ON, Canada

Jill Willis 🆔
Queensland University of Technology
Kelvin Grove, QLD, Australia

Bronwen Cowie 🆔
University of Waikato
Hamilton, New Zealand

Christine Harrison 🆔
King's College London
London, UK

Andrew Coombs 🆔
Queen's University
Kingston, ON, Canada

ISSN 2524-5562 ISSN 2524-5570 (electronic)
Teacher Education, Learning Innovation and Accountability
ISBN 978-981-99-6201-3 ISBN 978-981-99-6199-3 (eBook)
https://doi.org/10.1007/978-981-99-6199-3

© The Editor(s) (if applicable) and The Author(s), under exclusive license to Springer Nature
Singapore Pte Ltd. 2023

This work is subject to copyright. All rights are solely and exclusively licensed by the Publisher, whether
the whole or part of the material is concerned, specifically the rights of translation, reprinting, reuse
of illustrations, recitation, broadcasting, reproduction on microfilms or in any other physical way, and
transmission or information storage and retrieval, electronic adaptation, computer software, or by similar
or dissimilar methodology now known or hereafter developed.
The use of general descriptive names, registered names, trademarks, service marks, etc. in this publication
does not imply, even in the absence of a specific statement, that such names are exempt from the relevant
protective laws and regulations and therefore free for general use.
The publisher, the authors, and the editors are safe to assume that the advice and information in this book
are believed to be true and accurate at the date of publication. Neither the publisher nor the authors or
the editors give a warranty, expressed or implied, with respect to the material contained herein or for any
errors or omissions that may have been made. The publisher remains neutral with regard to jurisdictional
claims in published maps and institutional affiliations.

This Springer imprint is published by the registered company Springer Nature Singapore Pte Ltd.
The registered company address is: 152 Beach Road, #21-01/04 Gateway East, Singapore 189721,
Singapore

Paper in this product is recyclable.

Foreword

When I was asked to write the foreword to this book, there were two things that convinced me straight away. First, I saw the names of the authors; Christopher DeLuca, Jill Willis, Bronwen Cowie, Christine Harrison, and Andrew Coombs. These people do not only represent the leading research in their respective countries, Canada, Australia, New Zealand, and England; they are all in the forefront of international research in the field of assessment. A book written by such competent people must be worthwhile reading.

Second, the title attracted me: *Learning to Assess, Assessment Capacity in Teacher Education.* Personally, I have striven to learn to assess throughout my whole career, from being a teacher in primary and secondary school to becoming a teacher educator, leader of teacher education, doctoral supervisor, and researcher. I have never found the right answer, and will probably not, as I believe there is no one right way to assess. Good assessment will always be context and situation dependent. However, learning by experience, collaborating with national and international colleagues, engaging in research, and reading the literature has taken me a huge step forward. So has this book, by introducing to me an unknown concept, assessment capacity.

The authors define assessment capacity "*as a teacher's capacity to continually learn about their assessment practice – through relationships, adaptation, reflection, collaboration, and inventiveness – to imagine new possibilities for assessment in schools*" (Chapter 1).

The concept has, as I understand it, an infinite dimension to it. Assessment capacity describes a process which is dynamic, ongoing, never ending. A person who holds assessment capacity is mindful (McEvilley, 2002), engaged in a continuous self-monitored learning process, however, will never achieve a definite product which ends the learning process. This perception of an ongoing strive to improve assessment to support the learner aligns with my own pursuit to become a better assessor throughout my career. This book has provided me with a construct to define the never-ending search, assessment capacity.

The book focuses on four jurisdictions, all Commonwealth countries. This is a huge geographical spread, yet the shared educational history, even though it has taken various directions in the four jurisdictions, might suggest the jurisdictions have comparable assessment cultures. Chapter 2 gives an overview of the similarities and differences, which provides the reader from other countries with an understanding of the contexts of the student teachers' reflections. As a reader coming from a very different history, culture, and approach to education, it took me some time to see the relevance of the book to my own context and practice. However, when reading on, I would claim, that the book is relevant to a wide international audience, mainly because the presented model of assessment capacity is universal.

In the following there are three main issues related to assessment capacity I would like to highlight. First, my understanding of assessment capacity is that teachers become agents of their personal professionalism, and especially how it relates to dialogues with students about learning and assessment. Second, assessment capacity is discussed in relation to teacher education and the multiple functions of assessment in teacher education. Third, I will share some thoughts around the new concept in relation to the other discourses presented in Chapter 3.

Assessment Capacity as Personal Professionalism Practiced in Dialogue with Students

Education, including assessment, is still strongly influenced by tradition and culture, and not least, international politics. OECD, and the many international tests dictate decisions made not only in the four Commonwealth countries which are the backdrop of this book, but in a wider international context. Increasingly, we find that external accountability measures harm teacher agency and teachers' personal professionalism. Political professionalism takes over, with central control and explicit standards of teaching. Teachers are in danger of becoming technicians, being told not only what to teach, but also how to teach. This makes it difficult for teachers to develop their personal professionalism. When teachers have the opportunity to adapt their teaching and assessment to the learner and the situation, they practice Aristotles' concept of phronesis (Kinsella, 2021) which is a combination of knowledge, practical skills, and understanding of the context, the situation, and the learner. The aim is to support student learning, and for this to happen, teachers must engage in genuine dialogues with the students about the instructional encounter (Smith, 2001).

However, student voice and student agency are not taken sufficiently seriously, even though this is a key issue discussed when assessment researchers/educators/ policymakers meet in international forums; for example, in the last meeting of The International Educational Assessment network (IEAN) meeting in Slovenia in June, 2023. Furthermore, the principles of the UN Declaration, The Rights of the Child (1989), is often reflected in international and national policy documents. In the general plan of the Norwegian Educational Framework, it says: "*The school must be a place where children and young people experience democracy in practice. Pupils must experience that they are listened to in everyday school life, that they have a real influence, and that they can impact what concerns them*" (Ministry of Knowledge, 2017).

Unfortunately, the translation of the letter to the spirit and practice seems to be challenging, especially if it is being upscaled to a nation-wide practice. The reason, I believe, is that being open to an assessment practice in which students are in the centre and actively engaged in their own learning and assessment, depends, first and foremost, on the individual teacher and on the teacher's assessment capacity. Engaging in dialogues with students about learning and assessment might be scaring to teachers, as they are afraid of losing control, and the normative power balance in the classroom is being challenged. Assessment is sometimes used as a control, and even as a disciplinary measure, but the question is if such a (mis)use of assessment strengthens students' learning? More than two decades ago Jean Rudduck (1999) claimed that listening to the students and acting on what they say, might be useful in the strive to improve learning and instruction. In a later publication from 2007, Ruddock presents this model for how consulting with the students might improve learning and instruction, or the instructional encounter (Smith, 2001). Consulting students is beneficial to the school, the teachers, and the learners.

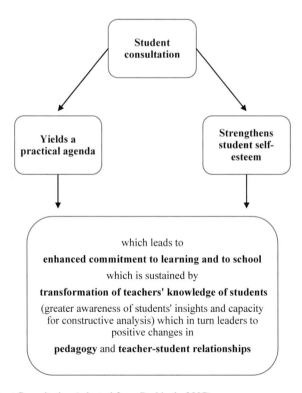

Fig. F.1 Student Consultation (adapted from Ruddock, 2007)

In a more recent Australian study, Finefter-Rosenbluh et al. (2021) found that when students were listened to and their suggestions for changes implemented, motivation for learning as well as learning outcomes improved. I would say that the same goes for assessment, consulting the students about how to improve assessment is likely to provide the teacher with useful information. Engaging in a dialogue with the students about assessment requires strong teachers, teachers who are in a constant search for improving learning and assessment, teachers who have developed assessment capacity and are confident to practice their personal assessment practice theory (Box et al., 2015).

Assessment Capacity and the Functions of Assessment in Teacher Education

Cultivating capacity in teacher education is complex and challenging for the reason that assessment takes on multiple functions in teacher education. All of them contribute, positively or less positively, to future or practicing teachers' understanding and practice of assessment.

An integrated part of teachers' work is to assess students' learning for summative as well as for formative purposes. Initial and in-service teacher education is where students of teaching (which here refers to students in initial as well as in-service education) learn the profession, including how to assess learning. However, students of teaching are also learners, and their learning is subject to assessment. During teacher education they are exposed to a variety of assessment activities, as well as assumptions about assessment. Subsequently, assessment serves multiple functions in teacher education which makes cultivating assessment capacity a challenging and complex task. To add to the complexity, there are a several assessors of learning in teacher education—external evaluators, university-based teacher educators, mentors, and practicing teachers—that preservice teachers meet during the practical component of their education. They all play a role in teaching how to assess, yet they do not all share the same beliefs, practices, and assessment criteria. Some of the roles assessment plays in teacher education are briefly discussed below, with the purpose of showing the complexity.

Gatekeeping

Biesta (2009) talks about three aims of education; qualification, socialisation, and subjectification. Gatekeeping serves the first aim, who is qualified to be a teacher and who is not? How gatekeeping assessment takes form, differs from context to context, including who the assessors are. In some jurisdictions, the gatekeepers are external to the academic institution who often assess according to a list of standards. In other contexts, the gatekeeping responsibility lies solely with the academic institution, or in collaboration with school-based mentors. The gatekeeping role is summative in character, and as such, it is high stakes for the learners. A similar function would summative assessment in content courses have, if the students pass or fail the course. Students of teaching are subject to this summative function of assessment during their education, and it is likely to impact their learning about, and later practice of, assessment accordingly.

Exposure to Assessment: Modelling by Teacher Educators

Biesta's (2009) second goal of education is socialisation. Students of teaching are socialised into specific assessment cultures practiced in teacher education. Teacher educators will always act as models to student teachers, thus modelling serves as a more implicit, yet not less important function of assessment in teacher education. How do teacher educators model assessment in their teaching? Do they model forms of assessment they would like their students to practice as teachers? Do teacher educators model assessment capacity? Personally, I believe that the importance of how assessment is practiced, and how it is modelled in teacher education, is a topic that deserves more attention when discussing how assessment can promote learning in schools. What models are students of teaching exposed to? What is the assessment competence of teacher educators? Do they really enact assessment capacity, continuously searching to improve assessment, to think the unthinkable?

The importance of modelling in teacher education is not new (Loughran and Beery, 2005; Swennen et al., 2010). Most modelling of assessment will be implicit and embodied, it refers to the way teacher educators provide feedback, written as well as oral, to the assignments they give, and in general, their behaviour towards their students. However, Loughran and Beery (2005) emphasise the importance of explicit modelling; teacher educators explaining and describing their assessment approaches to the students. When relating explicit modelling to assessment capacity, it also requires that teacher educators articulate their questions, challenges, worries, and constant search for innovative approaches to assessment. I would argue that this can be done by teacher educators in all subjects, not only in specific assessment courses. Moreover, the assessment practice students of teaching observe when they are placed in schools, will impact their own assessment practice when they start teaching. Assessment practice in schools is formed by the school's assessment culture, which again is shaped in accordance with local or national regulations. However, the most powerful model is the assessment practice by the individual teacher or mentor. School-based teacher educators have, therefore, a huge responsibility to explain their and the school's assessment practice to the students. For many practicing teachers it might be difficult to articulate their tacit knowledge (Smith, 2005), and perhaps it is even more problematic to talk about assessment capacity, as it is a state of being.

Specific Courses in Assessment

When I was a student of teaching, I had to take a course called 'Measurement and Evaluation.' I learned the psychometrics of testing, how to write good multiple-choice questions, how to look for the bell curve in a test, and to calculate the standard deviation to see the homogeneity in my class. The lower the standard deviation, the better. Well, when I started teaching it did not take me long before I understood there was much more to assessment than statistics, and I tried my own ways which at that time were rather innovative, such as self-assessment and portfolio assessment. The learners could choose their own entries in the portfolio, assignments they were proud of, but also assignments they were less happy with. Each entry had an explanatory text in which the students reflected on why they had chosen to include the entry. I remember the principal told me that 'such assessment approaches are unthinkable,' but he let me be as long as the students did ok in the summative matriculation exams. That was what really mattered to him and the school.

When I became the head of the same teacher education programme, I had studied myself, the evaluation course was replaced with a course titled 'Assessment as a Pedagogical Tool' in which the relation between assessment and motivation was emphasised. Learning and motivation theories underpinned the approaches to assessment discussed and explored. The guiding principle in the course was that assessment shall promote and not hinder learning. The individual teacher must find the optimal way to assess depending on the context and the situation. This I would relate to Biesta's (2009) third goal of education, subjectification, and the teacher enacts personal professionalism because it serves students' learning. This was in many ways thinking the unthinkable in a traditional and hierarchy context.

When I moved to other jurisdictions, I was surprised to learn that many teacher education programmes did not have a specific assessment course, at the most there was a lecture or two on assessment. Teaching about assessment seems not to be of importance in all teacher education programmes, unfortunately.

To sum up the functions of assessment in teacher education, the goal must be clear. If the aim is to develop assessment capacity in students of teaching, they need to be exposed to the concept in their own education, in the ways their learning is subject to assessment, through implicit and explicit modelling, and in specific assessment courses. My question is, or I can go so far and say that my worry is, that many teacher educators do not have the knowledge, the interest, the curiosity, and confidence to teach about assessment. We, teacher educators, should embrace the concept assessment capacity also with reference to our own learning.

Assessment Capacity in Relation to Other Assessment Discourses

I have in the beginning of this foreword said that to me assessment capacity has an indefinite dimension which makes it challenging to form a concrete construct to work with. However, I found Chapter 3 useful in understanding that assessment capacity is not a random concept, but it draws on leading discourses in assessment, *assessment competence, assessment literacy, assessment capability, and assessment identity.* These are all well-known concepts, and much is written about how to develop either or all in various professional development programmes for teachers. The chapter includes multiple references which the interested reader will find useful.

In Norway assessment for learning (AfL) is enforced by law, and in 2010 a nation-wide programme was initiated aiming at schooling teachers in the principles and practice of AfL, developing their assessment competence in relation to AfL. After four years, Hopfenbeck et al. (2015) examined the impact of the large-scale project as perceived by various stakeholders of education; national and local policymakers, school-leaders, teachers, and students. They found that successful implementation depended on communication and trust between the stakeholders, including the students. However, when the policy was perceived as a control device, the implementation was more challenging. A surprising finding was that student achievement did not seem to improve (Hopfenbeck et al., 2015), suggesting that schooling teachers does not automatically lead to better learning outcomes. My own thoughts are that the translation from the letter to practice is a three-stage process in teachers' learning, (a) a clear understanding of AfL (the letter), (b) accepting, internalising, and developing ownership of the underlying principles of AfL (spirit), and (c) translating teachers' personal understanding of AfL into personalised practice which serves their own students' learning. This is a time-consuming process, especially phase two, and I have seen too often that professional development programmes go from stage one to three, ignoring the importance of stage two, the internalisation of the principles of AfL, resulting in little effect on students' learning outcome. Changes become cosmetic and technical instead of being rooted in teachers' epistemology and pedagogical beliefs.

Returning to the Norwegian study, the authors conclude that *"successful implementation of the AfL programme was found in schools where factors such as trust, dialogue and higher levels of teacher agency were present"* (Hopfenbeck et al., 2015, p. 57).

The above conclusion made me reflect on how the well-known discourses thoroughly described in Chapter 3 relate to the new concept, assessment capacity. Whereas the definitions of assessment competence, literacy, capability, and identity might suggest a definite goal which the teacher can possibly achieve through professional development initiatives, successful implementation of AFL seems to be dependent on trust, dialogue, and teachers activating their personal professionality, agency. The indefinite dimension to assessment capacity seems to me to align with the factors found in the Norwegian study (Hopfenbeck et al., 2015).

Assessment capacity has been operationalised in the expansive model which breaks the concept into four sub-capacities:

- **Epistemic capacity,** learning and knowing
- **Embodied capacity,** emotional and physical wellbeing
- **Ethical capacity,** fairness and social justice
- **Experiential capacity,** everyday practices in school contexts.

The sub-capacities represent four central areas of teachers' professional development and concerns related to assessment. The concept, assessment capacity, is a rather abstract concept, it is a state of being, and therefore the sub-capacities are clarifying and help making the concept more concrete and manageable for the users. A separate chapter is devoted to a thorough explanation of each sub-capacity which facilitates the comprehension of the value of the expanded model. I found the guiding questions helpful when reflecting on my own assessment capacity. Thus, the elaborated model of assessment capacity presented in the book has the potential to become a useful tool for teacher educators to cultivate assessment capacity in initial as well as in-service teacher education, and it is likely to be helpful to practicing teachers who are searching for ways to improve teaching and assessment in striving to strengthen students' learning.

Conclusion

I find the book, and specifically the expanded model of assessment capacity with the thorough explanations of the sub-capacities, to be valuable for teacher educators to enrich their perception of assessment as well as to discuss the model with students of teaching. The underpinning understanding is that there is no right approach to assessment, no definite body of knowledge about assessment that needs to be learned. It is a state of mind which constantly seeks more knowledge and experience about assessment, to be concerned with students' and teachers needs and wellbeing during the learning process, striving to be fair to each individual student and the society as a whole. Finally, teachers and teacher educators must pursue ways to implement all of the above in practicing assessment, not being afraid being innovative. The importance of an open and reflective approach to assessment, to start thinking the unthinkable, is increasing now when artificial intelligence changes education, teaching, learning, and not least, assessment. The mindful and reflective approach to learning about assessment as presented in this book will become more and more relevant.

A final comment, I have often compared my own learning of assessment to my interpretation of Marc Chagall's paintings. Every time I look at his work, I find motifs I have not seen before, new understandings and interpretations, fascinated by how Chagall could think the unthinkable when he painted. His art shows the indefinite possibilities that open up when crossing the boundaries of traditions, norms, cultures, and preconceptions. This book, *Learning to Assess: Cultivating Assessment Capacity in Teacher Education,* has the potential to help teacher educators, teachers, and student teachers to cross boundaries in learning about assessment.

Kari Smith
Professor Emerita, Department
of Teacher Education NTNU,
Norwegian University of Science
and Technology

References

Biesta, G. (2009). Good education in an age of measurement: On the need to reconnect with the question of purpose in education. *Educational Assessment, Evaluation and Accountability (formerly: Journal of Personnel Evaluation in Education), 21*(1), 33–46.

Box, C., Skoog, G., & Dabbs, J. M. (2015). A case study of teacher personal practice assessment theories and complexities of implementing formative assessment. *American Educational Research Journal, 52*(5), 956–983.

Finefter-Rosenbluh, I., Ryan, T., & Barnes, M. (2021). The impact of student perception surveys on teachers' practice: Teacher resistance and struggle in student voice-based assessment initiatives of effective teaching. *Teaching and Teacher Education, 106*, 103436.

Hopfenbeck, T. N., Flórez Petour, M. T., & Tolo, A. (2015). Balancing tensions in educational policy reforms: Large-scale implementation of assessment for learning in Norway. *Assessment in Education: Principles, Policy & Practice, 22*(1), 44–60.

Kinsella, E. A. (2012). Practitioner Reflection and Judgement as Phronesis: A Continuum of Reflection and Considerations for Phronetic Judgement. In E. A. Kinsella, & A. Pitman (Eds.), *Phronesis as professional knowledge: Practical wisdom in the professions* (Vol. 1). (pp. 35–52). Springer Science & Business Media.

Kunnskapsdepartementet. (2017). *Overordnet del – verdier og prinsipper for grunnopplæringen.* Fastsatt som forskrift ved kongelig resolusjon. Læreplanverket for Kunnskapsløftet 2020.

Loughran, J., & Berry, A. (2005). Modelling by teacher educators, *Teaching and Teacher Education, 21*(2), 193–203.

McEvilley, T. (2002). The ethics of imperturbability. *The shape of ancient thought: Comparative studies in Greek and Indian philosophers*, 595–641.

Rudduck, J. (1999). Teacher practice and the student voice. In M. Lang, J. Olson, H. Hansen & W. Bunder (Eds.), *Changing Schools/Changing Practices: perspectives on educational reform and teacher professionalism* (pp. 41–54). Graant.

Rudduck, J. (2007). Student voice, student engagement, and school reform. In D. Thiessen & A. Cook-Sather (Eds.), *International handbook of student experience in elementary and secondary school* (pp. 587–610). Springer.

Smith, K. (2001). Children's rights, assessment and the digital portfolio: Is there a common denominator? In A. Pulverness (Ed.), *IATEFL 2001 Brighton Conference Sections* (pp. 55–68). University of Cambridge and IATEFL.

Smith, K. (2005). Teacher Educators' professional knowledge- How does it differ from teachers' professional knowledge? *Teaching and Teacher Education, 21*, 177–192.

Swennen, A., Jones, K., & Volman, M. (2010). Teacher educators: their identities, sub-identities and implications for professional development, *Professional Development in Education, 36*(1–2), 131–148, https://doi.org/10.1080/19415250903457893

United Nations. (1989). UN Convention on the Rights of the Child. https://www.ohchr.org/en/instruments-mechanisms/instruments/convention-rights-child

Contents

1 Cultivating Teacher Assessment Capacity 1
  1.1 Addressing the Challenge of Assessment Education 2
  1.2 What Do We Mean by Capacity? 8
  1.3 Drawing on Bernstein to *Think the Unthinkable* 10
  1.4 Developing Our Framework: Listening to Teachers as They
       Learn to Assess 12
  1.5 Conclusion 14
  References 15

2 The Landscape of Assessment Education 19
  2.1 Bernsteinian Perspective on the Assessment Landscape 20
  2.2 Mapping Similarities in Assessment Education Across Four
       Countries 24
       2.2.1 Assessment Is Strongly Framed Through Shared
              Education Foundations 25
       2.2.2 Assessment Is Strongly Framed by International
              Policies 27
       2.2.3 Assessment as Weakly Framed in Response to Student
              Voice and Student Agency 28
       2.2.4 Assessment Education Framing Is Occurring Within
              and Beyond Teacher Education 30
  2.3 Mapping Differences Between Assessment Education Policy
       Contexts 33
       2.3.1 England 33
       2.3.2 Australia 34
       2.3.3 Canada 36
       2.3.4 New Zealand 38
  2.4 Differences in the Classification and Framing of Assessment
       Education 40

2.5		Assessment Education Curriculum: Complex, Ever-Changing Decisions	42
	2.5.1	Conversations Across Contexts as Stories of Possibility	42
	References		43

3 The Constellation of Assessment Capacity Discourses ... 49
3.1 Assessment Learning Discourses ... 50
    3.1.1 Assessment Competence and Assessment Literacy: Foundational Discourses ... 51
    3.1.2 Competence Versus Literacy: A Narrow Distinction ... 53
    3.1.3 Assessment Capability: A Marked Shift ... 57
    3.1.4 Assessment Identity: A Turn Towards the Personal ... 58
3.2 From Competence to Identity ... 59
3.3 Towards Assessment Capacity ... 61
References ... 64

4 Epistemic Assessment Capacity ... 71
4.1 What Is Epistemic Assessment Capacity? ... 72
4.2 Preservice Teachers' Epistemic Learning Experiences ... 75
    4.2.1 Awareness of Knowledge, Learning, and Assessment Concepts and How They Change ... 76
    4.2.2 Awareness of Disciplinary Orientations ... 78
    4.2.3 Exploring Epistemic Awareness, Curiosity, and Flexibility ... 81
4.3 Developing Epistemic Assessment Capacity in Teacher Education ... 84
4.4 Conclusion ... 84
References ... 85

5 Embodied Assessment Capacity ... 89
5.1 What Is Embodied Assessment Capacity? ... 90
5.2 Preservice Teachers' Embodied Learning Experiences ... 92
    5.2.1 Awareness That Assessment Is an Emotional Rollercoaster ... 93
    5.2.2 Embodied Assessment Occurs In Situ with Materials and Spaces ... 98
    5.2.3 Learning to Manage Competing Demands Through Reflexive Agency ... 101
5.3 Developing Embodied Assessment Capacity in Initial Teacher Education ... 103
5.4 Conclusion ... 104
References ... 104

6 Ethical Assessment Capacity ... 109
6.1 What Is Ethical Assessment Capacity? ... 111
    6.1.1 What Is Being Valued in Assessment? ... 114
    6.1.2 Assessment as Identity Work ... 116

	6.1.3	Being Critically Aware of How Assessment Contributes to Broader Ideas of Social Justice	118
6.2		Developing Ethical Assessment Capacity in Initial Teacher Education	122
6.3		Conclusion	123
		References	124

7 Experiential Assessment Capacity 129

7.1		What Is Experiential Assessment Capacity?	130
	7.1.1	Assessment Experiences and Events as a Student	132
	7.1.2	Assessment Experiences and Events Within Preservice Teacher Programmes	134
	7.1.3	Assessment Experiences and Events Within Schools	136
7.2		Preservice Teachers' Experiential Assessment Capacity	140
7.3		Developing Experiential Assessment Capacity in Initial Teacher Education	144
7.4		Conclusion	145
		References	145

8 Learning to Assess 149

8.1		Thinking the Unthinkable: The Assessment Capacity Framework	151
	8.1.1	Interconnections	156
8.2		Developing Assessment Capacity: Direction for Teacher Education	160
8.3		Assessment That *Will Be*	163
		References	164

About the Authors

Christopher DeLuca is an Associate Dean at the School of Graduate Studies and Postdoctoral Affairs and Professor in Educational Assessment at the Faculty of Education, Queen's University (Ontario, Canada). He leads the Classroom Assessment Research Team and is Director of the Queen's Assessment and Evaluation Group. Website: www.cdeluca.com.

Jill Willis is an Associate Professor in the Faculty of Education at Queensland University of Technology (Brisbane, Australia). Her research focuses on reflexivity and agency in classroom assessment and evaluation processes. She currently leads research on accessibility in assessment and student evaluations of vertical schools.

Bronwen Cowie is Associate Dean Research Te Kura Toi Tangata, Division of Education, University of Waikato (Hamilton, New Zealand). Her research interests include assessment and assessment education, science education, and preservice and beginning teacher experiences. She has a particular interest in collaborative classroom-based research that includes student voice.

Christine Harrison is a Professor of Science Education at King's College (London, UK). Her research interests are in assessment and science education, especially the ways teachers deal with the interplay between assessment and teaching. She is currently working on how assessment and teaching play out in science practical lessons in primary and secondary schools.

Andrew Coombs is a Teaching Assistant Professor at Memorial University (Newfoundland & Labrador, Canada). Andrew's research focuses on understanding the factors shaping early career teachers' assessment practices and assessment learning needs. His quantitative and qualitative research methods, curriculum theory, and classroom assessment. Website: www.ACoombs.ca.

xix

Chapter 1
Cultivating Teacher Assessment Capacity

Abstract Assessment is one of the most complex activities in classrooms today. Every day, teachers need to negotiate and navigate historical, political, social, emotional, ethical, relational, and consequential assessment contexts and decisions to effectively support students' learning and wellbeing. In this chapter, the challenge of assessment and assessment education across jurisdictions is explicated. Simultaneously, the chapter begins to build an argument for the necessity and structure of a novel assessment learning framework, premised on the idea of *assessment capacity and notions of horizontal and vertical knowledge systems*. The chapter concludes with an initial articulation of the *Thinking the Unthinkable Assessment Capacity Framework* and how it was conceptualised.

Keywords Classroom assessment · Assessment capacity · Teacher education · Assessment literacy · Assessment competence · Assessment identity · Preservice teachers · Teacher learning

Assessment in education is a polarising topic. Whether the topic of conversation around a dinner table, in a Facebook group, or in a policy think tank, it does not take long before differences of opinion about assessment surface, often underscored by strong emotions. It seems that everyone has a stake in assessment debates, which is unsurprising as everyone has been shaped by the powerful force of assessment. Whether measuring one's developmental progress from birth, achievement in school, performance at work, or aptitude for college admission, assessment informs much of our self-perceptions and are the gatekeepers for work and life opportunities. As Stobart (2008) stated so simply, assessment shapes "how we see ourselves and how we learn" (p. 1). It is for this reason that continually striving to improve how we assess students in schools is so important.

Assessment has become a watchword of the twenty-first century, not just in schools but in society more generally. We assess just about everything from restaurants, hotels, and movies to doctors and teachers to cities and schools, all made easier through apps and online review platforms. Accountability mandates across sectors have brought the processes of them into vogue, using assessment as the engine for data to show progress, achievement, and growth, or the opposite. Assessment has become

© The Author(s), under exclusive license to Springer Nature Singapore Pte Ltd. 2023
C. DeLuca et al., *Learning to Assess*, Teacher Education, Learning Innovation
and Accountability, https://doi.org/10.1007/978-981-99-6199-3_1

a popular public discourse and an instrument of public policy that values higher scores over lower ones, comparisons with others, and continuous linear progress. These values might be powerful for making judgements and decisions within our public spheres but run counter to what many understand and value about personal development, growth, and learning—yet too often, these same values are applied to schools, classrooms, and students.

Assessment in schools ideally serves 'good' learning purposes. It can be an opportunity for students to show what they know and can do, and it can guide teachers, families, and schools to respond in ways that support and extend students' learning. Assessment performance provides evidence for individuals, helping them gain access to other opportunities, such as work or further study. As a form of pedagogy, formative assessment is rich in feedback and reflection opportunities, fosters community building, and supports students' agency in their learning. For schooling systems, collective assessment evidence can inform strategic decisions to bring about more equitable social change in schools and classrooms.

When assessment is discussed in the public arena, it is often not these stories of assessment achieving good outcomes that prevail. Rather, stories in the public and social media often focus on ways that assessment can go wrong for our students and our schools, with an accompanying message attached that 'it needs to be fixed,' highlighting gaps in achievement or differences between groups. Finding the parts to fix or change in current assessment practice is not easy. Assessment policies and practices are embedded into all layers of schooling and are among the most entrenched practices in schools today. It can seem too daunting and expensive to consider overhauling an entire schooling system. Very often, the focus of change is on the teachers as the people who can make the change. Hence, our book is about teachers as assessors and how mentor teachers and teacher educators can support teachers' *assessment capacity* for more sound and inclusive practice in schools.

1.1 Addressing the Challenge of Assessment Education

Teachers and Teacher Educators: This Book Is for You

Deciding what to teach about assessment in initial teacher education is not easy. The research has consistently shown that teacher candidates leave their preservice programmes hesitant in their assessment knowledge and skills (Volante & Fazio, 2007; Xu & Brown, 2016). This consistent finding is not surprising as assessment has not been a focus area for many preservice programmes over the decades. While regulating bodies articulate requirements for teachers to be 'assessment literate,' assessment has historically not occupied a prominent place in teacher education. In some contexts, teacher educators often find themselves responding to long lists created by accreditation and regulatory agencies, which might include topics in assessment, without sufficient time and access to resources or expertise to develop assessment education programmes (Richmond et al., 2019). Teacher educators have

1.1 Addressing the Challenge of Assessment Education

also expressed ambitious assessment learning goals for their preservice teachers (Coombs et al., 2021, pp. 16–17):

"We want them to be able to identify and reflect on their beliefs and understandings of our assessment."
"I want them to be able to effectively create assessment tools that align with good assessment practices."
"I want them to show me how they're understanding those practices, giving me examples of where they've used those practices, and then analyzing for me how those practices are going to inform their pedagogical decision making."

Assessment priorities can seem overwhelming, particularly given short preservice programme lengths, and it can be challenging to coordinate coherent conversations about assessment across institutions, as different faculty members hold vastly different views towards assessment (Gallagher et al., 2022). The challenge to effectively educate teacher candidates about assessment is further heightened because learning to assess is often a dual act of unlearning and relearning, as teacher candidates come to their preservice programmes with deeply entrenched views about assessment. Deep interrogation of these views takes time and perspective-shifting experiences (DeLuca et al., 2013, 2021a).

As a group of teacher educators and assessment researchers, we were compelled to investigate these challenges. This book is the result of our investigation, which has involved data collection and analysis from teacher candidates who were learning to assess across four countries (Australia, Canada, England, and New Zealand), policy reviews, interrogation of teacher education and assessment literature, and conversations over four years. Our investigation has resulted in the articulation of a novel ***Assessment Capacity Framework*** (see Fig. 1.1). The aim of this framework is to direct preservice and in-service teachers and teacher educator attention to four fundamental capacities that are critical in learning to assess. At the centre of this framework is the idea of *assessment capacity*. Assessment capacity is defined as a teacher's capacity to continually learn about their assessment practice—through relationships, adaptation, reflection, collaboration, and inventiveness—to imagine new possibilities for assessment in schools. Anchoring the framework on assessment capacity, with a focus on continuous professional learning, reorients previous conversations in the field about assessment literacy, competency, and capability, which largely seek to define teachers' assessment work and articulate their roles, responsibilities, and professional practices related to assessment in classrooms. As teachers work to expand their assessment capacity (i.e., as they learn to assess), they do so by engaging with four specific capacities:

- Learning and knowing, which we have called **epistemic capacity**.
- Emotional and physical wellbeing, which we have called an **embodied capacity**.
- Fairness and social justice, which we have called **ethical capacity**.
- Everyday practices in school contexts, which we have called **experiential capacity**.

Fig. 1.1 Four assessment capacities: epistemic, embodied, ethical, and experiential

These four assessment capacities (i.e., the four 4Es)—epistemic, embodied, ethical, and experiential—are essential capacities that underpin teacher learning in assessment and a beginning teacher's assessment decision-making. They are interrelated and inform one another. Yet, they are different enough from one another to provide a novel perspective for reflection and assessment learning.

This book takes a deep dive into what these capacities look like for preservice teachers and teacher educators, with each capacity explored in a separate chapter. To introduce how these capacities are evident, we start with an example from a preservice teacher's reflection. We can see the four assessment capacities evident here as a preservice teacher from our study reflects on their assessment learning experience. Reflections like this one were gathered from preservice teachers across teacher education programmes in Australia, Canada, England, and New Zealand in the process of this research project:

> I'm feeling very conflicted [about how to respond to a female student who has been absent with medically diagnosed anxiety and has not been able to contribute to a group assessment task] … The scientist in me weighs heavily on the side of reliability. But the social justice side of me is desperate for equity particularly because science itself as a discipline is far from equitable (selects against women, minority groups, racial diversity)… I'm keen to see that change and wonder if I could contribute to that in my high school science classes. I've been thinking a lot about equity and providing flexibility/choice in my assessment tasks for students. (Australian preservice teacher)

In working through a fairly common classroom assessment dilemma, the preservice teacher in this case has drawn on *epistemic* knowledge of how assessment in science has traditionally prioritised reliability. However, they have also recognised that assessment has a role to play in *ethical* and fair outcomes and that there are equity implications for the student and potentially for broader and longer-term social justice outcomes in terms of their participation in science. The preservice teacher is articulating how being an assessor creates *embodied* engagement for them and the student as they express feelings of conflict, desperation, and wonder. The resolution of the dilemma begins to be worked out, drawing in the *experiential* capacity, where they start to question what flexibility and choice might look like in assessment tasks for their own students.

1.1 Addressing the Challenge of Assessment Education

Awareness of the four capacities enables preservice teachers to think through and articulate their reasoning across everyday assessment situations. Similar to the three dimensions of assessment literacy proposed by Pastore and Andrade (2019)—conceptual, socio-emotional, and praxeological—our work adds an ethical dimension. The four assessment capacities provide an orientation at a meta-level, above a focus on skills and knowledge, to recognise the situated aspects of being an assessor. To be of benefit, we explore how these concepts might assist teacher educators in their course design and how our framework might be a schema for instruction in teacher education courses. The central chapters of this book focus on each of the concepts (i.e., epistemic, embodied, ethical, and experiential) to provide an in-depth discussion with examples to support teacher educators.

Preparation to be an assessor means always having a learning orientation and being prepared to reflect and inquire. Learning to be an assessor doesn't just take place at a university or in a teacher preparation course. It starts well before and continues well after. Assessment education begins early. Teachers begin learning about assessment when they are students and continue learning as professionals, parents, and community members, with their own experiences informing their orientations to teaching and assessment (Looney et al., 2018; Smith et al., 2014; Willis & Cowie, 2022). These layers of learning are illustrated by some more reflection data from preservice teachers collected in this project, showing that the preservice teachers' own layers of being parent, student, and teacher collectively inform experiences of learning to assess:

> I'm a bit worried at the moment about some of my kids' activities that needed to be completed by next week at school. My eldest daughter is presenting a speech in her mother tongue this Saturday and I just have been informed this morning. I want to complete my [university] assignment to the best of my ability but I also want to help my kids with their schoolwork as well. (New Zealand preservice teacher)

> I started teaching this week, team teaching year 8, teaching my first A-Level lesson and teaching the first lesson of my other year 8 class. Having not taught 'live' since before Christmas, I was feeling very apprehensive ahead of the first lesson. (English preservice teacher)

In preservice teacher programmes, assessment is a topic of learning as well as a process of learning. Preservice teachers learn about assessment theory and activities, and they are assessed themselves. Teacher education assessment tasks can confirm for preservice teachers that they are on the right path, confound previous beliefs or expectations of success, and credential an emerging teacher identity through government policies with registration requirements established through culminating and certifying assessment tasks. Teacher educators help to shape preservice teacher expectations as they emphasise various assessment messages in their course design or commentary. Similarly, mentor teachers in schools (also called host teachers or associate teachers) induct preservice teachers into the mysteries of working with students through assessment, managing multiple accountabilities and implications of policies for assessment in schools. Preservice teachers integrate the layers of learning to assess at university and in school-based learning placements as evident in these reflections:

> This week professional experience in school has been great timing for assessment. I will be marking Maths assessments this week and I looked through the previous assignments work which my supervising teacher explained is a new assessment task/style. Torrance (2017) described the change in assessment to include 21st century knowledge and skills and this was evident in the new Maths assessment; a portfolio of expenditure and savings for a trip to Bali upon graduation - a real-life example. (Australian preservice teacher)

> One notable challenge I faced was remaining objective and consistent in my grading: doing so through 25 submissions proved more difficult than I had imagined. More specifically, awarding and withholding points, analyzing the merit of certain arguments, and working with a lack of rubric were just some of the unique difficulties posed by assessment. Moving forward, with the help of insights provided by my AT as well as the natural progression in my own comfort and skill, my capacity to evaluate effectively and efficiently will be honed. (Canadian preservice teacher)

Continual development of assessment expertise is also essential for teachers, as assessment contexts and policies are always in flux (DeLuca et al., 2019d). Disruptions like the global pandemic of 2019 onwards meant that teachers and schools had to rapidly reconsider what was possible and important in assessment practices. In some nations, long-standing summative assessment practices were abandoned altogether (Cooper et al., 2022). Every teacher had to contemplate how assessment might be possible through unpredictable conditions and unfamiliar technologies. Moreover, teachers had to consider the fairness of assessment when students or families had their lives overturned. The global pandemic was a reminder that teacher educators are always looking ahead as part of their remit to prepare beginning teachers. An overarching schema is one way to guide beginning teacher assessors and teacher educators who need to design assessment programmes through assessment uncertainty and be prepared to reflect and inquire.

Learning to be an assessor means preparing teachers to be ready to engage with the challenges of assessment that *was*, assessment that *is*, and assessment that *might be*. Much more research is needed to identify how to support students, preservice teachers, teacher educators, early career and experienced teachers, school leaders, and systems navigating new assessment terrains. This book is a response to that need and an invitation to continue the assessment conversation across countries.

Assessment Researchers: This Book Is for You

To prepare teachers for the challenges of assessment that *might be*, more timely assessment research that connects principles from the assessment field to the educational research influencing teaching and learning is needed. As the comprehensive review of assessment literacy research outlined in Chapter 3 indicates, there is evidence that the assessment research field is deeply interested in identifying the rich and diverse types of learning needed for teachers to be effective and principled assessors. This book acknowledges the work occurring in the field and draws together some of the big ideas to inform future conversations and research. It contributes to scholarship by engaging assessment researchers from across the globe through a collaborative project that extends the field of assessment education and research.

While four capacities are proposed in this book around the central concept of assessment capacity, we acknowledge that future researchers may argue from additional research that could extend, expand, or reframe the presented capacities.

Assessment research that brings together multiple country contexts is needed to continue the tradition of learning from and with our jurisdictions to construct robust and culturally relevant assessment theory. Working together across four country contexts has led us to wrestle with assessment terminology in productive ways. As a result, we have been able to see similarities and differences across our contexts and have been able to recognise more clearly some of the assessment strengths and blind spots in our own understanding and in our assessment systems.

The four nations that feature in this book are Australia, Canada, England, and New Zealand. The shared colonial, Anglophone educational heritage of these four nations provides for some interesting comparisons, yet there are interesting contrasts as well. Canada and England are from the Global North, and Australia and New Zealand are from the Global South. England and New Zealand are geographically small island nations, and Australia and Canada are geographically large federations of states, provinces, and territories. England's population in 2022 of over 67.5 million people is much larger than New Zealand's population of 5.12 million people, Australia's population of around 26 million people, and Canada's population of over 38.5 million people. We acknowledge that the four countries featured in this book are not a global representation, so in the assessment ideas represented in the following chapters, there is an inherent invitation to create new and different connections by drawing in additional country conversations. In these chapters, we hope to highlight some possibilities for new assessment research and teacher education directions.

Professional Developers and Policymakers: This Book Is for You

The way that assessment education is framed, either by professional learning facilitators or by policymakers, represents assessment in particular ways. As Chapter 2 outlines, assessment is currently framed in many contexts as both a problem and solution, with teachers and teacher educators being given both blame and responsibility. When assessment is positioned as strongly associated with learning and inquiry (Wyatt-Smith & Adie, 2021) or as part of the cultural funds of knowledge (Cowie & Trevethan, 2021; Cowie et al., 2011), new possibilities for students and their teachers are *thinkable*. The inquiry at the heart of this book and the proposed principles can provide a framework for action and collaborative evaluation.

Preservice Teachers: This Book Is for You

If you are a preservice teacher, you may have picked up this book for an assessment task for your teacher preparation qualification. Some of the literature or thinking in this book will help you get that done. Or you may be wondering if you have been doing assessment 'right.' We hope you recognise your learning in the examples in these pages, as our thinking has been guided by the experiences and reflections of hundreds of preservice teachers as they have been learning to become assessors. In attending to preservice teachers' experiences, we also hope to model our shared epistemic stance of assessment in the service of learning, with student experiences at the centre. We believe that it is possible to create assessment change through classroom practices to improve equitable outcomes and to honour the embodied experiences of teacher educators, teachers, and students as they engage with assessment.

1.2 What Do We Mean by Capacity?

> Capacity suggests wideness, not narrowness; openness; space for possibilities not yet even imagined, or if imagined, done so with a tremble. Capacity puts aside the correcting mind...capacity holds room for unknowingness and peculiarity. Capacity is fearless in its embrace of the other inner side of things. (Doll, 2005, p. 21)

Multiple constructs have been used to describe the work, roles, and responsibilities of teachers in relation to assessment. Notably, these are assessment literacy, competency, capability, and identity. Previously, we have each written about these constructs: assessment literacies (Coombs et al., 2018, 2020, 2022; DeLuca et al., 2016, 2018, 2019a, 2019b, 2019c, 2021b; Edwards et al., 2022; Gareis et al., 2020; Harrison, 2005; Schneider et al., 2021; Wiliam et al., 2004; Willis et al., 2013) and assessment capability (DeLuca et al., 2019d; Willis & Cowie, 2022). In this book, we acknowledge the importance of these previous constructs in shaping teacher assessment education and understandings of how to support teacher learning in assessment. Chapter 3, in particular, delves deeply into each construct and how it contributes to our thinking and field of inquiry.

While assessment literacy, competency, capability, and identity have been instrumental to the field, we assert the need and value of articulating a new framing for how teachers learn to assess: *assessment capacity*. We make this assertion because previous characterisations of teachers' assessment work have been largely rooted in defining standards of practice or speaking to the immediate assessment actions of the present (i.e., what teachers need to do in their classrooms to engage in daily assessment activities with students). Through our novel characterisation of assessment capacity, we point to the future of assessment in schools by emphasising the crucial role teacher learning and teacher agency play in transforming classroom assessment experiences. For us, capacity inherently involves learning and development, as in the learning and development of educators in their roles as assessors. We see this learning and development not as a prescriptive act but rather as one rooted in relationships, adaptation, and inventiveness—a "space for possibilities not yet even imagined" (Doll, 2005, p. 21).

Previous conceptualisations of assessment literacy and capability involve "situated professional judgement, that is the ability to draw on learning and assessment theories and experiences to purposefully design, interpret, and use a range of assessment evidence in the service of student learning" (DeLuca et al., 2019d, p. 5). These capabilities are developed through preservice teacher experiences within teacher education programmes and in practice contexts such as those with mentor

1.2 What Do We Mean by Capacity?

teachers in schools. By drawing on accepted assessment capabilities, newly graduating teachers mostly learn to guide their students over familiar assessment territory with well-marked signposted paths to follow, with school processes clearly laid out. Ideally, new teachers integrate and leverage the range of assessment theories and practices they learned in their teacher preparation courses to facilitate learning through assessment as well as evaluate and report on student learning. Assessment capable teachers support students to achieve trusted credentials and become discerning, self-monitoring learners. As they enact assessment in capable ways, teachers also generate trustworthy and reliable evidence of student learning for school systems. Robust assessment capabilities equip teachers to contribute to current assessment practices that reflect cultural stories about student achievements and aspirations.

We now argue that teachers need more than assessment literacy and capability. While assessment capability prepares teachers for assessment that *once was* and *currently is* in schools, assessment capacity prepares teachers to consider future assessment possibilities—what assessment *will be*. Teachers have a professional responsibility to look up from familiar signposted assessment pathways to ask: *Where are we going?*—to notice how assessment is shaping the education landscape for their students and to challenge and change practices that are no longer inclusively supporting their students' learning. For example, the ways that assessment processes are linked to accountability shape the educational landscape teachers and students traverse. When the educational assessment landscape has well-marked features to do with accountability processes, capability would emphasise current skills and processes that can help teachers feel secure about their direction. Capacity opens up possibilities for new directions. For example, student data walls can be visible records that serve accountability functions or, depending on how the teacher makes use of them, can support a capacity for inquiring into student performance to consider how assessment may be more equitable. Assessment capacity encourages a learning and learner orientation to assessment work; it invites teachers to be curious about assessment practices and their impact on students, schools, and society. Most importantly, assessment capacity encourages teachers to use assessment information to transform systems of assessment while paying attention to the epistemic, embodied, ethical, and experiential facets of assessment decisions. Doing so opens new pathways and practices for assessment. Assessment capacity is fundamentally about empowering teachers to think differently about assessment in ways more congruent with their students' needs and those of their community.

Accountability and assessment systems based on teacher professionalism are in contrast to unintelligent accountability approaches that rely on standardised assessment reports or data that flow upwards to be aggregated before decisions flow down to practice. Such surveillance systems tend to have the opposite effect of an intention to support quality practice. They often create distrust and additional workloads that take professionals away from their primary roles of supporting student learning (O'Neill, 2013; Ozga et al., 2011). When assessment is used within accountability systems that are remote from the classroom, there are well-documented, concerning, and unwanted consequences. Narratives of failing schools; increased stress for students, teachers, and principals; narrowed curriculum; perverse incentives; and increased inequities as 'difficult' students are excluded are some of the consequences noted around the world (Klenowski & Wyatt-Smith, 2012; Spina, 2019). Preservice teachers are often made aware of these inequities in their teacher education courses and encouraged to be reflexive and take action. Yet, the assessment pathways in our systems are so deeply entrenched that taking action can be seen as daunting, if not impossible.

This book is based on the premise that teachers have a professional responsibility to look up from familiar assessment pathways, to notice how assessment is shaping the education landscape, and to ask: *Where are we going and why?* The book provides a framework and narratives for challenging assessment assumptions as we follow teacher candidates who are learning to assess. Our focus on assessment capacity highlights that agentic teachers can forge new ways of assessment in contexts of emerging educational agendas and imperatives. To contribute to assessment changes, preservice teachers will need assessment capacities to inquire into their own practice and be empowered with tools and ideas for taking action. Assessment capacity suggests that teacher educators and their preservice teachers engage with assessment that *is* and are also open to new possibilities and to thinking about what *might be* in order to be able to think about what is as yet *unthinkable* in current assessment practice.

1.3 Drawing on Bernstein to *Think the Unthinkable*

The idea that there is *thinkable* and *unthinkable* knowledge comes from the educational theories and language of educational sociologist Basil Bernstein (2000, 2003). Bernstein highlighted how assessment, along with curriculum and pedagogy, forms part of the interrelated message system that communicates cultural relationships of power in classrooms, schools, and societies. For example, messages about what knowledge is valued and who can access that knowledge are created and circulated through assessment practices (Gipps & Murphy, 1994). As preservice teachers move through initial teacher education programmes and cultivate their assessment capacity, they learn what is valued assessment knowledge and practice and become part of the transmission and enculturation process with their students. Their initial teacher education (ITE) programme, experiences as preservice teachers in school-based learning, and ITE assessment experiences create and maintain an order of meaning through the materials and how ideas, activities, and expected outputs are organised and explained. These orders of meaning simultaneously position people and regulate relationships, yet at the same time, create the space for the possibility of change in relationships.

Change in assessment occurs as teachers actively contextualise and recontextualise, or reshape, disciplinary ways of knowing through their assessment practices. Teachers—whether teacher educators, classroom teachers, or preservice teachers—are active agents who link the official production of assessment knowledge, often at the policy level, with pedagogical practices. Through classroom assessment and pedagogy, students develop their knowledge of themselves as learners, knowers, and doers in various aspects of the curriculum and through what their teachers prioritise. Teachers, through their assessment practices, establish what is *thinkable* or *unthinkable*. Everyday practice creates a form of consciousness about what it means to be an effective knower and learner as part of the culture of schooling.

In the realm of assessment, assessment capacity enables teachers to challenge and change the status quo, to equip teachers to ask fundamental questions about: *Where are we now in our assessment practices? How did we get here? And what is possible?* In doing so, they are agents in the (re)construction, maintenance, and transformation of the social order that assessment reifies (Bernstein, 2000, p. xxi). In developing our framework of assessment capacity, we recognise the forces and influences that shape teachers in their assessment work. We draw on Bernstein to provide a structure for how assessment learning and practice are framed to understand the message systems through which *thinkable* assessment knowledge is transmitted and enacted, and its boundaries are maintained or transgressed. We position our 4Es—epistemic, embodied, ethical, and experiential—in relation to Bernstein's vertical and horizontal knowledge systems (Bernstein, 2000, 2003). *Vertical knowledge* represents that which is official, codified, and canonical. In contrast, *horizontal knowledge* represents craft, practical, and local understandings. Applied to assessment—and learning within each of the four core capacities—vertical and horizontal knowledges continually shape teachers' assessment decisions and work (see Fig. 1.2). Navigating these knowledge systems, which are often not in alignment but rather orthogonal, is at the heart of learning to assess.

To realise the possibility for agency that teachers have in reshaping learning futures, reflexive awareness of the culture of schooling is needed. Without knowing about the big picture of policy and practice in assessment, teacher educators and the preservice teachers they work with will not fully be able to know why they do what they do or to appreciate the consequences of their context. In Chapter 2, some

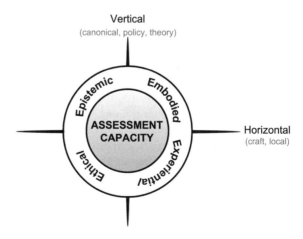

Fig. 1.2 Assessment capacity framework with vertical and horizontal knowledge axes

of the current assessment policy landscapes within and across the four countries in this study are highlighted so that teacher educators and their preservice teachers can consider how to make sense of assessment. In Chapter 3, the literature about assessment literacies, identity, capability, and capacity is explored in more detail, giving a big picture of the historical way the assessment research field has represented these topics.

1.4 Developing Our Framework: Listening to Teachers as They Learn to Assess

> The fundamental aim of our Assessment Capacity Framework—and indeed this book—is to advocate for, promote, and advance a theory for cultivating teacher assessment capacity across time and contexts, one that encourages teachers to challenge and change existing assessment practices to work in service of all students' learning.

Learning to assess is a complex process shaped by horizontal (i.e., craft, embedded, practical knowledge) and vertical (i.e., policy, public, theory, and canonical knowledge) systems (Bernstein, 2000, 2003). We propose that teacher candidates learn to assess by engaging in four fundamental capacities—epistemic, embodied, ethical, and experiential—which we frame through a discourse of *assessment capacity*. Our framework was born from the experiences of teacher candidates who were learning to assess, in combination with reviews of assessment literature, policy, and practice. In the four countries studied, each member of our research team collaborated with teacher educators who were teaching an assessment course. Specifically, we collected data from teacher candidates via ongoing reflections throughout their preservice programmes in Australia, Canada, England, and New Zealand and through surveys on their approaches to assessment. Teacher candidates were invited from one teacher education programme in each of the focal countries for participation in this study.

Preservice Teacher Reflections

Preservice teachers were invited to complete ongoing written reflections about their assessment learning through an online digital journal while they completed an assessment course in their teacher training. The collection of 1630 reflections from 374 preservice teachers in 4 countries was analysed using an abductive analysis process based on Charles S. Peirce's late nineteenth-century work on abductive reasoning and pragmatism. Abductive processes are a systematic way for researchers to construct theory that enables new perspectives by inquiring into empirical findings that are surprising in the light of existing theories (Timmermans & Tavory, 2012). The process involves attending to experiences, hunches, and data that are not easily explained, going back and forth between theorising, and then checking whether the

1.4 Developing Our Framework: Listening to Teachers as They Learn to Assess

data supports the argument. Timmermans and Tavory (2012) highlight that ongoing intense dialogue between colleagues in a community of inquiry is an essential part of this rigorous process of data exploration and theory development.

We used an abductive analysis process to interpret the data collected through this study in relation to broader policies and extant literature. Data analysis occurred over several years and stages—through conversations in Toronto in early 2019, in Brisbane later in 2019, and on Zoom many times from 2020 through 2023. The extended timeframe and multiple data representations were an important part of the process, enabling us to engage in seeing beyond what was previously *thinkable* or not visible. Our usual qualitative social analysis and quantitative survey analysis approaches were also supplemented with computational analysis in a process of *defamiliarisation*—looking at the data in new ways to try and overcome habitual readings (Timmermans & Tavory, 2012). This socio-technical process was based on previous work (Gibson & Willis, 2020; Willis & Gibson, 2020), where social analysis and computational technical analysis inform one another.

Key data extracts from preservice teacher reflections were analysed and discussed as a collective, leading to an initial theorisation about the capacities. Computational analysis was used to answer the question: *Is there evidence of these capacities across the preservice teacher reflections?* A list of the top 5% of n-grams (n = 687) was generated, an n-gram being a collection of words that frequently occur across the reflections (in this instance, groups of 1–5 words). Three of the researchers coded these n-grams and proposed four initial categories of emotion, cognition, temporality, and socio-materiality (that is, referring to social relationships or materials as contexts for assessment); however, the cognition list seemed to include some more epistemic traces like "belief" and "know," while some action-oriented phrases were fitting within emotion and cognition. After discussion, new theoretical categories were proposed by the research team—phenomenal (relating to experience, including emotion and culture), epistemic (relating to knowledge or knowing, including thinking and learning), corporeal (referring to tangible or physical things, including the environment), and teleological (referring to purpose or intent, including future action). The computational analysis then tested these categories for co-occurrence and frequency, and it was apparent that there was evidence of the high frequency of the categories. After some more experimentation, four more-fit-for-purpose computational combinations were identified and aligned with future-focused capacities reflected in our review of teacher education literature and teacher education policy reviews, resulting in the four capacities—epistemic, embodied, ethical, and experiential.

Importantly, our analysis shows that the resulting categories of epistemic, embodied, ethical, and experiential capacities within our framework were interrelated but also distinct. The extent of their appearance across the reflections could be represented in a computational visualisation (see Chapter 8), and relevant reflections were identified across the large dataset to illustrate each capacity for readers. Through this process, we explored the evidence of what mattered most to preservice teachers as they learned to be assessors. Their voices are represented as data in the four chapters about assessment capacities.

Preservice Teacher Survey
Preservice teachers were also invited to complete the Approaches to Classroom Assessment Inventory survey (ACAI) to self-assess their assessment orientations (DeLuca et al., 2016). The ACAI is a scenario-based survey based on 15 contemporary assessment standards across five geographic regions. The ACAI helps teachers identify and understand their approaches to 12 assessment dimensions across four categories: Assessment Purpose (Assessment for Learning, Assessment as Learning, Assessment of Learning), Assessment Process (design, use/scoring, communication), Assessment Fairness (standard, equitable, differentiated), and Assessment Theory (consistent, contextual, balanced) (DeLuca et al., 2016). In total, 489 preservice teachers completed the ACAI across the participating countries towards the end of their preservice programme to gain information on teacher candidates' approaches to assessment upon completion of their assessment education. Data from the survey were statistically analysed using descriptive statistics and analysis of variance. Results from the ACAI pertain most directly to the experiential capacity and are therefore presented in Chapter 7 of this book.

1.5 Conclusion

Assessment capacity is a big concept, and it is ambitious to consider the interplay between global and local contexts and priorities for assessment across four countries. In the remaining chapters of this book, you will read about the current teacher education landscape (Chapter 2) and existing assessment discourses (Chapter 3). Chapters 2 and 3 present the 'building blocks' for thinking about assessment capacity, describing both the foundation of assessment work that has been conducted previously as well as providing the philosophical basis for our Assessment Capacity Framework.

In Chapters 4–7, we present our four capacities—epistemic, embodied, ethical, and experiential—drawing on preservice teacher data, literature, and analysis to describe each capacity and its foundational characteristics. In these chapters, preservice teachers' learning about assessment is brought to life through narratives and reflections across the four country contexts, Australia, Canada, England, and New Zealand. In some cases, the same reflective excerpt is used in multiple chapters. This repetition occurs with intention. It signals the interconnection between the four capacities, and the complexity of learning to assess. These rich reflection narratives provide a strong foundation for learning from our preservice teachers as they learn to assess.

In the final chapter, we bring the arguments presented throughout this book together in a consolidated articulation of our novel *Assessment Capacity Framework*, with expressed implications and direction for teacher education programming. We underscore that this text is a beginning point in the assessment capacity conversation—more stories, more contexts, and more imaginings are needed—to advance assessment education within, across, and beyond teacher education programmes, to ultimately support more ambitious, inclusive, and radical thinking about assessment in schools.

References

Bernstein, B. (2000). *Pedagogy, symbolic control, and identity: Theory, research, critique* (Vol. 5). Rowman & Littlefield.

Bernstein, B. (2003). *Class, codes and control: Applied studies towards a sociology of language* (Vol. 2). Psychology Press.

Coombs, A. J., DeLuca, C., LaPointe-McEwan, D., & Chalas, A. (2018). Changing approaches to classroom assessment: An empirical study across teacher career stages. *Teaching and Teacher Education, 71*, 134–144.

Coombs, A. J., DeLuca, C., & MacGregor, S. (2020). A person-centered analysis of teacher candidates' approaches to assessment. *Teaching and Teacher Education, 87*. https://doi.org/10.1016/j.tate.2019.102952 (online).

Coombs, A. J., Ge, J., & DeLuca, C. (2021). From sea to sea: The Canadian landscape of assessment education. *Educational Research, 63*(1), 9–25.

Coombs, A. J., Rickey, N., DeLuca, C., & Lui, S. (2022). Chinese teachers' approaches to classroom assessment. *Educational Research for Policy and Practice*. https://doi.org/10.1007/s10671-020-09289-z (online).

Cooper, A. J., DeLuca, C., Holden, M., & MacGregor, S. (2022). Emergency assessment: Rethinking classroom practices and priorities amid remote teaching. *Assessment in Education: Principles, Policy & Practice, 29*(5), 534–554.

Cowie, B., Otrel-Cass, K., Glynn, T., Kara, H., Anderson, M., et al. (2011). *Culturally responsive pedagogy and assessment in primary science classrooms: Whakamana tamariki*. Teaching & Learning Research Initiative Nāu i Whatu Te Kākahu, He Tāniko Taku.

Cowie, B., & Trevethan, H. (2021). Funds of knowledge and relations as a curriculum and assessment resource in multicultural primary science classrooms: A case study from Aotearoa New Zealand. *International handbook of research on multicultural science education* (pp. 1–32). Springer.

DeLuca, C., Chavez, T., Cao, C., & Bellara, A. (2013). Changing conceptions of assessment: Pedagogies for pre-service assessment education. *The Teacher Educator, 48*(2), 128–142.

DeLuca, C., Coombs, A. J., & LaPointe-McEwan, D. (2019a). Assessment mindset: Exploring the relationship between teacher mindset and approaches to classroom assessment. *Studies in Educational Evaluation, 61*, 159–169.

DeLuca, C., Coombs, A. J., MacGregor, S., & Rasooli, A. (2019b). Toward a differential and situated view of assessment literacy: Studying teachers' responses to classroom assessment scenarios. *Frontiers in Education, 4*. https://doi.org/10.3389/feduc.2019.00094 (online).

DeLuca, C., Ge, J., Searle, M., Carbone, K., & LaPointe-McEwan, D. (2021a). Toward a pedagogy for slow and significant learning about assessment in teacher education. *Teaching and Teacher Education, 101*. https://doi.org/10.1016/j.tate.2021.103316 (online).

DeLuca, C., LaPointe-McEwan, D., & Luhanga, U. (2016). Approaches to classroom assessment inventory: A new instrument to support teacher assessment literacy. *Educational Assessment, 21*(4), 248–266.

DeLuca., C., Rickey, N., & Coombs, A. J. (2021b). Exploring assessment across cultures: Teachers' approaches to assessment in the U.S., China, and Canada. *Cogent Education, 8*(1), 1–26.

DeLuca, C., Schneider, C., Coombs, A. J., Pozas, M., & Rasooli, A. (2019c). A cross-cultural comparison of German and Canadian student teachers' assessment competence. *Assessment in Education: Principles, Policy & Practice, 27*(1), 26–45.

DeLuca, C., Valiquette, A., Coombs, A. J., LaPointe-McEwan, D., & Luhanga, U. (2018). Teachers' approaches to classroom assessment: A large-scale survey. *Assessment in Education: Principles, Policy & Practice, 25*(4), 355–375.

DeLuca, C., Willis, J., Cowie, B., Harrison, C., Coombs, A. J., Gibson, A., & Trask, S. (2019d). Policies, programs, and practices: Exploring the complex dynamics of assessment education in teacher education across four countries. *Frontiers in Education, 4.* https://doi.org/10.3389/feduc.2019.00132 (online).

Doll, M. A. (2005). Capacity and currere. *Journal of Curriculum Theorizing, 21*(3), 21–28.

Edwards, F., Cowie, B., & Trask, S. (2022). Using colleague coaching to develop teacher data literacy. *Professional Development in Education.* https://doi.org/10.1080/19415257.2022.208 1247

Gallagher, J., Willis, J., & Spina, N. (2022). Method as an opportunity for collaborative agency: An Australian Delphi inquiry into teacher educators' priorities in assessment education. In *Reconstructing the work of teacher educators* (pp. 197–221). Springer.

Gareis, C., Barnes, N., Coombs, A. J., DeLuca, C., & Uchiyama, K. (2020). Exploring the influence of assessment courses and student teaching on beginning teachers' approaches to classroom assessment. *Assessment Matters, 14*, 5–41.

Gibson, A., & Willis, J. (2020). Ethical challenges and guiding principles in facilitating personal digital reflection. In C. Burr & L. Floridi (Eds.), *Ethics of digital well-being: Philosophical study series* (Vol. 140, pp. 151–173). Springer.

Gipps, C. V., & Murphy, P. (1994). *A fair test? Assessment, achievement and equity.* Open University Press.

Harrison, C. (2005). Teachers developing assessment for learning: Mapping teacher change. *Teacher Development, 9*(2), 255–263.

Klenowski, V., & Wyatt-Smith, C. (2012). The impact of high stakes testing: The Australian story. *Assessment in Education: Principles, Policy & Practice, 19*(1), 65–79.

Looney, A., Cumming, J., van Der Kleij, F., & Harris, K. (2018). Reconceptualising the role of teachers as assessors: Teacher assessment identity. *Assessment in Education: Principles, Policy & Practice, 25*(5), 442–467.

O'Neill, O. (2013). Intelligent accountability in education. *Oxford Review of Education, 39*(1), 4–16.

Ozga, J., Dahler-Larsen, P., Segerholm, C., & Simola, H. (Eds.). (2011). *Fabricating quality in education: Data and governance in Europe.* Routledge.

Pastore, S., & Andrade, H. L. (2019). Teacher assessment literacy: A three-dimensional model. *Teaching and Teacher Education, 84*, 128–138.

Richmond, G., Salazar, M. D. C., & Jones, N. (2019). Assessment and the future of teacher education. *Journal of Teacher Education, 70*(2), 86–89.

Schneider, C., DeLuca, C., Pozas, M., & Coombs, A. J. (2021). Linking personality to teachers' literacy in classroom assessment: A cross-cultural study. *Educational Research and Evaluation, 26*(1–2), 53–74.

Smith, L. F., Hill, M. F., Cowie, B., & Gilmore, A. (2014). Preparing teachers to use the enabling power of assessment. In *Designing assessment for quality learning* (pp. 303–323). Springer.

Spina, N. (2019). 'Once upon a time': Examining ability grouping and differentiation practices in cultures of evidence-based decision-making. *Cambridge Journal of Education, 49*(3), 329–348.

Stobart, G. (2008). *Testing times: The uses and abuses of assessment.* Routledge.

Timmermans, S., & Tavory, I. (2012). Theory construction in qualitative research: From grounded theory to abductive analysis. *Sociological Theory, 30*(3), 167–186.

Torrance, H. (2017). Blaming the victim: Assessment, examinations, and the responsibilisation of students and teachers in neo-liberal governance. *Discourse: Studies in the Cultural politics of Education, 38*(1), 83–96.

References

Volante, L., & Fazio, X. (2007). Exploring teacher candidates' assessment literacy: Implications for teacher education reform and professional development. *Canadian Journal of Education, 30*, 749–770.

Wiliam, D., Lee, C., Harrison, C., & Black, P. (2004). Teachers developing assessment for learning: Impact on student achievement. *Assessment in Education: Principles, Policy & Practice, 11*(1), 49–65.

Willis, J., Adie, L., & Klenowski, V. (2013). Conceptualising teachers' assessment literacies in an era of curriculum and assessment reform. *The Australian Educational Researcher, 40*(2), 241–256.

Willis, J., & Cowie, B. (2022). Teacher educators preparing assessment capable pre-service teachers in Australia and New Zealand—Agents and authors within assessment policy palimpsests. In *Reconstructing the work of teacher educators: Finding spaces in policy through agentic approaches—Insights from a research collective* (pp. 179–196). Springer Nature Singapore.

Willis, J., & Gibson, A. (2020). The emotional work of being an assessor: A reflective writing analytics inquiry into digital self-assessment. In J. Fox, C. Alexander, & T. Aspland (Eds.), *Teacher education in globalised times* (pp. 93–113). Springer.

Wyatt-Smith, C., & Adie, L. (2021). The development of students' evaluative expertise: Enabling conditions for integrating criteria into pedagogic practice. *Journal of Curriculum Studies, 53*(4), 399–419.

Xu, Y., & Brown, G. T. (2016). Teacher assessment literacy in practice: A reconceptualization. *Teaching and Teacher Education, 58*, 149–162.

Chapter 2
The Landscape of Assessment Education

Abstract This chapter outlines the landscape of assessment education across jurisdictions, namely Australia, Canada, England, and New Zealand. Rooted in a Bernsteinian Perspective of knowledge codification (i.e., vertical and horizontal knowledge systems), assessment learning is structured in relation to strongly and weakly classified knowledge. Comparisons across assessment in schools and preservice teacher education programmes in each of the four focal countries are explored. The result of these comparisons is a cross-country mapping of assessment and assessment education that presents a layered and complex context for assessment learning that is always in flux.

Keywords Teacher education · Preservice teachers · Assessment · Comparative education · Assessment education · Assessment literacy

Assessment education occurs in landscapes that are shaped by policies, priorities, and practices of diverse groups of people who have an interest in education and are informed by layers of assessment learning. Some of these layers may be visible and evident in current policy, but others are invisible, bringing with them cultural values from long-forgotten contexts. For teachers, learning to assess is part of an ongoing process. It is continuously shaped by the contexts, cultures, and resources where their learning is occurring. Assessment practices in schools are not neutral, with schools and systems responding differently to education priorities, accountability mandates, and international assessment programmes (Hardy et al., 2021). Assessment priorities are impacted by historical trajectories in individual countries that encompass multiple "competing political readings of desirable forms of schooling" (Lingard et al., 2006, p. 87). This chapter focuses on four country contexts—Australia, Canada, England, and New Zealand—to illustrate the similarities and differences across the contexts and how these countries situate and shape assessment education that aims to develop preservice teacher assessment capacity.

The notion of *assessment capacity* suggests that teacher educators and their preservice teachers need to be equipped to engage with assessment that *was*, and *is*, but also be open to new and agentic possibilities about assessment that *might be*. Being aware of the cultural context of assessment is an essential foundation for responsive and

© The Author(s), under exclusive license to Springer Nature Singapore Pte Ltd. 2023   19
C. DeLuca et al., *Learning to Assess*, Teacher Education, Learning Innovation
and Accountability, https://doi.org/10.1007/978-981-99-6199-3_2

rigorous assessment capacity. When teachers and teacher educators become aware of why certain assessment practices are preferred over others and what alternatives there are, they develop the reflexive awareness that is necessary to take responsive and innovative action. We propose that teacher educators can draw on the four framing concepts in this book to prepare preservice teachers for their roles as reflexive, agentic assessors by focusing on how assessment is connected to:

- Learning and knowing, which we have called **epistemic capacity**.
- Emotional and physical wellbeing, which we have called an **embodied capacity**.
- Fairness and social justice, which we have called **ethical capacity**.
- Everyday practices in school contexts, which we have called **experiential capacity**.

The four capacities are an extension of assessment literacy recommendations that have informed teacher education over the last century and that are explored in detail in Chapter 3. Capacity focuses on the big picture of assessment as a means of understanding and hence changing or finding space for something new at the classroom level. This chapter takes a bird's eye view of assessment policy and practice across four countries to understand some of the cultural messages that shape the landscape of assessor learning and teacher educator assessment education work.

Firstly, we draw on some of Bernstein's (2000) theoretical concepts to describe some new ways of seeing the territories of assessment education. Then, we compare assessment policy contexts in the four countries we as authors hail from, Australia, Canada, England, and New Zealand. Finally, we offer some practical propositions for teacher educators developing assessment capacity with preservice teachers.

2.1 Bernsteinian Perspective on the Assessment Landscape

The dimensions of epistemic, embodied, ethical, and experiential assessment capacity are proposed to enable teacher educators and preservice teachers to think about what is and what is not yet *thinkable* in current assessment practice. As outlined in Chapter 1, we draw on Bernstein's (2000) ideas of assessment, pedagogy, and curriculum as three message systems that communicate what may be represented, accepted, and reproduced within social institutions like schools and universities as *thinkable* or accepted knowledge. Assessment tasks and the achievements they represent are a form of gatekeeping that can enable or deny access to other cultural forms of knowledge, power, and privilege (Lingard et al., 2006). In order to consider how assessment can be thought of in the service of learning for *all* learners, teachers as assessors need to be equipped to ask: *Where are we now? How did we get here? And what is possible?* In asking these questions, they are then able to consider who has the opportunity to participate in the construction, maintenance, and transformation of social order (Bernstein, 2000, p. xxi). In addition to Bernstein's analytical language of *vertical* (canonical) and *horizontal* (local) knowledge explored in Chapter 1, we introduce in this chapter the additional Bernsteinian concepts of *classification* and *framing.* Understanding how assessment policy has been classified and framed is one way of perceiving the message system through which *thinkable* assessment knowledge is transmitted and enacted, and its boundaries are maintained. Recognising what is *thinkable* is an important step for teacher educators to help prepare their preservice teachers to develop a critical perspective and preparedness to problematise the 'naturalness' of the status quo.

Bernstein's (2000) codes of classification and framing are used to help us, as authors, talk about the patterns of assessment knowledge across the four country contexts and how they occur within vertical, or official, and horizontal, or local, discourses. When knowledge is strongly classified, it has clear boundaries, an internal order, and specialised languages that fence the knowledge off and serve to keep it apart and separate from neighbouring ideas. Strongly classified knowledge can appear to be natural and not open to question, and it can also be reproduced readily by those with access to the specialised knowledge and language. The *Standards for Educational and Psychological Testing* (2018) developed by the American Educational Research Association, American Psychological Association, and National Council on Measurement in Education would be an assessment example of strongly classified knowledge. Weakly classified knowledge is less specialised, more integrated, and relies less on clearly defined traditions and texts. Weakly classified knowledge brings ideas from different specialisations together, is less singular, and is more of an integration. Assessment for Learning (AfL) is an example of weakly classified knowledge as it depends on disciplinary knowledge and may not be easily distinguished from pedagogy. Preservice teachers learn which AfL practices are valued and viable in different disciplines and contexts through interactions with teacher educators, mentor teachers in professional practice in schools, students, and colleagues within professional development networks. The theoretical concept of framing refers to how the knowledge is organised and packaged for a learner, either into discrete (strongly framed) or negotiated (weakly framed) curriculum and associated pedagogy. Framing is realised through the social organisation and regulation of learning.

Assessment education, when it is conceptualised as encompassing learning experiences associated with being assessed and how to act as an assessor, is somewhat unique in its framing because nearly everyone will experience some form of assessment education, both in and out of a school setting. The various practices we experience may come to be taken for granted as familiar and commonplace, making them invisible and alternatives hard to imagine. Questioning the naturalness of some assessment practices may generate conflict. Some policymakers or mentor teachers may deride how assessment education is framed by teacher educators as irrelevant to the 'real world' without recognising that real-world assessment is always discursively constructed. Teacher educators have important roles as *framers* who can articulate the *why*, the *how*, as well as the *what* of assessment beyond any list of accepted strategies or purposes. Teacher educators can frame learning about assessment and learning through assessment in ways that make visible some of the often invisible social, emotional, and ethical aspects of being an assessor.

What do the ideas of classification and framing mean for understanding how teacher educators can help preservice teachers learn to be assessors? To illustrate how these theoretical ideas might be helpful to understand assessment practices in action, we share two examples from previous work. The first example brings together assessment practices from teachers at the classroom level, and the second example brings together teacher education practices across nations.

Example 1: Teachers managing tensions across multiple assessment policies

Learning to be an assessor is a continuous process for teachers, especially as new assessment policies and practices are introduced, often at the same time. In this example, teachers in Queensland, Australia were coping with three new assessment policies that were being introduced simultaneously. All of the policies were influencing new teacher assessment practices, but none of the policies referred to the other (Willis et al., 2013). The first policy involved teachers learning new assessment practices to moderate student work in an online community. Teachers had to learn to bring together disciplinary ideas from mathematics that are strongly classified with their weakly classified local understandings of what denotes quality in terms of student justification and reasoning. At the same time, teachers in the second of the studies were working with Indigenous students to prepare them for national numeracy tests. At first, they did not seek out the advice of local Indigenous cultural advisors to learn how the strong classification and framing around mathematics knowledge could be made more culturally accessible. When they did, the teachers were able to recontextualise the learning and assessment to draw on the students' funds of knowledge, a deliberate weakening of the framing. The third assessment policy context involved teachers developing an awareness of AfL practices. Teachers each had different framing and classification practices from one another. Some teachers' AfL practices were being strongly framed through daily learning goals and a self-assessment revision quiz around a strongly framed and classified disciplinary understanding of science. Other teachers positioned the students as decision-makers within comparatively weak framing and classification of social studies. When considered side by side, the theoretical language of classification and framing helped make visible the complex assessment learning that teachers were expected to do. Teachers needed more than assessment knowledge and skills; they needed to actively negotiate and work with assessment ideas in their local contexts. They needed to recontextualise vertical assessment knowledge and use their capacities to establish a local, or horizontal, discourse that could expand their capacity to offer productive learning and assessment opportunities to students.

Example 2: Assessment education in four country contexts

How preservice teachers learn to be an assessor in teacher education courses is influenced by how the assessment programmes are framed. Some of the differences were evident in a 2018 review of a sample of teacher education programmes across Australia, Canada, England, and New Zealand (DeLuca et al., 2019).

Even though the assessment curriculum topics were quite similar, the descriptions showed how they were either strongly framed within a stand-alone course on assessment theory or weakly framed and integrated as part of a curriculum discipline focus. For example, assessment education in Australian programmes was more frequently represented as part of a teaching and learning cycle. That is, it was weakly classified and often taught within curriculum or discipline units. This finding may mean that discipline-informed perspectives on assessment are taught as instructor's horizontal knowledge of assessment practices is foregrounded. Assessment may be positioned as only a minor focus with little theory, and assessment may not be fully developed as a distinct field of knowledge. In contrast, in the initial teacher education courses reviewed in Canada, England, and New Zealand, assessment was often strongly classified as a course of study where the emphasis was on assessment theory and assessment strategies. In these cases, assessment may be insufficiently contextualised to take advantage of the affordances of the different disciplines/learning areas. Since that review, many of these teacher education courses have changed, as have the regulatory environments and the university and schooling experiences, due to COVID-19 and advances in technology. The challenges of integration or specialisation are topics of ongoing inquiry in assessment education (Oo et al., 2022).

Assessment knowledge is always changing. Nonetheless, the way that assessment knowledge is packaged in initial teacher education courses as either separate or integrated is part of the *cultural relay* that Bernstein identified.

Teacher educators have an important role within the cultural relay of the vertical knowledge system about educational practice. Teacher educators relay ideas as they design courses to teach and evaluate preservice teachers, recontextualising research and professional codes of practice and policies. Bernstein proposed that it is possible to trace how power is also relayed through knowledge systems and ask in whose interest is knowledge kept apart or is integration maintained (2000, p. 11). For example, when teacher educators in Australia design ways to build preservice teacher assessment knowledge based on the *Australian Professional Standards for Teachers* (AITSL, 2011) outlined in national *Standard 5: Assess, provide feedback and report on student learning*, they work with a series of strategies and practices that are strongly classified, as assessment is featured as a separate standard from other aspects of teaching. The framing of assessment as separate knowledge keeps assessment apart from some concepts like student agency or curriculum, and neutral language smooths out any hint that these are contestable or would vary in different contexts. In contrast, in England, the Initial Teacher Training (ITT) Framework (The Crown, 2019) includes statements in *Standard 6: Make accurate and productive use of assessment* that are strongly framed like: "Good assessment helps teachers avoid being over-influenced by potentially misleading factors, such as how busy pupils appear" (p. 26). There is a clear message of what 'proper' or strongly classified knowledge of assessment looks like, and the language does not invite debate. In New Zealand's professional standards, the integration is maintained with the same professional standard descriptors applying to experienced and newly qualified teachers; the only difference being the qualifying phrase that graduates will demonstrate the standards 'with support.' Such weakly framed statements of standards have meant that New Zealand teacher educators have needed to engage in many discussions about the meaning of this phrase to create the horizontal forms of knowledge to inform their course designs. How power is relayed through these knowledge systems and others, like codes of ethics in teaching, is made easier to see when expectations are compared between countries.

In this cultural relay of knowledge, teacher educators are always engaged in recontextualising vertical and horizontal knowledge, challenging and adjusting framing in response to contextual requirements. Indeed, teacher educators are also researchers who are creating new knowledge as part of the cultural relay. Assessment capacity is, therefore, a type of ongoing inquiry (Delandshere, 2002). It is ideally reflexive and oriented towards the service of learning.

> The four capacities—epistemic, embodied, ethical, and experiential—are new ways of framing the way that knowledge and curriculum systems are currently operating, opening up assessment education to an ongoing inquiry orientation.

Epistemic and ethical assessment capacities invite educators to ask: *Whose interests are, and are not, being well served by current assessment systems?* Embodied and experiential assessment capacities invite teachers to consider new possibilities by asking: *What are the experiences of students and teachers?* The four capacities can underpin preservice teachers' criticality in a way that can equip them to be agentic in their own classroom; that is, to recognise the discursive power of assessment policy and recontextualise it. Recognition informs action.

2.2 Mapping Similarities in Assessment Education Across Four Countries

In this next section, we map out some more of the similarities in assessment education and policy across the four countries. These sketch outlines are only some of the policies informing teacher education and schooling contexts in Australia, Canada, England, and New Zealand. There are also historical policy settlements and sedimentations, as well as new assessment features on the horizon. We acknowledge that curriculum and assessment policies are always in flux, with changes occurring as we write. Our aim in charting the concept of assessment education across four countries is to point to some familiar patterns appearing in all the countries before the orientations that are striking in their differences. These patterns highlight how assessment education experiences and assumptions are culturally ordered—and, being culturally ordered, are open to question and change.

2.2.1 Assessment Is Strongly Framed Through Shared Education Foundations

The schooling and teacher assessment education landscapes in Australia, Canada, and New Zealand share similar broad foundations with England. Historical colonial governments established by the British Empire imported schooling and assessment traditions from England that ignored and overrode long-standing Indigenous cultural knowledges, worldviews, and approaches to education. Education prior to colonisation had been conducted as a community and family matter, with assessment taking place in culturally embedded ways (Kerr & Averill, 2021; Rameka, 2021). Colonisation meant that formal schooling systems outside of the family and community were established for some young people, with other young people excluded from formal education. Government and church-run schools were established soon after colonisation. There was a formal signing of treaties between England and tangata whenua (Indigenous people)—in New Zealand in the Treaty of Waitangi in 1840, and in England and France and the 364 First Nations in Canada in 70 historic treaties signed between 1701 and 1923 (Government of Canada, 2023). Australia is the only Commonwealth country without a treaty with Aboriginal and Torres Strait Islander people and colonial governments (Burney, 2018), despite ongoing activism for constitutional representation and treaty, including the *Uluru Statement from The Heart* (National Constitutional Convention, 26 May 2017). Assessment histories in these countries are shaped by these colonial beginnings.

The traditions of schooling from England during the eighteenth and nineteenth centuries, with the emergence of mass schooling, reach forward into current assessment practices. The systems of education that had previously occurred in small parish schools, in homes, or through vocational learning could not keep pace with social changes occurring through rapid industrialisation and urbanisation in England. Mass schooling was created through the advocacy of competing interest groups, including those who saw benefits of economic utilitarianism, evangelical religious groups interested in moral development, and workers' collectives interested in human rights (McKay & Firmin, 2008). The mix of government and church education systems drew from a White and Western scientific epistemic paradigm of how individual children are inducted into mastery of formal school knowledge, traditionally by progressing from simple and concrete examples to more abstract general principles.

The education systems in England and the three colonies of Australia, Canada, and New Zealand have typically been designed around strongly classified discipline areas like mathematics, English, science, history, geography, and music, and strongly framed assessment tasks that emphasise standardised ways of representing knowledge, so it appears uncontested and authoritative (McArthur et al., 2022). For much of the twentieth century, assessment functioned as a process of exclusion by sorting students into professions through competition for restricted further education or preferred employment places (Shepard, 2000; Torrance, 2017). Access to opportunity depended on a student's culture, gender, race, and dis/ability, as assessment examinations reflected the cultural values of those who had power, which typically were those with a male upper- and middle-class view of knowledge (Gipps & Murphy, 1994; Stobart, 2008). Assessment was most frequently conducted through examinations (Shepard, 2000).

Assessment has been associated with some devastating consequences for Indigenous peoples; for example, Indigenous students were often excluded from education or, if given access to formal education, were excluded from the assessment activities that could enable them to gain qualifications. Restricting access to credentials or even opportunities to progress to the next grade of schooling through education added to the cumulative effect of dispossession of family, land, language, and identity. For example, the Truth and Reconciliation Commission of Canada's (2015) inquiry into residential schools documented the poor quality of education in these schools and how Indigenous parents were forced to send their children to residential schools by the Indian Act of 1896. Low expectations, overcrowded classrooms, and an emphasis on memorisation meant that students were often not offered the curriculum, pedagogy, and assessment opportunities they needed to progress through schooling or achieve educational credentials. Rameka (2021) writes that the traditional Western assessment practices in New Zealand often led to restricted educational opportunities for Māori children. Assessment is still being experienced in ways that exclude many First Nations learners. In Australia and New Zealand, assessment data is used to construct narratives of deficits about 'achievement gaps,' locating problems within the learner and not problematising wider systems (Shay et al., 2022) or assessment tasks and processes (Hardy, 2015). Yet, recognition of the cultural impact of assessment, and the epistemic assumptions that underpin assessment practices, is also more positive, leading to some possibilities for change. For example, in New Zealand, te reo Māori is an official language, and students are able to complete formal assessment tasks in te reo Māori. NZQA, as the formal exit assessment agency, is developing 'aromatawai' as Kaupapa Māori perspective on assessment (NZQA, 2022). In Ontario, Canada, Indigenous education—including Indigenous history, culture and traditions, and current issues facing Indigenous peoples —is now part of the core curriculum with additional course offerings in secondary education context (e.g., Indigenous languages). Similarities in colonial foundations also inform assessment education more broadly.

Even though cultural values and power relationships have become more diverse in the twenty-first century, many of these early assessment systems and assumptions reach forward into current practice. For instance, even now, assessment is often seen as synonymous with examinations that are conducted without support resources and under time constraints, reflecting value priorities of individualism, competition, and efficiency associated with early industrial schooling (Tai et al., 2022). These values can be reflected in initial teacher education courses and assessment education that equate assessment education with a focus on individual assessment and making sure preservice teachers can prepare their students for examinations and how to grade reliably. We would argue that assessment capacity includes an awareness of these educational epistemic foundations and assessment purposes that have traditionally underpinned summative examinations. It also includes an awareness of how assessment is strongly framed by international policies.

2.2.2 Assessment Is Strongly Framed by International Policies

From the 1980s onwards, assessment policy systems in the four countries have advocated for both formative assessment activities during teaching and learning and summative assessment activities at the end of curriculum units. Teacher education courses have reflected this change of focus in their assessment education to include a greater emphasis on formative assessment or Assessment for Learning (AfL), with this shift occurring to a greater extent in England, Canada, and New Zealand than in Australia. Additionally, from the 2000s onwards, national and international high-stakes assessment regimes like PISA (Programme for International Student Assessment) have had increasing influence (Hardy et al., 2021). PISA's proliferation globally has been enabled by big data computational systems that provide fast, sophisticated analysis of large data sets that have resulted in international comparisons and league tables, meta-data on test-taking actions being captured, and online and dynamic assessment being facilitated (Sellar, 2015). Assessment education and expertise have broadened beyond the education profession to include data infrastructure engineers, learning analytics systems, and edu-businesses which have created new spaces and relations of, and for, educational governance through measurement of the performance of schools in different national systems. Large-scale assessment data has contributed to greater public faith in numbers and made visible persistent inequities in participation and outcomes for some student groups. This has allowed for more strategic resource allocations; however, when there has been little critical analysis in policymaking, this has led to deficit framing of some groups and positioned achievement gaps as a lack in students or teachers rather than a structural issue (Selwyn et al., 2022). Critique and analysis of assessment equity within international and digital assessment regimes require more than teaching to a test (Stobart, 2005); however, such critique is part of the yet-to-be fully realised capacities to be developed through most teacher preparation courses of assessment education. To enable critique, there is a need for more teacher educator knowledge of quickly evolving assessment technologies and collaboration with data infrastructure engineers and others to contribute to equitable assessment infrastructures that are evolving at speed.

The nature of equitable assessment and equitable education is explored further in Chapter 6 and is sketched out here as it is a shared influential assessment focus across the four countries outlined in this book. The UNESCO report *Learning: The Treasure Within* (Delors, 1996) put forward an expansive agenda of four pillars of education—Learning to know, Learning to do, Learning to live together, and Learning to be. In many ways, this report could be seen as providing a lead for equitable national agendas through its holistic focus on lifelong learning, knowledge and action, the collective, and identity, the latter encapsulated in the phrase "learning to be." An agenda of equity through education is evident in several international declarations, including the *United Nations Convention on the Rights of the Child* (UN, 1989), the *Declaration on the Rights of Indigenous Peoples* (UN, 2007), and the *Convention on the Rights of Persons with Disabilities* (UN, 2006). More recently, the United Nations launched *Transforming Our World: The 2030 Agenda for Sustainable Development* (UN, 2015). The UN Sustainable Development Goals aim to provide a "shared blueprint for peace and prosperity for people and the planet, now and into the future" (see https://sdgs.un.org/goals). Within these goals, Goal 4 states that education aims to: *Ensure inclusive and quality education for all and promote lifelong learning.* Equitable assessment, access, and outcomes are everyday and real concerns for teachers and teacher educators who ask:

> How can we address current systemic inequities? How can assessment practice respond to the increasing diversity of classrooms as a result of globalisation, where this diversity includes the presence of refugee and migrant children who may have experienced trauma, recognition of the impacts of colonisation on Indigenous peoples, and of COVID-19?

These questions are why assessment education is more than a list of skills. Rather, it is important work for teacher educators who critically inquire, conduct research, and develop the field so that they can share their knowledge with their preservice teachers. These teachers can then be supported to critically inquire into their own practice and the experiences of their students and plan for more equitable assessment practices.

2.2.3 Assessment as Weakly Framed in Response to Student Voice and Student Agency

Another shared policy framing of assessment that is starting to feature is that of student agency within the assessment process. The OECD 2030 *Education Futures Learning Compass* places student agency and co-agency with others as the central concern for schools for the future. The website for this policy sets out student voices from across the globe, critiquing how traditional assessment is not fit for students' current experiences or their future needs where knowledge is always expanding (OECD, 2022). Authentic assessment practices are represented by the OECD as opportunities to contribute to personal and community wellbeing, future problem-solving, and economic innovation. This emphasis on students' more active role in assessment and curriculum is reflective of the concept of respecting students' funds of knowledge and aspirations (Cowie et al., 2010; Zipin et al., 2015). Assessment that respects, responds to, and fosters children's funds of knowledge and aspirations is framed as more than an economic imperative. It is deeply connected to how children

2.2 Mapping Similarities in Assessment Education Across Four Countries

invest in learning: "When a child's worldview is left unvalued and expressionless in an educational setting, what should we expect in terms of engagement, investment and learning from that child?" (Calabrese Barton et al., 2011, p. 4). A challenge for assessors and for assessment education will be to reconcile that not everything that students know and are learning can be, or needs to be, fully assessed and communicated. To respond to this practicality, assessment may need to be accepted as weakly classified—that is, integrated within the knowledges and ways of expression of local communities—and weakly framed—associated with learning and the child's identity as a learner.

Teacher educator awareness of how assessment is framed is one way to bring these ideas to life for teachers. For example, framing assessment as enabling student voice and agency will impact whether knowledge is presented as constructed or received (see Chapter 4). When students only experience strongly classified knowledge, any mystery about the development of new knowledge, or the contestability of disciplinary knowledge, has been removed (Bernstein, 2000). Cultural and community knowledges are made invisible and *unthinkable* by strongly framed knowledge construction and assessment processes that highlight Western scientific traditions (Kerr, 2014; Shay & Lampert, 2022). Ideals of collaboration and student agency invite teachers to question the assumptions that all valued learning is individual and objective, that all valued learning takes place in schools, and that assessment is always a formal, individual process. Shay et al. (2022, p. 2) powerfully argue for a future of collaborative educational policy construction where "what counts as evidence should privilege Indigenous voices, intellectualism, sovereignties, strengths, and aspirations" (p. 2). An example of this intent can be found in the current refresh of the curriculum in New Zealand, which aims to provide equal status to Mātauranga Māori (i.e., Māori knowledge and worldviews) (New Zealand Government, 2022). Making these kinds of aspirational assessment changes to enable student agency may seem like a big task for teacher educators and teachers; however, teacher educators are critical and important framers of assessment possibility.

Teachers across the four country contexts are also engaging in the affordances of digital data as a responsive assessment opportunity. Instead of being one summative task, assessment is being reconstituted as digitally integrated activities in response to local needs or the personal interests of the learner. Digital data compiled through school learning management systems and teacher and student portfolios is transforming assessment from a traditional, strongly framed, and classified process to being something that is more horizontal and occurring through the accumulation of small data points gathered through collaborative, exploratory learning (Cope & Kalantzis, 2016). In Australia, such representations are evident in Big Picture schools and the New Metrics for Success project (Melbourne Graduate School of Education, 2023) that aim to capture more complex capabilities. The Records of Learning in New Zealand (Te Tāhuhu o te Mātauranga | Ministry of Education, 2023) aims to provide holistic, strengths-based records of learning that show the progress of each learner. Simultaneously, teacher educators need to be wary of the way that digital big data can promulgate assessment and assessment results as objective and valid measures of the quality of education systems and schools, and what counts as a 'good' teacher (Selwyn et al., 2022), rather than representations that invite critical inquiry.

Another future-oriented assessment similarity in the four focus countries is occurring in the way that curriculum is being framed. There is a similarity in the way that policies are being framed to argue that students need to be prepared for the future (or, as we have represented in this book, to *think the unthinkable*) as we face global uncertainties and unknown futures. Lists of lifelong and lifewide learning skills have emerged as transversal competencies that span the breadth of the curriculum. New thinking is evident in how some previously strongly classified curriculum areas are becoming more weakly classified. Language studies now may include literature, semiotics, media studies, and cultural production of texts. Science, technology, and mathematics are often now integrated as STEM (science, technology, engineering, and mathematics) and, with the addition of art, as STEAM. Interestingly, this shift has led to the need for students to understand the epistemological aspects of the different disciplines that are being integrated through STEM as an overarching goal that offers both distinction and coherence to the concepts and practices of interest (Elby, 2022). Yet, alongside increasing innovation, there are increasing conservative calls for more prescription within traditional disciplines. Such neo-traditional calls can be attractive, as deliberately weakly framed curriculum can be more demanding on teachers as they make more decisions about what to teach, when, and where. Neo-traditional forms of curriculum thinking do not necessarily require many changes to assessment education, as assessment traditions have been slow to transform to accommodate weakly classified knowledge. Yet there are shared concerns about how traditional forms of assessment are impacting student wellbeing (Cho & Chan, 2020) and the impact of traditional assessment practices like feedback, grading, and reporting on teacher wellbeing and teacher workloads (Stacey et al., 2023). Changes towards transdisciplinary and multimodal knowledge making may feel messy for teachers or teacher educators. Weakly framed curriculum approaches have the potential to enable previously *unthinkable* ideas. As ways of communicating new ideas become enticingly *thinkable* through new media and technologies, there are also new possibilities relating to assessment practice and potential. Teacher educators can prepare newly qualified teachers to engage with these currently *unthinkable* trends early in their careers, even if it is just articulating how, as teachers, we are always learning and can be part of the reframing of assessment within the profession.

2.2.4 Assessment Education Framing Is Occurring Within and Beyond Teacher Education

An additional similarity in policy across the four countries is how the decision of what assessment education is needed and how to teach it is no longer just the domain of teacher educators. Assessment education is increasingly being shaped by a wide range of decision-makers, including government, policy and professional bodies, regulators, university administrators, researchers, mentor teachers, and preservice teachers themselves. Increasingly in each country, community groups, parents, media, global edu-businesses, and assessment organisations are policy actors who are influencing the directions for students and teacher assessment education. In New Zealand, the national qualifications authority makes exemplar tasks available to teachers, and NZCER (New Zealand Council for Educational Research) produces standardised multiple choice tests in school Years 3–10 in mathematics, reading, and writing. In Australia, the initial teacher education literacy and numeracy benchmark assessment tasks are produced and scored by ACER (Australian Council for Educational Research), a private assessment company. While teacher education is less driven by external agencies across Canadian provinces, the policy landscape and accreditation agencies promote essential content. For example, in Ontario, *Growing Success: Assessment, Evaluation and Reporting in Ontario Schools (2010)* is an expected and necessary text within teacher education programmes, structuring a strongly vertical learning context (Ontario Ministry of Education, 2010).

In all four countries, teacher educators from university and tertiary settings have traditionally prepared teachers in partnerships with mentor teachers where preservice teachers do practical placements in school classrooms. However, the pre-eminence of teacher educators and established patterns of university-school partnerships in support of teacher education are being challenged. The ongoing removal of teacher education from universities to take place fully in school sites is a long-term trend in England that is the result of ongoing government deregulation. Another common and recent trend in teacher education in each of the countries is a movement from a policy focus on auditing teacher education programme plans and inputs (e.g., programme design, learning outcomes, and tasks) to auditing outputs; that is, whether programme assessment tasks allow preservice teachers to demonstrate prescribed programme outcomes. These outcomes of teacher education programmes are often linked to nationally established and monitored criteria for practice (Pullin, 2017). In England and Australia, the growing mistrust in teacher judgement and teacher education (Mockler & Stacey, 2021) is reflected in the increasing regulation of teacher education, with government policies like the *ITT Core Content Framework (2019)* in England and *Accreditation of Initial Teacher Education Programs in Australia: Standards and Procedures (2015)* (Mayer & Mills, 2021). The Australian Government introduced Literacy and Numeracy Tests for Initial Teacher Education Students (LANTITE) in 2016 and the Graduate Performance Assessment task as requirements for graduation by 2019. These policies are the latest within an increasing accountability culture that uses managerial approaches through compliance with standards, inspections, and data known as the Global Education Reform Movement (GERM). Sahlberg (2016) traces the origins of GERM from Hargreaves' early work and in policy through the 1988 Education Reform Act in England, a market logic of policy standards, increased competition between schools, and more public information and accountability provided by standardised national and international testing of students. The Programme for International Student Assessment (PISA), Trends in International Mathematics and Science Study (TIMSS), and Progress in International

Reading Literacy Study (PIRLS) large-scale assessments have directed the focus of governments through fast policy borrowing (Hardy et al., 2021). Teacher performance conditions are also a focus of international measurement and comparison through TALIS, the OECD Teaching and Learning International Survey. Together these trends represent a shifting dynamic for the role of teacher educators whose work is mediated by a growing network of policy actors.

For example, whether as a result of GERM or other policy borrowing, it is evident in the OECD TALIS data from 2018 that there is a similar focus across the four countries on how teachers are expected to use assessment (OECD, 2019), with assessment practices outlined in Table 2.1

. Canadian provinces each decide whether to participate in TALIS, with the province of Alberta's responses included in the table as indicative data. These items reflect an attempt to strengthen the policy framing of assessment practice in classrooms as they do not focus on teachers' knowledge *about* assessment but rather on *how* teachers integrate assessment into learning. By being a measure and comparison of assessment practice, the measure then also works to create an expected standard for teacher assessment practice and, therefore, teacher education in assessment.

These data suggest there are strong similarities across the four countries of the teacher's role in assessment, with some intriguing small differences. Teachers frequently report that they monitor student progress and provide feedback, an indication that AfL is a familiar policy in the four country contexts. What is not clear is whether teachers interpret these broad concepts in similar ways, as assessment terms that use similar words may be understood as quite different across contexts, as highlighted in the next section.

Across the four countries, some of the strong similarities in assessment education that have been raised so far include that assessment is:

- strongly classified and framed through shared similar education foundations;
- strongly framed through shared current commitments in international policies;
- weakly classified when integrating more student voice and collaboration; and

Table 2.1 Teacher reported assessment practices from the TALIS survey (2018)

Assessment survey items from the TALIS survey (2018)	OECD average (%)	Australia (%)	Alberta, Canada (%)	England (%)	New Zealand (%)
Teachers routinely assess their students' progress by observing them and providing immediate feedback	79	89	87	88	89
Teachers report administering their own assessments to their student	77	74	94	76	73
Teachers frequently let students evaluate their own progress	41	44	42	69	49

- changing from being framed substantially by teacher educators to being framed by policy.

The following short overviews of policies now point to a few key differences between assessment education cultures in the four countries to highlight capacities for change and the potential for new liberating assessment microstructures and landscapes.

2.3 Mapping Differences Between Assessment Education Policy Contexts

We begin our description of the country context with England as the 'mother' country for the education systems in the other three countries, while acknowledging how each country has evolved in response to local circumstances.

2.3.1 England

In England, what preservice teachers learn about assessment is deeply influenced by a culture of accountability and audit to a pervasive extent, a clear difference between the four countries. Summative assessment of student learning is linked to the assessment of teachers and schools through national curriculum, assessment, and the school inspection system. Assessment is strongly framed as a neutral and accurate measure of teaching even more than student learning, with official policy documents proposing that teachers and schools are "properly accountable to pupils, parents and the taxpayer for the achievement and progress of every child, on the basis of objective and accurate assessments" (Gove, 2010, para 3). The 1988 Education Reform Act introduced a prescriptive national curriculum with an assessment system based on external testing at the end of key stages at ages 7, 11, 14, and 16. The Act also introduced the publication of school performance tables which incentivised schools to maximise their results on the assumption parents would select the 'best' school for their children. Even when, in 2014, a new national curriculum was introduced into primary schools—extending greater freedom to teachers in curriculum and assessment to meet expectations for the end of each key stage—teacher performance descriptors were developed to monitor teacher assessment alongside external tests.

With more than 13 different pathways to becoming a teacher in England (Whiting et al., 2018), teacher educators and university-based initial teacher education (ITE) courses have a rapidly reducing influence on assessment preparation. Hartley (1998) noted that the centralised prescription of curriculum and assessment in schools was paralleled by government prescription of initial teacher education. Prescription has been coupled with continuous government reforms that have privileged the increasing role of schools as the site for teacher preparation, most recently following the Carter review of initial teacher training (ITT) (Carter, 2015). The development of *Core Content for Initial Teacher Education* (The Crown, 2019) reflects the tension between increasing devolution of responsibility for teacher education to schools and increasing regulatory oversight (Mutton et al., 2017). School-based contexts are weakly classified, reflecting a policy philosophy of learning to teach through apprenticeship. Preservice teachers experience assessment as a form of auditing and accountability, resulting in what Mayer and Mills (2021) describe as a *technical* and *craft* view of teaching.

The assessment culture created by these policies inevitably informs and regulates teachers' and students' assessment practices. Since 1992, the Office for Standards in Education (OFSTED) has had inspectors report on student achievement, the quality of the teaching, the quality of leadership, and student management in schools. A school's overall performance is judged as one of the following: outstanding, good, requires improvement, or inadequate. Along with school visits, the inspection process involves the distribution of questionnaires to parents, students, and school staff. OFSTED also regulates assessment education by providing standards and reviews of ITE providers. Preservice teachers are judged by OFSTED during their practical placements in schools, with the performance of the preservice teacher in their first year used to make judgements about the ITE programme in terms of its quality and partnership with schools.

The English assessment system is high stakes and highly regulated, with seemingly limited freedom for teachers to make decisions about curriculum, pedagogy, and assessment. Yet, within this restricted assessment education context, there has also been a formidable focus on Assessment for Learning (AfL) since 1998, through the advocacy and work of teacher educators and assessment researchers in successive teacher action research projects (Assessment Reform Group, 1999; Black & Wiliam, 1998; Harrison, 2005). AfL is a response to restrictive assessment cultures and emphasises the role of teachers and students learning together through day-to-day classroom assessment practices. This initiative illustrates that innovation is possible even in an apparently closed system, opening up the need to prepare teachers to look for opportunities to work within systems for students.

2.3.2 Australia

An informative distinction in Australia's assessment education landscape is in the way that assessment is caught between the remits of a federal government that provides funding to schools and universities and uses assessment data for quality assurance; the six state and two territory governments that retain constitutional responsibility for schooling, and three schooling choices each with different governance and decision-making systems (State, Catholic, and Independent). Assessment is most often referred to in public discourse in a strongly classified way as providing data for league tables that inform policy and system reforms or as an

2.3 Mapping Differences Between Assessment Education Policy Contexts

outcome of schooling to be used for university entrance. For example, the Australian federal government introduced a national assessment sampling scheme in literacy and numeracy (NAPLAN) in 2008, before a national curriculum for Prep to Senior (Year 12) was introduced in 2010. NAPLAN was intended as a low-stakes assessment task for students to be used formatively by schools as it was not a measure of specific school curriculum but rather a generalised sample of cross-curricular literacy and numeracy levels of students in Years 3, 5, 7, and 9. Even though it was weakly framed and classified, it quickly had the effect of being a high-stakes assessment process. A national website, MySchool, enabled parents to compare schools based on NAPLAN results, among other data, with the media regularly creating league tables to rank schools. As a result, many schools began to focus on NAPLAN preparation with the effect that it began to strongly frame and direct the curriculum (Klenowski, 2015), and teachers, leaders, and students experienced greater performance pressures (Howell, 2017; Spina, 2019). The accountability discourse associated with NAPLAN echoes that of England with school choice and data-driven accountability decision-making but differs in some essential ways. In Australia, the assessment national testing accountability network does not include a single prescriptive curriculum, multiple high-stakes summative assessment tasks, or a reinforcing inspectorate from within a single authority.

Assessment policy is not clearly articulated at a national level in Australia beyond the NAPLAN testing discourse and some broad assessment standards expressed in *The Australian Curriculum Framework, Prep to Senior (Year 12)* in 2010. Rather, assessment is strongly classified by each state, territory, and employer group, and each takes responsibility for articulating policy that impacts practice. Each state and territory has a curriculum and assessment authority that interprets the national standards into local syllabi and assessment guidelines and policies for schools and teachers to apply. These broad guidelines have the effect of enabling Australian teachers to continue a long history of having a great deal of autonomy in assessment design, grading, and responsibility for teachers' social moderation of results for most school year levels (Adie et al., 2012). The variety of schooling systems means that levers for national regulation of schools are diffused through state agreements and national frameworks, such as the *Australian Professional Standards for Teachers* (AITSL, 2011). However, assessment education is being increasingly strongly classified and framed through the Australian federal government, which has the power to regulate teacher education.

It is not surprising that teacher education is seen as an arena for national education change when teacher education institutions are funded and regulated by the Australian federal government. After the federal Dawkins review of 1988, teacher preparation in Australia shifted from colleges to university degrees, currently either 4-year undergraduate or 2-year post-graduate courses offered in over 400 courses from 40 higher education providers. Universities in Australia are not-for-profit, receive most of their funding from the federal government, and are regulated by the federal government through accreditation and review cycles. The pervasiveness of the federal government using teacher education as a lever to intervene in education is demonstrated by the fact that there have been over 100 government reviews of teacher education conducted since the 1970s (Louden, 2008), the latest having been commissioned in September 2022 (Clare, 2022). Assessment of preservice teachers increasingly features in these reviews. For example, the *Action Now: Classroom Ready Teachers* (2014) review required teacher graduates to produce teaching portfolio assessments (TPAs) of evidence from their teaching practice that show "positive impact on student learning" (AITSL, 2015, p. 45). National regulations give the rationale that "robust assessment of teacher education students is vital to giving schools and families the confidence that graduates are classroom ready" (Australian Government, February 2015, p. 8). Assessment of preservice teachers is associated with quality assurance, with teacher educators facing greater restrictions in their course design (Churchward & Willis, 2019). However, teacher educators still have a high degree of agency in the framing of assessment education as they integrate assessment education most frequently through discipline-based courses, supporting preservice teachers to learn to design, enact, grade, and moderate school-based assessment (DeLuca et al., 2019; Gallagher et al., 2022). A direct result of an increase in government regulation has been that preservice teachers experience the tensions of having high-stakes assessments govern their teacher preparation experiences while, at the same time, being prepared to have a great deal of agency in their assessment practices as teachers.

Teachers having a great deal of assessment responsibility is not new in Australia, but the cultural pressure associated with assessment is new. Cultural conditions include persistent government policy narratives that blame teacher educators and teachers for falling PISA results, media narratives criticising teachers more than any other profession (Mockler, 2022), and increasing data-driven accountability without additional time for the work (Stacey et al., 2023). These conditions have created a climate of teacher stress that is fuelling a national teacher shortage (Australian Government, December 2022). While teachers and teacher educators are the policy actors who experience the tensions, they are also the agents who still have some freedom to interpret the effects of the intersections of these policies. In the middle of these tensions, there remains some opportunity to carefully attend to *what is* and think of *what next* in assessment and assessment education.

2.3.3   Canada

A point of difference in assessment education in Canada is the decentralised but collaborative approach to assessment policy design. Provincial education has been established since 1867 and the British North America Act, with the result that Canada does not have a national office of education. The ten provinces and three territories regulate all aspects of primary school through to post-secondary education (Smyth & Hamel, 2016). While separate in jurisdictions, the various provincial and territorial perspectives on assessment are relatively consistent. Education policy is driven through ministries of education that engage professional and academic organisations, enabling a consistent emphasis on standards-based education and the use of assessment to support student learning, including principles associated with assessment, AfL, and test development (DeLuca et al., 2017). The culture of collaboration and standards-based principles of education somewhat reflects Canada's geographic proximity to the USA, with its strong psychometric tradition of assessment standards (DeLuca et al., 2016), and the negotiation required to navigate cultural diversity inherent in Canada with English and French colonial traditions.

Similarly, teacher education is guided by ministries of education, provincial accreditation agencies, and principles developed through a democratic process of collaboration from the 62 member institutions within the Association of Canadian Deans of Education (ACDE) network, representing every province in Canada (Magnusson et al., 2016). The *Deans' Accord on Initial Teacher Education* (Collins & Tierney, 2006), for example, deliberately avoids the concepts of standards, instead identifying 12 principles to guide individual institutions in teacher education programme development and accreditation, a form of purposeful weak framing. Each province has separate certification requirements, and teachers' professionalisation and teacher education are governed either by the provincial government or by self-regulating bodies.

Teacher education in Canada has not seen a relatively heavy focus in policy arenas; yet, the tensions of neo-liberal emphases on student and parental choice, individual freedoms, competition, and accountability are evident alongside the activism "from teacher education institutions and the profession itself for more autonomy and respect, with a desire for greater professionalization and self-regulation" (Walker & von Bergmann, 2013, p. 87). Assessment is strongly framed as a social and political act by the ACDE principles. For example, the second principle "envisions the teacher as a professional who observes, discerns, critiques, assesses, and acts accordingly" (p. 1). Preservice teacher education in assessment is designed by teacher educators who are recognised as highly influential role models, advocates, and provocateurs (DeLuca et al., 2018). However, within teacher education, assessment has played a comparatively marginal role until recently, when more teacher education programmes are endorsing dedicated courses to assessment (DeLuca & Bellara, 2013). Importantly, DeLuca notes that preservice teacher programmes can act as a pivotal point-of-change from largely summative conceptions of assessment towards more learning-oriented conceptions and skills; however, positive orientations towards fairness for students through assessment need to be supported by more comprehensive understandings of the complexities of assessment in theory and practice in Canadian schools (Rasooli et al., 2022). With an emphasis on fairness and classroom-based assessment, a high level of assessment capability is expected of Canadian teachers.

There is "surprising consistency" of assessment expectations within the provincial and territory policies that teachers will "implement continuous assessments to facilitate, track, and report on student learning in relation to curriculum expectations" (DeLuca et al., 2018. p. 172). Assessment in schools involves teachers in all stages of the development of regional, provincial, and national tests and the associated materials such as scoring guides, rubrics, and the choosing of exemplars for use in scoring.

Professional development in assessment is largely offered at the school district level. However, evidence of GERM and assessment used for accountability purposes is noted in provincial policy and in teacher assessment practices (Copp, 2019). For example, in Ontario, the desire for accountability and data to inform system improvement led to the creation of mid-stakes testing by the Education Quality and Accountability Office (EQAO). Assessment results were made public for parental choice of school and for district directors and superintendents to inform interventions but were not used for more punitive outcomes like school closures, as has been evident in the USA and England. Hargreaves (2020) identified how the EQAO policy has had both positive and negative impacts, prompting current concerns about how assessment can be more inclusive, how to attend to effects on student wellbeing, and how continued focus on test preparation reduces possibilities for innovation. The integrated framing of assessment as related to student learning, supported by long-term investment in teacher professional learning and collaborative inquiry in assessment, has led to a developmental assessment approach that expects teachers to be highly assessment literate and capable throughout their careers.

2.3.4 New Zealand

New Zealand's education system is distinctive in that, while there is a single national Ministry of Education, schools are 'self-managing.' State schools are governed by Boards of Trustees, which include the school principal, a staff member elected by the school staff, a student representative, and several trustees elected by the parents of current students. Teachers and English-medium schools have considerable freedom and flexibility to develop teaching programmes that best suit their students within the broad framework of the *New Zealand Curriculum* (Ministry of Education, 2007). Te Marautanga o Aotearoa (Ministry of Education, 2007) provides the curriculum framework for Māori medium schools and is also used by some English-medium schools. National assessment policy has placed substantial significance on teachers' use of formative assessment over a sustained period of years (Crooks, 1988, 2011; New Zealand Department of Education, 1989; New Zealand Ministry of Education, 1994, 2007, 2011, 2020; Nusche et al., 2012). Schools are charged with and trusted to develop their own more formal assessment and reporting systems.

Ministry documents across time reiterate that students should be at the centre of the assessment process, ideally taking an active role in using assessment to evaluate and advance their own learning. Assessment is positioned as strongly framed by these policy documents, foregrounding student learning but also having a role in sharing information with a range of stakeholders in a manner that is consistent with education as a system that learns. Assessment is construed as weakly classified (not separated) as it is seen as highly integrated with curriculum, lifelong student learning, and teacher and family contributions. Family and whānau are positioned as partners in the assessment process through a process of *ako*, teaching and learning as reciprocally related.

2.3 Mapping Differences Between Assessment Education Policy Contexts

The notion of teacher assessment capability was introduced to define the assessment expertise that teachers need to possess in the 2009 *Directions for Assessment in New Zealand* report (Absolum et al., 2009) and has been further developed by Hipkins and Cameron (2018). These documents endorse the priority and value accorded to the centrality of students to the assessment process and assessment as a partnership between teachers and families. They reiterate the focus on the role of assessment in a system that learns. Overall, a cultural preference for integrated and responsive assessment policy—or weak classification and framing—is evident in the distinctive feature that New Zealand has no comprehensive assessment system for students from school entry to Year 10. National standards in reading, writing, and mathematics for primary-aged students were introduced at the beginning of the 2010 school year and withdrawn in 2017 with a change of government. System-level data has been generated through light sampling as part of the National Monitoring Study of Student Achievement (NMSSA, formally the National Education Monitoring Project) since 1995. These national and international assessment regimes have provided evidence of equity concerns related to the participation and achievement of Māori and Pasifika students and students from lower socioeconomic backgrounds (e.g., May, 2019). This issue has been addressed in a suite of policies that offer guidance on culturally responsive pedagogy (New Zealand Ministry of Education, 2020) that includes an emphasis on teachers generating and using a range of data to inform and monitor student learning and portray the two-way exchange of information with families and whānau as central to helping students learn.

Senior secondary students (school Years 11, 12, and 13) are assessed by a combination of internally and externally assessed achievement standards via the National Certificate of Educational Achievement (NCEA) exit qualification. Teachers are responsible for designing teaching programmes and developing and marking tasks that assess the internal achievement standards, with a sample of data moderated (Hipkins et al., 2016). There is some evidence that teachers may limit their practice of formative assessment to preparing for formal internal assessment tasks (Hume & Coll, 2009; Moeed, 2015). On the other hand, some teachers have exploited the flexibility across NCEA and the curriculum to design senior secondary teaching programmes that increase the study options available to their students (Trask & Cowie, 2022). The New Zealand curriculum refresh *Te Mātaiaho* is shifting the curriculum and assessment landscape as all learning areas become structured around *Understand* (the big ideas), *Know* (rich contexts for exploring the big ideas), and *Do* (practices that bring rigour to learning). Within the refresh, equal status is accorded to mātauranga Māori (Māori knowledge). *Te Mātaiaho* has introduced an approach to progression that replaces year levels with five phases of learning (Y1–3, Y4–6, Y7–8, Y9–10, and Y11–13) intended to act as signposts that guide student learning pathways. This development is complemented by a refresh of the Māori medium curriculum and of *aromatawai* as a process grounded on Māori values, aspirations, and practices that is similar but not the same as *assessment* in the conventional sense.

Preservice teacher education is situated within the seven national universities and a number of private providers, 27 institutions in total. All providers are required to meet specific requirements as set out in the *ITE Programme Approval, Monitoring and Review Requirements* (New Zealand Teaching Council, 2019). The requirements include that programmes provide opportunities for preservice teachers to engage with *Our Code, Our Standards/ Ngā Tikanga Matatika Ngā Paerewa* (Education Council, 2017). In line with international trends, the 2019 ITE requirements shifted the focus for accreditation of programme inputs (learning outcomes) to an audit of programme assessments, with these taken as evidence of what learning graduates would have demonstrated at graduation. At least some programme assessment tasks are required to be co-designed with teachers as part of provider and school/teacher partnership in support of teacher learning. Every programme assessment framework needs to include a 'culminating integrative assessment' that assesses the integration of theory and practice and the synthesis of student learning across the Code and Standards. Institutions are free to design their own curriculum and assessments within the frame of the ITE requirements. While not as strongly regulated by government policy as it is in England or Australia, there is evidence of emerging concern in New Zealand about this stronger classification in the university sector in relation to academic freedom (Couch et al., 2022). An earlier study by Smith et al. (2014), which investigated the development of 'assessment capable' teachers, identified that, in some instances, assessment education was a standalone campus-based course, and in others, it was embedded across courses; in all cases, it featured as part of preservice teachers' school-based practical requirements and evaluation. Teacher education also includes the first two years teachers are responsible for a class. During this time, their workload is reduced, they are assigned a mentor teacher, and they may meet in regional cohorts. Ongoing professional development related to effective assessment occurs via targeted programmes for teachers and principals (Crooks, 2011), with teacher assessment capability being a well-recognised foundation for all teachers.

2.4   Differences in the Classification and Framing of Assessment Education

Across the four countries, the differences in assessment education include some general patterns that demonstrate how knowledge is both strongly and weakly classified across the contexts (see also Fig. 2.1):

- In England, assessment education seems more strongly classified and strongly framed as the broader assessment system is high stakes and highly regulated. Assessment for Learning (AfL) guidance is also clearly, strongly framed and provides spaces for teacher action.
- In Australia, assessment education is nationally more strongly classified around accountability purposes, with states and territories providing the specialist shared assessment language and processes that guide teachers. General assessment strategies expressed in professional standards, initial teacher education regulations, and schooling systems' advice operate as a weak/moderate framing.

2.4 Differences in the Classification and Framing of Assessment Education

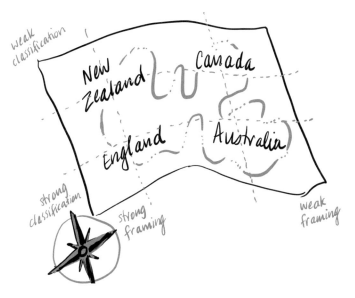

Fig. 2.1 Schematic representation of assessment classification (strong/weak) by country

- In Canada, assessment education is weakly classified as being integrated with learning at a provincial level, with highly integrated framing around assessment as a process of system and individual learning. Learning about assessment happens largely through short courses in preservice programmes and through school-based practical (i.e., practicum) experiences. For in-service teachers, school districts offer professional development opportunities, often within a framework of collaborative inquiry.
- In New Zealand, assessment is weakly classified; that is, it is positioned as integral to teaching and learning. While long-standing policy strongly frames Assessment for Learning (AfL) as a social good, there is evidence of deliberately weakening policy framing as collaborations with students and communities become an active priority.

The policy histories of the four countries reflect a British colonial heritage in their formal organisation of schooling and assessment that is mostly based on teachers designing tasks to evaluate disciplinary knowledge. Yet, the histories of each country have led to important differences. In New Zealand, there has been a consistent focus on students at the centre of assessment and policies that emphasise partnership and equity in assessment. In Canada and Australia, the relationships between federal and state/province governments have led to layered assessment policies, with Canadian provinces having autonomy through collaborative national accords and Australia increasing national regulation of teacher education, similar to the way assessment is being directed mainly towards national accountability purposes in England.

These are broad generalisations and are selected to highlight key differences in order to show how important the social and cultural contexts are for teacher assessment education. While assessment skills and practices may have the same names in different contexts, teachers come to learn about them in different ways. None of the contexts reflects an optimal blend of policies, but all of them offer opportunities for teacher action and agency in assessment. There is an overall trend to acknowledge the importance of student voice and wellbeing, to view student diversity as a resource to be considered and celebrated, and to recognise the challenges for teachers when assessment is used more for accountability than for learning purposes. The overviews are intended to offer perspectives for teacher educators to consider and to highlight the importance of learning from one another.

2.5 Assessment Education Curriculum: Complex, Ever-Changing Decisions

The assessment education landscape reflects assessment priorities that *were*—reflecting histories, that *are*—how and what assessment priorities are integrated into policies and practices, and that point to *what could be*. This chapter highlights the pivotal role of the teacher educator and the importance of understanding the broader landscape of assessment education.

2.5.1 Conversations Across Contexts as Stories of Possibility

As noted by DeLuca et al. (2019), assessment education "appears to almost always be in a state of responsive flux" (p. 87). Hardy et al. (2021) also note how valuable it is to compare contexts for initial teacher education to recognise the possibilities within seemingly similar prescriptive policy landscapes. It is not often that, as teacher educators, we get the luxury of exploring the assessment landscapes in other contexts. Yet, in conversations across the four country contexts about similarities and differences, the multiple perspectives have helped us look at our own assessment education contexts in new ways. We have been able to reflect on the ways that assessment and curriculum policy, and traditions in education organise our attention and sensitivities. Seeing how assessment priorities are culturally ordered and where assessment education is strongly or weakly classified or framed, and by whom, has led us to ask previously *unthinkable* questions. When it has seemed that what was *thinkable* about assessment education is increasingly governed by regulatory frameworks or restrictive policy, we have been able to explore what might be the horizons of possibilities. *What could we learn from our different legal and policy contexts and trajectories of concern about Indigenous achievement and education, from student and community voices, and from the voices of preservice teachers?* We wondered what might serve as a generative framework for thinking about assessment that would work and be informative across the four countries.

Assessment education that *is* was illustrated in this chapter through the contexts of assessment education policies and the realities of assessment courses in teacher education institutions. Assessment education is organised around strongly framed texts like school and teacher education policy mandates, accreditation, accountability, and long-standing enculturated practices that communicate the taken-for-granted assessment knowledge and skills that are seen as essential. While teacher educators are vital to the organisation and articulation of assessment education, it is rare that the teacher educator's voice and rationale behind assessment programs, either standalone or embedded, are made visible and or shared.

Teacher educators interpret the layers of school, university, and school-based policy imperatives into situated, highly integrated programmes where teacher educators, mentor teachers, and preservice teachers work at the intersections of each other's knowledge and practice. Importantly, teacher educators act as knowledge brokers. Yet, we would argue that teacher educators also have a role as knowledge makers, a role that enables preservice teachers to consider how they might respond to assessment that *will be*.

References

Absolum, M., Flockton, L., Hattie, J., Hipkins, R., & Reid, I. (2009). *Directions for assessment in New Zealand: Developing students' assessment capabilities.* Unpublished paper prepared for the New Zealand Ministry of Education.

Adie, L. E., Klenowski, V., & Wyatt-Smith, C. (2012). Towards an understanding of teacher judgement in the context of social moderation. *Educational Review, 64*(2), 223–240.

American Educational Research Association. (2018). *Standards for educational and psychological testing.* American Educational Research Association.

Assessment Reform Group. (1999). *Assessment for learning: Beyond the black box.* University of Cambridge School of Education.

Australian Government. (2015, February). *Students first. Teacher Education Ministerial Advisory Group: Action now: Classroom ready teachers: Australian Government response.* https://www.aitsl.edu.au/docs/default-source/default-document-library/150212_ag_response_-_final.pdf?sfvrsn=8c4ee33c_2

Australian Government. (2022, December). *National teacher workforce action plan.* https://www.education.gov.au/teaching-and-school-leadership/resources/national-teacher-workforce-action-plan

Australian Institute for Teaching and School Leadership (AISTL). (2011). *Australian professional standards for teachers.* AISTL.

Australian Institute for Teaching and School Leadership (AITSL). (2015). *Accreditation of initial teacher education programs in Australia.* AITSL. https://www.aitsl.edu.au/docs/default-source/national-policy-framework/accreditation-of-initial-teacher-education-programs-in-australia.pdf

Bernstein, B. (2000). *Pedagogy, symbolic control, and identity: Theory, research, critique* (Vol. 5). Rowman & Littlefield.

Black, P., & Wiliam, D. (1998). Assessment and classroom learning. *Assessment in Education: Principles, Policy & Practice, 5*(1), 7–74.

Burney, L. (2018). Taking 'a rightful place in our own country': Indigenous self-determination and the Australian people. *Australian Journal of Public Administration, 77*(S1), S59–S62.

Calabrese Barton, A., Basu, J., Johnson, V., & Tan, E. (2011). Introduction. In J. Basu, A. Calabrese Barton, & E. Tan (Eds.), *Democratic science teaching: Building the expertise to empower low-income minority youth in science* (pp. 1–20). Springer.

Carter, A. (2015) Carter review of initial teacher training (ITT), London: DfE. Retrieved from: https://www.gov.uk/government/publications/carter-review-of-initial-teacher-training

Cho, E. Y. N., & Chan, T. M. S. (2020). Children's wellbeing in a high-stakes testing environment: The case of Hong Kong. *Children and Youth Services Review, 109.* https://doi.org/10.1016/j.childyouth.2019.104694 (online).

Churchward, P., & Willis, J. (2019). The pursuit of teacher quality: Identifying some of the multiple discourses of quality that impact the work of teacher educators. *Asia-Pacific Journal of Teacher Education, 47*(3), 251–264.

Clare, J. (2022, September). *Teacher education expert panel.* https://ministers.education.gov.au/clare/teacher-education-expert-panel

Collins, A., & Tierney, R. (2006). Teacher education accord: Values and ideals of the teaching profession in Canada. *Education Canada, 46*(4), 73–75.

Cope, B., & Kalantzis, M. (2016). Big data comes to school: Implications for learning, assessment, and research. *AERA Open, 2*(2). https://doi.org/10.1177/2332858416641907 (online).

Copp, D. (2019). Accountability testing in Canada: Aligning provincial policy objectives with teacher practices. *Canadian Journal of Educational Administration and Policy, 188*, 15–35.

Couch, D., Devine, N., & Stewart, G. T. (2022). The Teaching Council and initial teacher education: False binaries and academic freedom. *New Zealand Journal of Educational Studies, 57*, 1–5.

Cowie, B., Jones, A., & Otrel-Cass, K. (2010). Re-engaging students in science issues of assessment, funds of knowledge and sites for learning. *International Journal of Science and Mathematics Education, 9*, 347–366.

Crooks, T. J. (1988). The impact of classroom evaluation practices on students. *Review of Educational Research, 58*(4), 438–481.

Crooks, T. (2011). Assessment for learning in the accountability era: New Zealand. *Studies in Educational Evaluation, 37*(1), 71–77.

Delandshere, G. (2002). Assessment as inquiry. *Teachers College Record, 104*(7), 1461–1484.

Delors, J. (1996). *Learning: The treasure within: Report to UNESCO of the International Commission on Education for the twenty-first century* (Delors report). http://hdl.voced.edu.au/10707/114597

DeLuca, C., & Bellara, A. (2013). The current state of assessment education: Aligning policy, standards, and teacher education curriculum. *Journal of Teacher Education, 64*(4), 356–372.

DeLuca, C., Braund, H., Valiquette, A., & Cheng, L. (2017). Grading policies and practices in Canada: A landscape study. *Canadian Journal of Educational Administration and Policy, 184*, 4–22.

References

DeLuca, C., Coombs, A., & Sherman, A. (2018). Preparing teachers for assessment in schools: The influence of teacher educators. In *Innovation and accountability in teacher education* (pp. 171–186). Springer.

DeLuca, C., LaPointe, D., & Luhanga, U. (2016). Teacher assessment literacy: A review of international standards and measures. *Educational Assessment, Evaluation, and Accountability, 28*(3), 251–272.

DeLuca, C., Willis, J., Cowie, B., Harrison, C., Coombs, A., Gibson, A., & Trask, S. (2019). Policies, programs, and practices: Exploring the complex dynamics of assessment education in teacher education across four countries. *Frontiers in Education, 4.* https://doi.org/10.3389/feduc.2019.00132 (online).

Education Council. (2017). *Our code our standards: Ngā Tikanga Matatika Ngā Paerewa.* Education Council and Ministry of Education. https://teachingcouncil.nz/assets/Files/Code-and-Standards/Our-Code-Our-Standards-Nga-Tikanga-Matatika-Nga-Paerewa.pdf

Elby, A. (2022). *Epistemology and learning in STEM education.* Oxford University Press.

Gallagher, J., Willis, J., & Spina, N. (2022). Method as an opportunity for collaborative agency: An Australian Delphi inquiry into teacher educators' priorities in assessment education. In *Reconstructing the work of teacher educators* (pp. 197–221). Springer.

Gipps, C. V., & Murphy, P. (1994). *A fair test? Assessment, achievement and equity.* Open University Press.

Gove, M. (2010, November 5). *Michael Gove announces review of Key Stage 2 testing.* https://www.gov.uk/government/news/michael-gove-announces-review-of-key-stage-2-testing

Government of Canada. (2023). *Treaties and agreements.* Retrieved 11 March 2023, from https://www.rcaanc-cirnac.gc.ca/eng/1100100028574/1529354437231

Hardy, I. (2015). Data, numbers and accountability: The complexity, nature and effects of data use in schools. *British Journal of Educational Studies, 63*(4), 467–486.

Hardy, I., Jakhelln, R., & Smit, B. (2021). The policies and politics of teachers' initial learning: The complexity of national initial teacher education policies. *Teaching Education, 32*(3), 286–308.

Hargreaves, A. (2020). Large-scale assessments and their effects: The case of mid-stakes tests in Ontario. *Journal of Educational Change, 21*(3), 393–420.

Harrison, C. (2005). Teachers developing assessment for learning: Mapping teacher change. *Teacher Development, 9*(2), 255–263.

Hartley, D. (1998). Repeat prescription: The national curriculum for initial teacher training. *British Journal of Educational Studies, 46*(1), 68–83.

Hipkins, R., & Cameron, M. (2018). *Trends in assessment: An overview of themes in the literature.* NZCER Rangahau Mātauranga o Aotearoa Press.

Hipkins, R., Johnston, M., & Sheehan, M. (2016). *NCEA in context.* NZCER Rangahau Mātauranga o Aotearoa Press.

Howell, A. (2017). 'Because then you could never ever get a job!': Children's constructions of NAPLAN as high-stakes. *Journal of Education Policy, 32*(5), 564–587.

Hume, A., & Coll, R. K. (2009). Assessment of learning, for learning, and as learning: New Zealand case studies. *Assessment in Education: Principles, Policy & Practice, 16*(3), 269–290.

Kerr, B. G., & Averill, R. M. (2021). Contextualising assessment within Aotearoa New Zealand: Drawing from mātauranga Māori. *AlterNative: An International Journal of Indigenous Peoples, 17*(2), 236–245.

Kerr, J. (2014). Western epistemic dominance and colonial structures: Considerations for thought and practice in programs of teacher education. *Decolonization: Indigeneity, Education & Society, 3*(2), 83–104.

Klenowski, V. (2015). Questioning the validity of the multiple uses of NAPLAN data. In *National testing in schools* (pp. 44–56). Routledge.

Lingard, B., Mills, M., & Hayes, D. (2006). Enabling and aligning assessment for learning: Some research and policy lessons from Queensland. *International Studies in Sociology of Education, 16*(2), 83–103.

Louden, W. (2008). 101 Damnations: The persistence of criticism and the absence of evidence about teacher education in Australia. *Teachers and Teaching: Theory and Practice, 14*(4), 357–368.

Magnusson, K., Frank, B., & Ellsworth, K. (2016). The ACDE accords: A case study in democratic leadership. In *Assembling and governing the higher education institution* (pp. 425–438). Palgrave Macmillan.

Mayer, D., & Mills, M. (2021). Professionalism and teacher education in Australia and England. *European Journal of Teacher Education, 44*(1), 45–61.

May, S. (2019). *PISA 2018 New Zealand summary report system performance & equity.* New Zealand Ministry of Education.

McArthur, J., Blackie, M., Pitterson, N., & Rosewell, K. (2022). Student perspectives on assessment: Connections between self and society. *Assessment & Evaluation in Higher Education, 47*(5), 1–14.

McKay, B., & Firmin, M. W. (2008). The historical development of private education in Canada. *Education Research and Perspectives, 35*(2), 57–72.

Melbourne Graduate School of Education. (2023). *New metrics for success: Transforming what we value in schools.* https://education.unimelb.edu.au/new-metrics-for-success

Mockler, N. (2022). Teacher professional learning under audit; Reconfiguring practice in an age of standards. *Professional Development in Education, 48*(1), 166–180.

Mockler, N., & Stacey, M. (2021). Evidence of teaching practice in an age of accountability: When what can be counted isn't all that counts. *Oxford Review of Education, 47*(2), 170–188.

Moeed, A. (2015). *Science investigation: Student views about learning, motivation and assessment.* Springer.

Mutton, T., Burn, K., & Menter, I. (2017). Deconstructing the Carter Review: Competing conceptions of quality in England's 'school-led' system of initial teacher education. *Journal of Education Policy, 32*(1), 14–33.

National Constitutional Convention. (2017, May 26). *Uluru Statement from the heart.* https://ulurustatement.org/the-statement

New Zealand Department of Education. (1989). *Assessment for better learning: A public discussion document.* Department of Education.

New Zealand Government. (2022). *What's changing with the refresh of the New Zealand curriculum?* https://curriculumrefresh.education.govt.nz/whats-changing; https://ncea.education.govt.nz/mana-orite-mo-te-matauranga-maori-equal-status-matauranga-maori-ncea; https://nzareblog.wordpress.com/2022/09/20/mana-orite/

New Zealand Ministry of Education. (1994). *Assessment policy to practice.* Ministry of Education. https://nzcurriculum.tki.org.nz/The-New-Zealand-Curriculum

New Zealand Ministry of Education. (2007). *New Zealand curriculum.* Ministry of Education. https://nzcurriculum.tki.org.nz/The-New-Zealand-Curriculum

New Zealand Ministry of Education. (2011). *Ministry of Education position paper: Assessment (Schooling sector).* Ministry of Education.

New Zealand Ministry of Education. (2020). *Assessment for learning—PLD priority.* https://pld.education.govt.nz/regionally-allocated-pld/pld-priorities/

New Zealand Teaching Council. (2019). *ITE programme approval, monitoring and review requirements.* New Zealand Teaching Council.

Nusche, D., Dany, L., John, M., & Paulo, S. (2012). *OECD reviews of evaluation and assessment in education: New Zealand 2011* (Vol. 2012). OECD Publishing.

NZQA. (2022). *Aromatawai and the principles of assessment.* NZQA.

Ontario Ministry of Education. (2010). *Growing success: Assessment, evaluation, and reporting in Ontario schools.* https://www.edu.gov.on.ca/eng/policyfunding/growsuccess.pdf

Smith, L. F., Hill, M. F., Cowie, B., & Gilmore, A. (2014). Preparing teachers to use the enabling power of assessment. In *Designing assessment for quality learning* (pp. 303–323). Springer.

Stobart, G. (2005). Fairness in multicultural assessment systems. *Assessment in Education: Principles, Policy & Practice, 12*(3), 275–287.

Stobart, G. (2008). *Testing times: The uses and abuses of assessment.* Routledge.

References

OECD. (2019). TALIS 2018 results (Volume I): Teachers and school leaders as lifelong learners. *TALIS*. https://doi.org/10.1787/1d0bc92a-en

OECD. (2022). *OECD future of education and skills 2030*. https://www.oecd.org/education/2030-project/

Oo, C. Z., Alonzo, D., & Asih, R. (2022). Acquisition of teacher assessment literacy by pre-service teachers: A review of practices and program designs. *Issues in Educational Research, 32*(1), 352–373.

Pullin, D. (2017). What counts? Who is counting? Teacher education improvement and accountability in a data-driven era. In J. Nuttall, A. Kostogriz, M. Jones, & J. Martin (Eds.), *Teacher education policy and practice: Evidence of impact, impact of evidence* (pp. 3–16). Springer.

Rameka, L. K. (2021). Kaupapa Māori assessment: Reclaiming, reframing and realising Māori ways of knowing and being within early childhood education assessment theory and practice. *Frontiers in Education, 6*. https://doi.org/10.3389/feduc.2021.687601 (online).

Rasooli, A., DeLuca, C., & Cheng, L. (2022). Beginning teacher candidates' approaches to grading and assessment conceptions—Implications for teacher education in assessment. *Educational Research for Policy and Practice, 22*, 63–90.

Sahlberg, P. (2016). The global educational reform movement and its impact on schooling. *The Handbook of Global Education Policy, 12*(4), 128–144.

Sellar, S. (2015). Data infrastructure: A review of expanding accountability systems and large-scale assessments in education. *Discourse: Studies in the Cultural Politics of Education, 36*(5), 765–777.

Selwyn, N., Pangrazio, L., & Cumbo, B. (2022). Knowing the (datafied) student: The production of the student subject through school data. *British Journal of Educational Studies, 70*(3), 345–361.

Shay, M., & Lampert, J. (2022). Community according to whom? An analysis of how indigenous 'community' is defined in Australia's *Through Growth to Achievement* 2018 report on equity in education. *Critical Studies in Education, 63*(1), 47–63.

Shay, M., Sarra, G., & Lampert, J. (2022). Indigenous education policy, practice and research: Unravelling the tangled web. *The Australian Educational Researcher, 50*, 73–88.

Shepard, L. A. (2000). The role of assessment in a learning culture. *Educational Researcher, 29*(7), 4–14.

Smyth, E., & Hamel, T. (2016). The history of initial teacher education in Canada: Québec and Ontario. *Educação & Formação, 1*(1), 88–109.

Spina, N. (2019). 'Once upon a time': Examining ability grouping and differentiation practices in cultures of evidence-based decision-making. *Cambridge Journal of Education, 49*(3), 329–348.

Stacey, M., McGrath-Champ, S., & Wilson, R. (2023). Teacher attributions of workload increase in public sector schools: Reflections on change and policy development. *Journal of Educational Change*, 1–23. https://doi.org/10.1007/s10833-022-09476-0

Tai, J., Ajjawi, R., Bearman, M., Boud, D., Dawson, P., & Jorre de St Jorre, T. (2022). Assessment for inclusion: Rethinking contemporary strategies in assessment design. *Higher Education Research & Development, 42*, 483–497.

Te Tāhuhu o te Mātauranga | Ministry of Education. (2023). *Records of learning*. https://conversation.education.govt.nz/conversations/curriculum-progress-and-achievement/what-you-said-5/records-of-learning/

The Crown. (2019). *Initial teacher training (ITT): Core content framework*. https://www.gov.uk/government/publications/initial-teacher-training-itt-core-content-framework

Torrance, H. (2017). Blaming the victim: Assessment, examinations, and the responsibilisation of students and teachers in neo-liberal governance. *Discourse: Studies in the Cultural politics of Education, 38*(1), 83–96.

Trask, S., & Cowie, B. (2022). Tight-loose: Understanding variability, trade-offs and felt accountability across the curriculum-pedagogy-assessment dynamic. *The Curriculum Journal, 33*(4), 587–601.

Truth, & Reconciliation Commission of Canada. (2015). *Canada's residential schools: The Final report of the truth and reconciliation Commission of Canada* (Vol. 1). McGill-Queen's Press-MQUP.

United Nations (UN). (1989). *Convention on the rights of the child* (1989). Treaty no. 27531. Treaty Series, 1577 (pp. 3–178). https://treaties.un.org/doc/Treaties/1990/09/19900902%2003-14%20AM/Ch_IV_11p.pdf

United Nations (UN). (2006). *Convention on the rights of persons with disabilities.* Treaty Series, Vol. 2515.

United Nations (UN). (2007). *Declaration on the rights of Indigenous peoples.* https://www.un.org/development/desa/indigenouspeoples/wp-content/uploads/sites/19/2018/11/UNDRIP_E_web.pdf

United Nations (UN). (2015). *Transforming our world: The 2030 agenda for sustainable development.* https://sdgs.un.org/2030agenda

Walker, J., & von Bergmann, H. (2013). Teacher education policy in Canada: Beyond professionalization and deregulation. *Canadian Journal of Education, 36*(4), 65–92.

Whiting, C., Whitty, G., Menter, I., Black, P., Hordern, J., Parfitt, A., Reynolds, K., & Sorensen, N. (2018). Diversity and complexity: Becoming a teacher in England in 2015–2016. *Review of Education, 6*(1), 69–96.

Willis, J., Adie, L., & Klenowski, V. (2013). Conceptualising teachers' assessment literacies in an era of curriculum and assessment reform. *The Australian Educational Researcher, 40*(2), 241–256.

Zipin, L., Sellar, S., Brennan, M., & Gale, T. (2015). Educating for futures in marginalized regions: A sociological framework for rethinking and researching aspirations. *Educational Philosophy and Theory, 47*(3), 227–246.

Chapter 3
The Constellation of Assessment Capacity Discourses

Abstract Over the past three decades, policy and professional standards have repeatedly called for teachers to integrate assessment continuously across their practice in various ways to identify, monitor, support, evaluate, and report on student learning. Educational researchers have conceptualised and operationalised multiple constructs to understand teachers' classroom assessment practice, including *assessment competency*, *assessment literacy*, and later, *assessment capability* and *assessment identity*. The result of these multiple constructs presents a constellation of assessment discourses, which have influenced contemporary educational policies and professional development practices across systems, shaping understandings of teachers' assessment work. This chapter critically maps the constellation of assessment capacity discourses through a scoping review methodology to examine how these related discourses have been conceptualised for preservice or in-service teachers. Across the chapter, the evolution of each construct is analysed over time (i.e., since the introduction of the construct into peer-reviewed literature) and space (i.e., geography), and in consideration for how the constructs contribute towards a current view of teachers' assessment work today.

Keywords Assessment literacy · Assessment competency · Assessment capability · Assessment identity · Assessment work · School assessment · Classroom assessment · Preservice teachers · In-service teachers

Over the past three decades, policy and professional standards have repeatedly called teachers to integrate assessment continuously in their practice to identify, monitor, support, evaluate, and report on student learning (e.g., *Standards for Teacher Competence in Educational Assessment of Students*—AFT et al., 1990; *The Classroom Assessment Standards for PreK-12 Teachers*—Klinger et al., 2015). This growing emphasis on teachers' assessment capacity is, in part, a result of the long-recognised strong relationship between high-quality teaching, classroom assessment, and student learning by educational researchers (e.g., Black & Wiliam, 2009; Fenstermacher & Richardson, 2005; Hattie, 2008; Herppich et al., 2018; Putnam & Borko, 1997). High-quality assessment practices have been shown to decrease achievement gaps (Stiggins & Chappuis, 2005), support students with diverse learning needs (Guskey, 2007),

© The Author(s), under exclusive license to Springer Nature Singapore Pte Ltd. 2023
C. DeLuca et al., *Learning to Assess*, Teacher Education, Learning Innovation and Accountability, https://doi.org/10.1007/978-981-99-6199-3_3

and positively influence students' motivation and self-esteem (Black & Wiliam, 1998). In addition to the mounting evidence on the importance of assessment for student learning, assessment is a core feature of standards-based educational systems, which are often coupled with accountability frameworks. Assessment remains the key evidentiary source to demonstrate students' attainment of standards and respond to accountability demands.

There has been a proliferation of theories, policies, and professional development practices to support teachers' classroom assessment work over the past several decades. This support has resulted in multiple, and at times, overlapping discourses to characterise teachers' roles and responsibilities in assessment. In this chapter, we map the constellation of discourses related to teacher assessment capacity, namely *assessment competence, assessment literacy, assessment capability*, and *assessment identity*, in order to provoke a more comprehensive conceptualisation of what it means for a teacher to effectively engage with assessment throughout their professional practice, from preservice to in-service.

The historical and contemporary evolution of the literature that characterises teachers' assessment work has contributed to a novel conceptualisation for cultivating teacher assessment capacity, which we articulate through four core capacities—epistemic, embodied, ethical, and experiential. The epistemic capacity explores how teachers learn and re-learn key philosophical and foundational assessment principles. Embodied capacity involves the social-emotional and physical aspects of teachers' assessment practice and assessment learning. Ethical capacity raises awareness of the intersection of assessment with the socio-cultural contexts of teaching, exploring the role and enactment of fairness and social justice in assessment for and among students. Finally, experiential capacity examines how teachers experience assessment practice as learning. In this chapter, we delve into assessment literacy and learning literature to sketch out previous characterisations of teachers' assessment work, roles, and responsibilities.

3.1 Assessment Learning Discourses

Researchers have conceptualised and operationalised multiple discourses to promote teachers' assessment learning and their subsequent classroom assessment practice. Discourses have included:

- *assessment competence* (e.g., Herppich et al., 2018; Schneider & Bodensohn, 2017; Smith, 2007),
- *assessment literacy* (e.g., Brookhart, 2011; Popham, 2004; Xu & Brown, 2016), and later,
- *assessment capability* (e.g., Booth et al., 2014; DeLuca et al., 2019c; Hill et al., 2010), and
- *assessment identity* (e.g., Looney et al., 2018; Wyatt-Smith et al., 2010).

3.1 Assessment Learning Discourses

These multiple discourses have influenced contemporary educational policies and professional development practices across systems, shaping understandings of teachers' assessment work.

3.1.1 Assessment Competence and Assessment Literacy: Foundational Discourses

The first mention of an assessment capacity discourse was *assessment competence* in the early 1990s peer-reviewed publication *Educational Measurement* (Stiggins, 1991a). This article discussed how Stiggins and Conklin (1992) "identif[ied] six specific dimensions of classroom assessment competence that teachers need to master if they are to assess the full range of valued achievement targets accurately and manage classroom assessment environments effectively" (p. 8). These dimensions included (a) teachers' knowledge of the purposes of assessment (e.g., to inform decisions, as teaching tools, and for classroom management); (b) possessing a clear and highly differentiated understanding of achievement targets and possible assessment practices to assess those targets; (c) understanding the attributes of high-quality assessments; (d) being skilled at the three forms of assessment for tracking student achievement (e.g., paper–pencil assessment instruments, observations, conversations with students); (e) understanding the interpersonal dynamics of classroom assessment (e.g., cultural differences of students); and (f) being able to deliver feedback, particularly in the form of report cards.

A citation map has been generated of peer-reviewed research ($n = 23$) related to assessment competence from 1991 to 2019 to create a constellation of assessment competence discourse research. Figure 3.1 shows the indirect influence of Stiggins (1991a) on the field and other related seminal publications (i.e., the 1990 *Standards*, Herppich et al., 2018). In the figure, arrow directions signify citation in publication (i.e., an arrow pointing from Publication A to Publication B means that Publication A cited Publication B in conceptualising assessment competence). Interestingly, there are many assessment competence articles that are not directly connected to Stiggins (1991a) or the *Standards* (AFT et al., 1990).

Despite the indirect connections between Stiggins (1991a) and the many assessment competence studies included in this review (40%), the idea of assessment competence as an enacted classroom practice is commonly employed by scholars (e.g., Gareis, 2007; Göçer, 2011; Marais et al., 2008). Ekström (2013) noted that "a central component of teachers' professional competence is the practice of evaluating and assessing their students' work and achievement" (p. 278), a sentiment echoed by Klug et al. (2018), who considered "assessment competence as a process, describing the actions teachers should take in each phase to create the best possible assessment" [p. 299]). While assessment competence studies may not have direct links to Stiggins (1991a), the ideas he advanced have permeated this discourse.

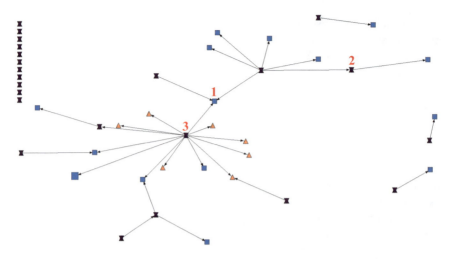

Fig. 3.1 Citation map for assessment competence. *Notes* Citation map includes assessment competence (black hourglass), assessment literacy (orange triangle), and non-peer-reviewed publications (blue box). 1 = *Standards* (AFT et al., 1990); 2 = Stiggins (1991a); 3 = Herppich et al. (2018). Only publications cited by Herppich et al. (2018) and included in this review are shown here

Since 1991, conceptualisations of assessment competence have evolved in two significant directions. First, the definition of assessment competence has transitioned from one focused on producing high-quality assessments to one focused on producing high-quality assessment practices *for explicitly supporting student learning*. As discussed above, assessment competence, as proposed by Stiggins (1991a), did not directly focus on supporting student learning but instead on accurately measuring student achievement, while many recent articles imply or directly state that assessment competence should focus on the use of assessment practices to support student learning (e.g., Andersson et al., 2019; Ekström, 2013; Jang & Sinclair, 2018; Jones, 2014; Mak, 2019; Matre & Solheim, 2015; Schneider & Bodensohn, 2017; Smith, 2011).

The second trend has been the increasing prominence of the context-dependent nature of assessment competence. DeLuca et al. (2019b) noted this shift: "Understanding of assessment competence has evolved from the learning of technical skills in assessment to a context-dependent, socially defined understanding encompassing a multitude of approaches to assessment" (p. 1). Other researchers (e.g., Hasse et al., 2014; Herppich et al., 2018) have conceptualised assessment competence as a "context-specific disposition" (p. 62). While there is a core commitment to assessment enactment in relation to contexts of practice, assessment competence has also maintained its strong connection to assessment standards in Europe and North America and how these standards present the purposes of assessment practices (e.g., Capperucci, 2019; Plake et al., 1993; Schneider & Bodensohn, 2017).

The conception of assessment competence, most commonly found in recent literature and primarily derived from authors associated with European institutions, is one in which teachers engage in high-quality assessment practice tailored to their teaching and learning context to support student learning. Aligning closely with this conceptualisation is the model of teacher assessment competence developed by Herppich et al. (2018). These authors conceptualised assessment competence as a "measurable cognitive disposition that is acquired by dealing with assessment demands in relevant educational situations and that enables teachers to master these demands quantifiably in a range of similar situations in a relatively stable and relatively consistent way" (p. 185). Encompassing much of the previous research on assessment competence and related fields, the authors present a multidimensional model possessing quantifiable dimensions where assessment is separated from other teacher competencies (e.g., instructional competencies).

3.1.2 Competence Versus Literacy: A Narrow Distinction

Assessment literacy appeared in peer-reviewed literature (Schafer, 1993) immediately after the emergence of assessment competence (Stiggins, 1991a). However, Schafer (1993) noted that "the purpose of this article is to consider the need for assessment literacy for teachers and the level of success now achieved in meeting that need. An attempt to measure teachers' understandings about assessment is described by Plake et al. [1993]" (p. 119). Plake et al. (1993) examined teachers' assessment literacy in relation to "assessment competencies" (p. 21), emphasising the close relationship these discourses shared. These authors drew on Stiggins' (1991b) article in *Phi Delta Kappen*, in which he outlined the dimensions of an assessment literate person, including (a) understanding the full range of possible achievement targets possible for students (i.e., subject matter, thinking skills, behaviours, and products); and (b) having the ability to carry out assessment methods (e.g., paper–pencil performance, and feedback). In short:

> Assessment literates know if and when an assessment appropriately reflects a clearly defined achievement target. They are sensitive to the appropriateness to the intended target of the sample of student performance being assessed. They can identify factors that may interfere with results and mislead decision makers. And they know whether or not they can use the results in the form produced. They also know that, if the appropriate conditions are not satisfied, achievement data may be rendered less useful, bad decisions may result, and students may be harmed. Assessment literates care about high-quality education and act assertively to prevent unsound assessment. (Stiggins, 1995, p. 537)

Interestingly, Stiggins' (1991b) description of assessment literacy aligned closely with his previously described characterisation of assessment competence (1991a). This is unsurprising as both conceptualisations were advanced by the same scholar in the same year, albeit in different publications.

Further highlighting the close alignment between assessment competence and assessment literacy is the influence of the *Standards for Teacher Competence in Educational Assessment of Students* (AFT et al., 1990) which, despite the title, has been cited more often within assessment literacy publications than assessment competence publications (e.g., Fan et al., 2011; Gu, 2014; Mertler, 2004; Muhammad et al, 2019; Quitter, 1999; Quitter & Gallini, 2000; Williams, 2015; Yastıbaş & Takkaç, 2018; Zwick et al., 2008). While direct reference to the *Standards* has diminished in more recent publications, there remain indirect references to this foundational publication (e.g., Howley et al. [2013] cite Mertler [2004], who cite AFT et al. [1990]). Importantly, this influential citation contributes directly to a strongly framed classification of assessment knowledge stemming from the United States (USA) context.

However, in 2011, Brookhart argued that the *Standards* no longer fully encapsulated the assessment realities of classroom teachers, noting three emerging trends: (a) the rise in assessment for accountability purposes, particularly within the USA; (b) the increasing importance of formative assessment; and (c) the highly diverse nature of contemporary teaching contexts. Accordingly, Brookhart called for a revision to the *Standards* and, more importantly, signalled that the field of assessment literacy needed to heed contemporary classroom assessment realities if it was to accurately reflect teachers' assessment work.

Since these initial publications (AFT et al., 1990; Brookhart, 2011; Schafer, 1993; Stiggins, 1991b) provided a noteworthy foundation for the field, assessment literacy has become the dominant discourse to describe teachers' assessment work. However, as noted by Popham (2011), "you will not find a whole flock of definitions for assessment literacy floating about in the educational literature" (p. 267) with "no standard definition of the concept of assessment literacy" (Walters, 2010, p. 318). That said, several key scholars have significantly shaped the field of assessment literacy or specific fields within assessment literacy (e.g., assessment literacy in physical education, language assessment literacy). The citation map for assessment literacy exhibits the substantial number of publications regarding assessment literacy, the high degree of interconnectedness between studies, and key publications (Fig. 3.2).

The influence of Stiggins (1991a, 1991b, 1995, 1997, 1999a, 1999b, 1999c, 2002a, 2002b, 2004, 2005, 2010, 2014; Stiggins et al., 2006, 2012; Stiggins & Duke, 2008) cannot be understated. His coining of the term *assessment literacy* in 1991 and continued publications on this construct have provided a body of work that has undeniably shaped scholars' conceptualisation of this construct (as evidenced by the large number of citations of his work). Popham (2004, 2005, 2006, 2008, 2009a, 2009b, 2011, 2013) has been an equal force in the field, conceptualising assessment literacy not as a set of dimensions or in direct relation to the *Standards* but as an "individual's understandings of the fundamental assessment concepts and procedures deemed likely to influence educational decisions" (Popham, 2011, p. 267). In 2013, Willis et al. marked an important shift in assessment literacy literature. They explicitly recognised that teachers' assessment work was directly influenced by socio-cultural conditions in classrooms and schools, defining assessment literacy as:

> Dynamic social practices which are context dependent and which involve teachers in articulating and negotiating classroom and cultural knowledges with one another and with learners, in the initiation, development and practice of assessment to achieve the learning goals of students. (p. 241)

3.1 Assessment Learning Discourses

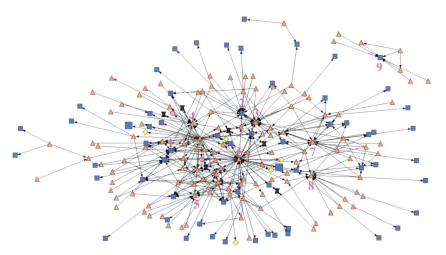

Fig. 3.2 Citation map for assessment literacy. *Notes* Citation map includes assessment literacy (orange triangles), assessment competence (black hourglass), assessment capability (pink circle), assessment identity (yellow diamonds), and publications not included in this review (blue box). 1 = *Standards* (AFT et al., 1990); 2 = Stiggins (1991b); 3 = Popham (2009a); 4 = Popham (2011); 5 = Willis et al. (2013); 6 = Xu and Brown (2016); 7 = Inbar-Lourie (2008); 8 = Fulcher (2012); 9 = Hay and Penney (2009). Only publications cited by these models and included in this review are shown here

This conceptualisation of assessment literacy has been taken up by a number of scholars, including Poskitt (2014), Clark (2015), Xu and Brown (2016), Baker and Riches (2018), DeLuca and colleagues (Coombs et al., 2018, 2020; DeLuca et al. 2019a), Adie et al. (2019), Ataie-Taber et al. (2019), and Pastore and Andrade (2019).

In 2016, Xu and Brown reviewed 100 articles to present a model of teachers' assessment literacy in practice. Their model consisted of six dimensions: knowledge base, teacher conceptions of assessment, institutional and socio-cultural contexts, teacher assessment literacy in practice, teacher learning, and teacher identity (re)construction as assessors. Despite its recent publication, this model has been highly influential, pointing towards the value of a multidimensional view of assessment literacy that includes assessment knowledge, teachers' conceptions and beliefs about assessment, teacher learning and identity, and consideration for the assessment context (Adie et al., 2019; Ayalon & Wilkie, 2020; Bijsterbosch et al., 2019; Firoozi et al., 2019; Gotch & McLean, 2019; Rasooli et al., 2018; Xu & Brown, 2016).

More recently, Pastore and Andrade (2019) completed a Delphi study to generate a three-dimensional model (conceptual, praxeological, and socio-emotional) to define assessment literacy. Their resulting overarching definition of assessment literacy encapsulates a similar conceptualisation to that of Xu and Brown's (2016) model: "the interrelated knowledge, skills, and dispositions that a teacher can use to design and implement a coherent and appropriate approach to assessment within the classroom context and the school system" (Pastore & Andrade, 2019, pp. 134–135).

The conceptual dimension encompasses that a "teacher needs to know what assessment is in terms of different models and methods. In this dimension, conceptions a teacher has of assessment, teaching, and learning play a fundamental role" (p. 135). The praxeological dimension is the practice of assessment in the classroom that "allows a teacher to integrate the assessment process with other teaching practices in order to monitor, judge, and manage the teaching–learning process. This dimension includes the main actions in which a teacher is involved when navigating multiple, and sometimes competing, assessment demands" (p. 135). The third dimension is the socio-emotional dimension, built upon the foundation that assessment is a social practice in which teachers "manage the social and emotional aspects of assessment, especially but not exclusively within the context of the classroom" (p. 136).

Within the broad field of assessment literacy, two subfields were prevalent in publications included in our review: language assessment literacy and physical education assessment literacy. Falsgraf (2005), Inbar-Lourie (2008, 2013), and Fulcher (2012) are core scholars shaping the language assessment literacy field, with Falsgraf (2005) defining assessment literacy "as the ability to understand, analyse, and apply information on student performance to improve instruction" (as cited in Inbar-Lourie [2008], p. 389). In addition, Inbar-Lourie (2008), following the trend towards understanding assessment literacy as socially and culturally dependent, "placed social context at the heart of assessment and assessment literacy" (Fulcher, 2012, p. 116).

Hay and Penney's (2009) model of physical education assessment literacy has not only shaped assessment literacy within physical education (DinanThompson & Penny, 2015; Leirhaug et al., 2016; Park, 2017; Starck et al., 2018) but also language assessment literacy (Koh et al., 2018; Sultana, 2019). Reflecting a social-constructivist paradigm, this model consists of conceptualising assessment literacy within physical education as "the development of knowledge and capacities to implement assessment and interpret the outcomes of assessment in a manner that is critically aware and that optimised the value of assessment for all students" (Hay & Penney [2009] as cited in Starck et al. [2018], p. 520).

In sum, assessment literacy emerged with a strong foundation rooted in the *Standards* (AFT et al., 1990) and seminal works by Stiggins (1991a, 1991b). This foundation described the standards of assessment practice teachers should meet to be assessment literate, with mastery at the heart of this conception of assessment work. Building on this foundation, the discourse has evolved towards multiple models, conceptualisations, definitions, and subfields. This evolution has recognised that assessment work involves more than knowledge and enactment of assessment standards—although these remain central to all models—and has now expanded to consider the socio-cultural and historical contexts that shape teachers' practices, conceptions/beliefs, and learning of assessment. Such an enlarged view has the potential to more effectively reflect the demands of distinct classroom contexts of assessment in which teachers' work yet continue to hold clearly discernable standards of practice for the field.

3.1.3 Assessment Capability: A Marked Shift

Unlike assessment literacy and assessment competence, peer-reviewed studies focused on *assessment capability* have only appeared recently. Published in 2010 in *Assessment Matters*, Hill et al. explore how preservice teachers could be prepared to be assessment capable. In doing so, they drew on the definition of assessment capability from Absolum et al. (2009), who defined assessment capability as:

> the orchestrators, encouragers, interpreters, and mediators of learning. They need to understand how students can use and value assessment as a powerful means of furthering their own learning. As the experts in the learning partnership, teachers need to take the lead in all assessment that students cannot manage without support. But they need to do so in ways that encourage students to feel deeply accountable for their own progress and support them to become motivated, effective, self-regulating learners. To do this, teachers clearly need to be knowledgeable about the curriculum and teaching, but they also require well developed assessment capabilities and the motivation to use these to forge learning partnerships with their students. (p. 24)

As seen in Figure 3.3, publications on assessment capability included in this chapter drew almost exclusively on the conceptualisation proposed by Absolum et al. (2009). As a consequence, conceptualisations of assessment capable teachers included here are quite similar, centring on the notation that assessment capable teachers: (a) possess the knowledge and skills to effectively utilise and modify their classroom assessment practices and (b) support students in becoming motivated, effective, and self-regulating learners.

A key distinction between assessment literacy and competence is noted by Hill et al. (2017): assessment competence and assessment literacy understand student involvement in assessment as "one key component" while assessment capable

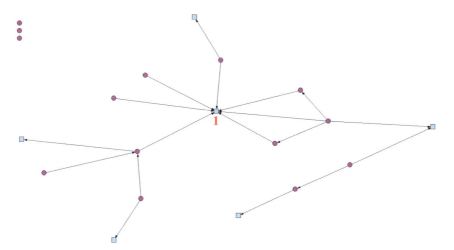

Fig. 3.3 Citation map for assessment capability. *Notes* Citation map includes assessment capability (pink circle) and publications not included in this review (blue box). 1 = Absolum et al. (2009)

teachers "have the curricular and pedagogical capability, and the motivation to engender assessment capability in their students" (p. 2). In this way, assessment capability speaks more to weakly classified knowledge of assessment. In essence, assessment capability is not limited to a teacher-centric characteristic (as with literacy and competence) but extends beyond the teacher to students' future learning and the capability of students to shape those learning experiences.

As an emerging discourse, assessment capability adds a new dimension to literacy and competence, one that focuses on the student (as opposed to assessment competence and literacy, which are focused primarily on the teacher). However, this discourse remains effectively used in New Zealand and has yet to spread substantially to other jurisdictions. Furthermore, given the highly connected nature of publications that utilise this discourse, it is unlikely that multiple conceptualisations and the rise of related subfields of research will arise in the near future.

3.1.4 Assessment Identity: A Turn Towards the Personal

Drawn from a similar line of logic as assessment capability, a discourse of *assessment identity* aimed to broaden the underpinning facets that contribute to teachers' and students' assessment work. First introduced into the peer-reviewed literature by Wyatt-Smith et al. (2010) and refined over nearly a decade, assessment identity is broadly conceptualised as a teachers' personal and professional identification with their assessment work—which includes curriculum knowledge and skills, knowledge of effective assessment practice, confidence enacting assessment practices, belief in the effectiveness of the assessment process—which is shaped by prior experience and context. As noted by Wyatt-Smith and Adie (2019) and echoed by other assessment identity scholars, "practice and identity may change, often innovatively and creatively, as the result of exposure to different artefacts or activities, and this may be different for each individual involved in the practice" (p. 6). One influence that shaped teachers' assessment identity "as a member of [a] community through moderation 'practice' where, through participation, a level of competence that is recognisable is established" (Wyatt-Smith et al., 2010, p. 64). Assessment identity reflects a recognition of the weak framing of assessment knowledge—that it is developed in various ways—and that assessment knowledge is also weakly classified—that it is integrated with other kinds of knowledge.

The dynamic, interconnected nature of assessment identity is articulated by Looney et al. (2018) in their model of teacher assessment identity (occupying a central node in the citation map; see Fig. 3.4). The model is comprised of five interrelated dimensions: (a) I know (knowledge of curriculum and assessment), (b) I feel (emotions towards assessment), (c) I believe (beliefs regarding assessment), (d) I am confident (self-efficacy in assessment), and (f) my role (agency and role as assessor within a context). While some of these dimensions appear similar to elements of assessment competence and assessment literacy models discussed previously, the foundation of assessment identity is primarily teacher identity literature

3.2 From Competence to Identity

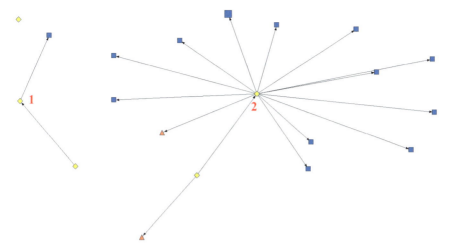

Fig. 3.4 Citation map for assessment identity. *Notes* Citation map includes assessment identity (yellow diamond), assessment literacy (orange triangle), and publications not included in this review (blue box). Similar to Figs. 3.1 and 3.2, the large blue box represents the large number of studies included by a publication that developed models of assessment identity (i.e., Looney et al., 2018). Only publications cited by this model and already included in this review are shown here. 1 = Wyatt-Smith et al. (2010); 2 = Looney et al. (2018)

(e.g., Connelly & Clandinin, 1999; Hargreaves & Goodson, 1996; Leavy et al., 2007; Mitchell & Weber, 1999; Mockler, 2011). In basing conceptualisations of assessment identity on a different literature base than much of the assessment competence, literacy, and capability research, the discourse surrounding assessment identity is markedly different. Assessment identity is always in the making, shaped by experiences within and beyond the classroom: assessment identity is "framed and reframed over a career and mediated by [the] context in which teachers work and live" (Looney et al., 2018, p. 446). Unlike how many researchers articulate enhancing assessment competence and literacy, assessment "identity development is neither simple nor linear: rather it is in response to events and circumstances" (p. 446).

3.2 From Competence to Identity

At the onset of the educational accountability movement, teachers were called to use assessment in new and more integrated ways. This movement resulted in the articulation of assessment as a core professional capacity for teachers and the spurring of new discourses for teachers' assessment work. The early emergence of these discourses pointed towards a mastery orientation, as seen in both assessment competence and literacy discourses, with teacher expectations for assessment practice clearly delineated. Such a view could deem a teacher assessment literate or competent or not, and, in this way, could support notions of teacher accountability in relation to assessment standards. When coupled with the growth of GERM neo-liberal accountability cultures (outlined in Chapter 2), the result naturally was implications for teacher evaluation and performance appraisal, remediation, and professional development. Teacher educators may well have designed assessment courses based on the strongly classified sense of assessment knowledge expressed in lists of core assessment capacities. However, as these discourses evolved, researchers recognised the multiple factors shaping teachers' assessment work and the challenges in building systemic assessment literacy across all standards and contexts. In short, it became clear that the practice of assessment is not as easy as it may seem.

By acknowledging the roles of teacher beliefs, contexts of practice, student diversity, and opportunities for professional learning, discourses of assessment literacy and competence enlarged to understand how enacted assessment expectations were shaped by teachers' socio-cultural contexts, leading towards a more complex view of assessment literacy and competence. This shift in focus has been gradual and may not be readily obvious to teacher educators who do not specialise in assessment research. Assessment capability and identity further position assessment work as a negotiated context-specific practice by recognising that assessment must be responsive to students (in fact, in the view of assessment capability, students are equal agents in the design and use of assessments) and that assessment is an integrative part of teachers' professional identity. There has been a deliberate weakening of the classification of assessment as a stand-alone practice as the importance of being responsive to students and contexts has grown.

In summary, assessment work, as represented by these discourses, has changed over time:

- Capability and identity are epistemologically different from earlier discourses as they prioritise students and teachers as the primary mediators of assessment knowledge, with agency and capacity to enact context-relevant assessment decisions.
- Each of the four discourses (competence, literacy, capability, and identity) presents a distinct pattern of evolution and contribute a unique—although at times overlapping—conception of assessment work.
- Combined, these discourses represent a complex picture of what it means for teachers to engage assessment with implications for practice and professional learning.

A further challenge contributing complexity to the field is that, despite their distinctive contributions, assessment discourses have been used interchangeably and often without clear definitions. As evident from our review of the literature, many scholars view these four discourses as either closely related or synonymous. As Edwards (2013) notes, "[assessment] capability is developed by teachers, students and other stakeholders over time, and has been alternatively described by some as assessment literacy" (p. 214). A similar sentiment is expressed by Schneider and Bodhensen (2017), "In contemporary literature on educational assessment in general and on teachers' assessment practice in particular, there is no doubt that assessment capacity, or assessment competence as we refer to it in this chapter, is a key feature for successfully enacting the teaching profession" (p. 127). Cowie et al. (2014) state, "assessment capability, also discussed as assessment literacy" (p. 2). This review of terms can help assessment researchers to carefully articulate assessment discourses. In this book, we propose the further development of the assessment research field and, in partnership with teacher educators, to develop teacher assessment capacity.

3.3 Towards Assessment Capacity

At present, multiple assessment discourses are in circulation, holding synergies and tensions that offer opportunities, but also confusion, for supporting classroom assessment practices and professional development. Importantly, regardless of discourse, the assessment research field to date has been largely preoccupied with conceptualising how assessment operates in teachers' professional practice and identities rather than on a future view towards how teachers develop their assessment capacity throughout their professional careers to envision new assessment realities in schools.

> We argue that to effectively support teachers in classroom assessment, we need an expanded discourse—one that creates space not only for what teachers need to know and be able to do in assessment now but, more importantly, for the complex realities of learning to assess and for imagining new assessment possibilities for classrooms of the future.

Such a discourse reinterprets the constellation of assessment discourses through a lens of teacher professional growth and development, premised on the understanding that teachers' assessment work is an act always in the making.

Introducing a new discourse is not intended to further fracture the field; in fact, the opposite. This new discourse is intended to unify the previous discourses within a professional learning framework—with a framework that seeks, as its primary motive, the continual development of teachers' assessment capacity. Our previous mapping of assessment discourses provides grounds for the intentional use of terms, the purposeful positioning of policies and standards, and the foundation for professional practices. Our framework acknowledges and builds from these previous discourses but makes a notable departure from them. While previous discourses have largely aimed to define teachers' assessment work, role, and responsibilities and prepare them for assessment that *was* and *is,* our framework serves a forward-looking function to support teachers' continuous professional growth in assessment. The fundamental aim of our framework—and indeed this book—is to advocate for, promote, and advance a theory for cultivating teacher assessment capacity across time and contexts, one that encourages teachers to challenge and change existing assessment practices to work in service of all students' learning.

We have turned purposefully to *capacity* as an overarching discourse, rooting specifically in Doll's (2005) notion that "capacity suggests wideness, not narrowness; openness; space for possibilities not yet even imagined" (p. 21). Capacity offers a generative discourse, without judgement, holding a learner- and learning-centred orientation. It is about embracing the "other inner side of things" (Doll, 2005, p. 21), encouraging teachers to dig deeply into what they do and why, and challenging ways of being towards more socially just and purposeful ends.

Applied to assessment, capacity invites a reconsideration of what it means to be 'assessment literate' or 'assessment competent'—to move beyond the acquisition of knowledge and skills in assessment. This shift from the 'known end' embraces teachers as continual learners of this complex field, interweaving with pedagogy, curriculum, student diversity, context, and identity. By negotiating learned knowledge in relation to the embodied and experiential dimensions of teachers' assessment work, assessment capacity acknowledges that teachers are called on to rationalise their assessment decisions and are the primary agents in creating new assessment possibilities for a constantly changing educational world.

The driving intention of our framework is to encourage continuous development of assessment thought and practice in classrooms (see Fig. 3.5). The framework articulates four core assessment capacities—epistemic, embodied, ethical, and experiential—that we propose provoke new possibilities for assessment in teachers' classrooms. The four capacities are centred around the idea of assessment capacity.

Drawing on Bernstein (2000, 2003), the four capacities are positioned upon two knowledge axes—vertical and horizontal assessment knowledge systems. The vertical knowledge system denotes strongly classified knowledge shaping teachers' assessment work and involves canonical, codified, theoretical, and policy-based

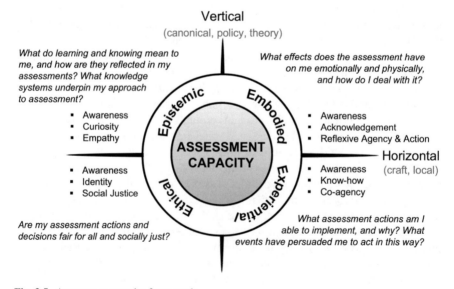

Fig. 3.5 Assessment capacity framework

3.3 Towards Assessment Capacity

knowledge systems. In contrast, horizontal knowledge involves craft knowledge about assessment, connoisseurship, and know-how cultivated through experience within schools and teacher communities of practice. As teachers learn to assess, they are always referencing, balancing, and negotiating knowledge across these axes, even as knowledge across these systems conflicts, contradicts, and counteracts one another. At the core of the framework is the idea of *assessment capacity*.

> *Assessment capacity* is defined as a teacher's capacity to continually learn about their assessment practice—through relationships, reflection, reflexivity, collaboration, inquiry, and inventiveness—to imagine and explore new possibilities for assessment in schools.

The four key capacities for learning to assess are: epistemic, embodied, ethical, and experiential. Each of these capacities enables contextualised reflection and decision-making about assessment thinking and practice through reflection on past experiences, analysis of present situations, and imagining of the yet-to-come. Each capacity is guided by central reflective questions and supported by foundational themes. The four capacities are as follows.

Epistemic capacity: The epistemic capacity is about reflecting on and challenging the knowledge systems that shape teaching, learning, and assessment activities. Guiding this capacity are the reflective questions: *What do learning and knowing mean to me, and how are they reflected in my assessments? What knowledge systems underpin my approach to assessment?*

Embodied capacity: The embodied capacity responds to the physical, emotional, and social-material experiences of assessment as felt within teachers' bodies as they learn about and implement assessment. The driving reflective question to attend to the embodied capacity is: *What effects does the assessment have on me emotionally and physically, and how do I deal with it?*

Ethical capacity: The ethical capacity asks teachers to consider how diversity in their classroom shapes their assessment practice. It considers how teachers plan, make decisions about, and create opportunities for and interpret student agency within and through assessment processes. It also involves socio-cultural considerations within assessment practices, fair distribution of resources for learning and assessment, procedural fairness, equity in assessment, and explicit consideration for the consequences of assessment actions on diverse students and the learning collective. Guiding teachers' ethical capacity development is the following reflection question: *Are my assessment actions and decisions fair for all and socially just?*

Experiential capacity: The experiential capacity is purposefully presented last, as it is the culmination of the previous three capacities in action. Experiential capacity involves constructing knowledge about assessment through first-hand experiences across contexts of practice. Fundamentally, teachers develop this capacity by reflecting on the questions: *What assessment actions am I able to implement, and why? What events have persuaded me to act in this way?*

In the next four chapters (Chapters 4–7), each capacity is explained in depth, drawing on preservice teacher data, analyses, and literature. In the final chapter of the book (Chapter 8), the *Assessment Capacity Framework* is revisited with consideration for how it directs teacher learning and teacher education (see Chapter 8 for full articulation of the framework). Overall, the framework invites teachers to question: *What am I thinking, feeling, and doing in assessment now? How did I get here? And what else is possible?* Leveraging the framework encourages teachers to be active agents in the (re)construction and transformation of the social order that assessment reifies in schools and society (Bernstein, 2000, p. xxi), advancing new possibilities for assessment in classrooms.

References

Absolum, M., Flockton, L., Hattie, J., Hipkins, R., & Reid, I. (2009). *Directions for assessment in New Zealand (DANZ): Developing students' assessment capability.* Ministry of Education. http://assessment.tki.org.nz/Assessment-inthe-classroom/Assessment-position-papers

Adie, L., Stobart, G., & Cumming, J. (2019). The construction of the teacher as expert assessor. *Asia-Pacific Journal of Teacher Education, 48*, 436–453.

American Federation of Teachers (AFT), National Council on Measurement in Education (NCME), & National Education Association (NEA). (1990). Standards for teacher competence in educational assessment of students. *Educational Measurement: Issues and Practice, 9*(4), 30–32.

Andersson, U. B., Löfgren, H., & Gustafson, S. (2019). Forward-looking assessments that support students' learning: A comparative analysis of two approaches. *Studies in Educational Evaluation, 60*, 109–116.

Ataie-Tabar, M., Zareian, G., Amirian, S. M. R., & Adel, S. M. R. (2019). A study of socio-cultural conception of writing assessment literacy: Iranian EFL teachers' and students' perspectives. *English Teaching & Learning, 43*(4), 389–409.

Ayalon, M., & Wilkie, K. J. (2020). Developing assessment literacy through approximations of practice: Exploring secondary mathematics pre-service teachers developing criteria for a rich quadratics task. *Teaching and Teacher Education, 89.* https://doi.org/10.1016/j.tate.2019.103011 (online).

Baker, B. A., & Riches, C. (2018). The development of EFL examinations in Haiti: Collaboration and language assessment literacy development. *Language Testing, 35*(4), 557–581.

Bernstein, B. (2000). *Pedagogy, symbolic control, and identity: Theory, research, critique* (Vol. 5). Rowman & Littlefield.

Bernstein, B. (2003). *Class, codes and control: Applied studies towards a sociology of language* (Vol. 2). Psychology Press.

Bijsterbosch, E., Béneker, T., Kuiper, W., & van der Schee, J. (2019). Teacher professional growth on assessment literacy: A case study of prevocational geography education in The Netherlands. *The Teacher Educator, 54*(4), 420–445.

Black, P., & Wiliam, D. (1998). Assessment and classroom learning. *Assessment in Education, 5*(1), 7–73.

References

Black, P., & Wiliam, D. (2009). Developing the theory of formative assessment. *Educational Assessment, Evaluation and Accountability, 21*, 5–13.

Booth, B., Hill, M. F., & Dixon, H. (2014). The assessment-capable teacher: Are we all on the same page? *Assessment Matters, 6*, 137–157.

Brookhart, S. M. (2011). Educational assessment knowledge and skills for teachers. *Educational Measurement: Issues and Practice, 30*, 3–12.

Capperucci, D. (2019). From competence curriculum design to assessment and certification of achievement: Two empirical models for TEFL. *Studi sulla Formazione/open Journal of Education, 22*(1), 147–175.

Clark, J. S. (2015). "My assessment didn't seem real": The influence of field experiences on preservice teachers' agency and assessment literacy. *Journal of Social Studies Education Research, 6*(2), 1–21.

Connelly, F. M., & Clandinin, D. J. (1999). *Shaping a professional identity: Stories of education practice.* Teachers College Press.

Coombs, A., DeLuca, C., LaPointe-McEwan, D., & Chalas, A. (2018). Changing approaches to classroom assessment: An empirical study across teacher career stages. *Teaching and Teacher Education, 71*, 134–144.

Coombs, A., DeLuca, C., & MacGregor, S. (2020). A person-centered analysis of teacher candidates' approaches to assessment. *Teaching and Teacher Education, 87*. https://doi.org/10.1016/j.tate.2019.102952 (online).

Cowie, B., Cooper, B., & Ussher, B. (2014). Developing an identity as a teacher-assessor: Three student teacher case studies. *Assessment Matters, 7*(6), 1–16.

DeLuca, C., Coombs, A., & LaPointe-McEwan, D. (2019a). Assessment mindset: Exploring the relationship between teacher mindset and approaches to classroom assessment. *Studies in Educational Evaluation, 61*, 159–169.

DeLuca, C., Schneider, C., Coombs, A., Pozas, M., & Rasooli, A. (2019b). A cross-cultural comparison of German and Canadian student teachers' assessment competence. *Assessment in Education: Principles, Policy & Practice, 27*, 26–45.

DeLuca, C., Willis, J., Cowie, B., Harrison, C., Coombs, A., Gibson, A., & Trask, S. (2019c). Policies, programs, and practices: Exploring the complex dynamics of assessment education in teacher education across four countries. *Frontiers in Education, 4*. https://doi.org/10.3389/feduc.2019.00132 (online).

DinanThompson, M., & Penney, D. (2015). Assessment literacy in primary physical education. *European Physical Education Review, 21*(4), 485–503.

Doll, M. A. (2005). Capacity and currere. *Journal of Curriculum Theorizing, 21*(3), 21–28.

Edwards, F. (2013). Quality assessment by science teachers: Five focus areas. *Science Education International, 24*(2), 212–226.

Ekström, A. (2013). Epistemic positioning and frameworks for participation: Learning to assess objects of craft in teacher education. *Learning, Culture and Social Interaction, 2*, 277–292.

Falsgraf, C. (2005, April). *Why a national assessment summit? New visions in action.* National Assessment Summit. Meeting conducted in Alexandria, VA.

Fan, Y. C., Wang, T. H., & Wang, K. H. (2011). A web-based model for developing assessment literacy of secondary in-service teachers. *Computers & Education, 57*(2), 1727–1740.

Fenstermacher, G. D., & Richardson, V. (2005). On making determinations of quality in teaching. *Teachers College Record, 107*(1), 186–213.

Firoozi, T., Razavipour, K., & Ahmadi, A. (2019). The language assessment literacy needs of Iranian EFL teachers with a focus on reformed assessment policies. *Language Testing in Asia, 9*(1), 1–14.

Fulcher, G. (2012). Assessment literacy for the language classroom. *Language Assessment Quarterly, 9*(2), 113–132.

Gareis, C. R. (2007). Reclaiming an important teacher competency: The lost art of formative assessment. *Journal of Personnel Evaluation in Education, 20*(17), 17–20.

Göçer, A. (2011). Evaluation of written examination question of Turkish language in accordance with Bloom's taxonomy. *Croatian Journal of Education, 13*(2), 161–183.

Gotch, C. M., & McLean, C. (2019). Teacher outcomes from a statewide initiative to build assessment literacy. *Studies in Educational Evaluation, 62*, 30–36.

Gu, P. Y. (2014). The unbearable lightness of the curriculum: What drives the assessment practices of a teacher of English as a Foreign Language in a Chinese secondary school? *Assessment in Education: Principles, Policy & Practice, 21*(3), 286–305.

Guskey, T. (2007). Using assessment to improve teaching and learning. In D. Reeves (Ed.), *Ahead of the curve: The power of assessment to transform teaching and learning* (pp. 15–29). Solution Tree Press.

Hargreaves, A., & Goodson, I. (1996). Teachers' professional lives: Aspirations and actualities. In I. Goodson & A. Hargreaves (Eds.), *Teachers' professional lives* (pp. 1–27). Falmer.

Hasse, S., Joachim, C., Bögeholz, S., & Hammann, M. (2014). Assessing teaching and assessment competences of biology teacher trainees: Lessons from item development. *International Journal of Education in Mathematics Science and Technology, 2*(3), 192–205.

Hattie, J. (2008). *Visible learning: A synthesis of over 800 meta-analyses relating to achievement.* Routledge.

Hay, P. J., & Penney, D. (2009). Proposing conditions for assessment efficacy in physical education. *European Physical Education Review, 15*(3), 389–405.

Herppich, S., Praetorius, A. K., Förster, N., Glogger-Frey, I., Karst, K., Leutner, D., Behrmann, L., Böhmer, M., Ufer, S., Klug, J., Hetmanek, A., Ohle, A., Böhmer, I., Karing, C., Kaiser, J., & Südkamp, A. (2018). Teachers' assessment competence: Integrating knowledge-, process-, and product-oriented approaches into a competence-oriented conceptual model. *Teaching and Teacher Education, 76*, 181–193.

Hill, M., Cowie, B., Gilmore, A., & Smith, L. F. (2010). Preparing assessment-capable teachers: What should preservice teachers know and be able to do? *Assessment Matters, 2*, 43–65.

Hill, M. F., Ell, F. R., & Eyers, G. (2017). Assessment capability and student self-regulation: The challenge of preparing teachers. *Frontiers in Education, 2*. https://doi.org/10.3389/feduc.2017.00021 (online).

Howley, M. D., Howley, A., Henning, J. E., Gilla, M. B., & Weade, G. (2013). Intersecting domains of assessment knowledge: School typologies based on interviews with secondary teachers. *Educational Assessment, 18*(1), 26–48.

Inbar-Lourie, O. (2008). Constructing a language assessment knowledge base: A focus on language assessment courses. *Language Testing, 25*(3), 385–402.

Inbar-Lourie, O. (2013). Guest editorial to the special issue on language assessment literacy. *Language Testing, 30*(3), 301–307.

Jang, E. E., & Sinclair, J. (2018). Ontario's educational assessment policy and practice: A double-edged sword? *Assessment in Education: Principles, Policy & Practice, 25*(6), 655–677.

Jones, J. (2014). Student teachers developing a critical understanding of formative assessment in the modern foreign languages classroom on an initial teacher education course. *The Language Learning Journal, 42*(3), 275–288.

Klinger, D. A., McDivitt, P. R., Howard, B. B., Munoz, M. A., Rogers, W. T., & Wylie, E. C. (2015). *The classroom assessment standards for PreK-12 teachers.* Kindle Direct Press.

Klug, J., Schultes, M. T., & Spiel, C. (2018). Assessment at school–teachers' diary-supported implementation of a training program. *Teaching and Teacher Education, 76*, 298–308.

Koh, K., Burke, L. E. C. A., Luke, A., Gong, W., & Tan, C. (2018). Developing the assessment literacy of teachers in Chinese language classrooms: A focus on assessment task design. *Language Teaching Research, 22*(3), 264–288.

Leavy, A. M., McSorley, F. A., & Boté, L. A. (2007). An examination of what metaphor construction reveals about the evolution of pre-service teachers' beliefs about teaching and learning. *Teaching and Teacher Education, 23*, 1217–1233.

References

Leirhaug, P. E., MacPhail, A., & Annerstedt, C. (2016). 'The grade alone provides no learning': Investigating assessment literacy among Norwegian physical education teachers. *Asia-Pacific Journal of Health, Sport and Physical Education, 7*(1), 21–36.

Looney, A., Cumming, J., van Der Kleij, F., & Harris, K. (2018). Reconceptualising the role of teachers as assessors: Teacher assessment identity. *Assessment in Education: Principles, Policy & Practice, 25*(5), 442–467.

Mak, P. (2019). Impact of professional development programme on teachers' competencies in assessment. *Journal of Education for Teaching, 45*(4), 481–485.

Marais, N., Niemann, R., & Kotzé, G. (2008). Leadership for redressing assessment competence in schools. *Education as Change, 12*(1), 151–167.

Matre, S., & Solheim, R. (2015). Writing education and assessment in Norway: Towards shared understanding, shared language and shared responsibility. *L1 Educational Studies in Language and Literature, (Scand. L1 Res.), 15*, 1–33.

Mertler, C. A. (2004). Secondary teachers' assessment literacy: Does classroom experience make a difference? *American Secondary Education, 33*(1), 49–64.

Mitchell, C., & Weber, S. (1999). *Reinventing ourselves as teachers: Beyond nostalgia.* Falmer.

Mockler, N. (2011). Beyond 'what works': Understanding teacher identity as a practical and political tool. *Teachers and Teaching, 17*, 517–528.

Muhammad, N., Hama, F., & Bardakçı, M. (2019). Iraqi EFL teachers' assessment literacy: Perceptions and practices. *Arab World English Journal (AWEJ), 10*(2), 431–442.

Park, Y. (2017). Examining South Korea's elementary physical education performance assessment using assessment literacy perspectives. *International Electronic Journal of Elementary Education, 10*(2), 207–213.

Pastore, S., & Andrade, H. L. (2019). Teacher assessment literacy: A three-dimensional model. *Teaching and Teacher Education, 84*, 128–138.

Plake, B. S., Impara, J. C., & Fager, J. J. (1993). Assessment competencies of teachers: A national survey. *Educational Measurement: Issues and Practice, 12*(4), 10–12.

Popham, W. J. (2004). Why assessment illiteracy is professional suicide. *Educational Leadership, 62*(1), 82–83.

Popham, W. J. (2005). *Classroom assessment: What teachers need to know.* Allyn and Bacon.

Popham, W. J. (2006). Needed: A dose of assessment literacy. *Educational Leadership, 63*, 84–85.

Popham, W. J. (2008). *Transformative assessment.* ACSD.

Popham, W. J. (2009a). Assessment literacy for teachers: Faddish or fundamental? *Theory into Practice, 48*(1), 4–11.

Popham, W. J. (2009b). *Is assessment literacy the "Magic Bullet"?* The Blog of Harvard Education Publishing. http://www.hepg.org/blog/19

Popham, W. J. (2011). Assessment literacy overlooked: A teacher educator's confession. *The Teacher Educator, 46*(4), 265–273.

Popham, W. J. (2013). *Classroom assessment: What teachers need to know* (7th ed.). Pearson.

Poskitt, J. (2014). Transforming professional learning and practice in assessment for learning. *Curriculum Journal, 25*(4), 542–566.

Putnam, R. T., & Borko, H. (1997). Teacher learning: Implications of new views of cognition. In *International handbook of teachers and teaching* (pp. 1223–1296). Springer.

Quitter, S. M. (1999). Assessment literacy for teachers: Making a case for the study of test validity. *The Teacher Educator, 34*(4), 235–243.

Quitter, S. M., & Gallini, J. K. (2000). Teachers' assessment literacy and attitudes. *The Teacher Educator, 36*(2), 115–131.

Rasooli, A., Zandi, H., & DeLuca, C. (2018). Re-conceptualizing classroom assessment fairness: A systematic meta-ethnography of assessment literature and beyond. *Studies in Educational Evaluation, 56*, 164–181.

Schafer, W. D. (1993). Assessment literacy for teachers. *Theory into Practice, 32*(2), 118–126.

Schneider, C., & Bodensohn, R. (2017). Student teachers' appraisal of the importance of assessment in teacher education and self-reports on the development of assessment competence. *Assessment in Education: Principles, Policy & Practice, 24*(2), 127–146.

Smith, K. (2007). Empowering school- and university-based teacher educators as assessors: A school–university cooperation. *Educational Research and Evaluation, 13*(3), 279–293.

Smith, K. (2011). Professional development of teachers: A prerequisite for AfL to be successfully implemented in the classroom. *Studies in Educational Evaluation, 37*, 55–61.

Starck, J. R., Richards, K. A. R., & O'Neil, K. (2018). A conceptual framework for assessment literacy: Opportunities for physical education teacher education. *Quest, 70*(4), 519–535.

Stiggins, R. J. (1991a). Relevant classroom assessment training for teachers. *Educational Measurement: Issues and Practice, 10*(1), 7–12.

Stiggins, R. J. (1991b). Assessment literacy. *Phi Delta Kappan, 72*, 534–539.

Stiggins, R. J. (1995). Assessment literacy for the 21st century. *Phi Delta Kappan, 77*(3), 238–245.

Stiggins, R. J. (1997). *Student centered classroom assessment*. Prentice Hall.

Stiggins, R. J. (1999a). Evaluating classroom assessment training in teacher education programs. *Educational Measurement: Issues and Practice, 18*(1), 23–27.

Stiggins, R. J. (1999b). Are you assessment literate? *The High School Journal, 6*(5), 20–23.

Stiggins, R. J. (1999c). Assessment, student confidence, and school success. *Phi Delta Kappan, 81*(3), 191–198.

Stiggins, R. J. (2002a). Assessment crisis: The absence of assessment for learning. *Phi Delta Kappan, 83*(10), 758–765.

Stiggins, R. J. (2002b). Learning teams for assessment literacy. *Journal of Staff Development, 30*(4), 5–7.

Stiggins, R. J. (2004). New assessment beliefs for a new school mission. *Phi Delta Kappan, 86*, 22–27.

Stiggins, R. J. (2005). From formative assessment to assessment for learning: A path to success in standards-based schools. *Phi Delta Kappan, 87*, 324–328.

Stiggins, R. J. (2010). Essential formative assessment competencies for teachers and school leaders. In H. L. Andrade & G. J. Cizek (Eds.), *Handbook of formative assessment* (pp. 233–250). Routledge.

Stiggins, R. J. (2014). Improve assessment literacy outside of schools too. *Phi Delta Kappan, 96*(2), 67–72.

Stiggins, R. J., Arter, J. A., Chappuis, J., & Chappuis, S. (2006). *Classroom assessment for student learning: Doing it right, using it well*. Educational Testing Service.

Stiggins, R. J., Arter, J. A., Chappuis, J., & Chappuis, S. (2012). *Classroom assessment for student learning: Doing it right, using it well*. Prentice Hall.

Stiggins, R. J., & Chappuis, J. (2005). Using student-involved classroom assessment to close achievement gaps. *Theory into Practice, 44*, 11–18.

Stiggins, R. J., & Conklin, N. F. (1992). *In teachers' hands: Investigating the practices of classroom assessment*. Suny Press.

Stiggins, R. J., & Duke, D. (2008). Effective instructional leadership requires assessment leadership. *Phi Delta Kappan, 90*, 285–291.

Sultana, N. (2019). Language assessment literacy: An uncharted area for the English language teachers in Bangladesh. *Language Testing in Asia, 9*(1), 1–14.

Walters, F. S. (2010). Cultivating assessment literacy: Standards evaluation through language-test specification reverse engineering. *Language Assessment Quarterly, 7*(4), 317–342.

Williams, J. C. (2015). "Assessing without levels": Preliminary research on assessment literacy in one primary school. *Educational Studies, 41*(3), 341–346.

Willis, J., Adie, L., & Klenowski, V. (2013). Conceptualising teachers' assessment literacies in an era of curriculum and assessment reform. *The Australian Educational Researcher, 40*(2), 241–256.

References

Wyatt-Smith, C., & Adie, L. (2019). The development of students' evaluative expertise: enabling conditions for integrating criteria into pedagogic practice. *Journal of Curriculum Studies, 53,* 399–419.

Wyatt-Smith, C., Klenowski, V., & Gunn, S. (2010). The centrality of teachers' judgement practice in assessment: A study of standards in moderation. *Assessment in Education: Principles, Policy & Practice, 17*(1), 59–75.

Xu, Y., & Brown, G. T. (2016). Teacher assessment literacy in practice: A reconceptualization. *Teaching and Teacher Education, 58,* 149–162.

Yastıbaş, A. E., & Takkaç, M. (2018). Understanding language assessment literacy: Developing language assessments. *Journal of Language and Linguistic Studies, 14*(1), 178–193.

Zwick, R., Sklar, J. C., Wakefield, G., Hamilton, C., Norman, A., & Folsom, D. (2008). Instructional tools in educational measurement and statistics (ITEMS) for school personnel: Evaluation of three web-based training modules. *Educational Measurement: Issues and Practice, 27*(2), 14–27.

Chapter 4
Epistemic Assessment Capacity

with Michael Holden

Abstract This book presents a novel framework, *Thinking the Unthinkable*, aimed at cultivating teacher assessment capacity. The framework includes four fundamental capacities: epistemic, embodied, ethical, and experiential. In this chapter, the epistemic capacity is explored through literature, preservice teacher reflections and narratives, and interpretive analysis. At its core, the epistemic capacity is about reflecting on and challenging the knowledge systems that shape teaching, learning, and assessment in classrooms and schools. Guiding this capacity are the reflective questions: *What do learning and knowing mean to me, and how are they reflected in my assessments? And, what knowledge systems underpin my approach to assessment?* The chapter concludes with guidance for developing epistemic capacity in initial teacher education.

Keywords Epistemic · Epistemology · Learning · Knowing · Epistemic curiosity · Epistemic empathy · Assessment · Knowledge systems · Teacher education · Teacher reflection · Teacher development

"I think that… I wonder if…It seems to me" are the kind of thinking and imagining that teacher educators enjoy hearing their preservice teachers say when they are learning about assessment. These comments are traces of *epistemic* assessment capacity. Preservice teachers develop epistemic capacity as they learn about theories of learning, knowing, and assessment that have changed over time and cultivate their curiosity about how different assessment practices are valued by different subject disciplines and cultures. In our study, with preservice teachers across four countries (Australia, Canada, England, and New Zealand), this developing epistemic assessment awareness was evident in preservice teacher reflections like:

> Throughout this unit I have found myself questioning if the quizzes that we are giving to the students are helping them in any way. I have been seeing a trend in the marks that those who have done poorly on the first test have often found similar results on other forms of assessment throughout the unit. … I often try to find a trend in the students' errors, but cannot always find one and therefore do not know what to provide them as formative feedback. But

> I also know that my check marks are not really teaching them anything. I have for sure been struggling with assessment in Organic Chemistry because the students do need practice – but I am not sure if constant quizzes are the best way to do this. (Canadian preservice teacher)

In this reflection, the preservice teacher wondered if the assessment practice of regular quizzes with "checkmarks" as feedback "is teaching them [students] anything." This query reflects an epistemic awareness of different orientations to assessment, such as the role of formative assessment and feedback, as they are aware that the purpose of these assessment practices is to help students improve. Teacher educators reading this reflection from a learning theory epistemic lens might also conclude that the preservice teacher adheres to a more behaviourist view of learning in that they see merit in practice as repeated revisiting of ideas. Awareness of the epistemic traditions of the discipline of Organic Chemistry might lead the educator to cast a different light on this. Subject-specific or disciplinary knowledge will influence what types of assessment patterns are valued and more commonly practised in each discipline (Heritage & Wylie, 2020). Organic Chemistry has a strong vertical organisation as a knowledge system, for example, with its agreed rules for naming compounds (Bernstein, 2000). The preservice teacher's interest in trends in student errors suggests that they consider there are likely to be patterns in student reasoning and consistent ideas underpinning student responses. Teacher educators engaging with this type of inquiry may point the preservice teacher towards identifying the patterns that are inconsistent with how organic chemists think so they could share these insights with students who could then use disciplinary epistemic ways of reasoning to inform their self-assessment thinking and action. It could be that the preservice teacher is already beginning to recognise that students need a breadth and depth of experience in the disciplinary rules across different problem contexts for them to build a robust understanding. In this short reflection, the preservice teacher is developing their epistemic assessment capacity through their questioning and is ready to explore the various epistemic foundations that inform assessment choices.

4.1 What Is Epistemic Assessment Capacity?

The *epistemic assessment capacity* represents a preservice teacher's learning to recognise, interpret, and interrogate the relationship between theories of knowing and learning and assessment. Teachers with strong epistemic assessment capacity examine the linkages between their beliefs about learning, knowledge, and knowing and their orientation to and practice of assessment. At its core, epistemic assessment capacity is about awareness, curiosity, and empathy about making sense of learning and knowing.

As highlighted in the core questions at the heart of this book (see Fig. 4.1), an epistemic assessment capacity brings these questions together as: *What does learning and knowing mean to me, and how are they reflected in my assessments? What knowledge systems underpin my approach to assessment?*

4.1 What Is Epistemic Assessment Capacity?

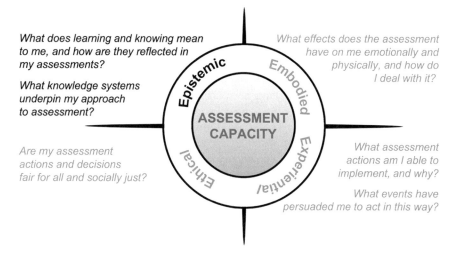

Fig. 4.1 Core questions with focus on the epistemic capacity

The epistemic capacity foregrounds the importance of ways of thinking about learning and knowing when assessing as part of supporting teachers and teacher educators as they develop their assessment decision-making.

Epistemology is concerned with the theory of knowledge and its philosophical study, how knowledge is constructed, and how knowledge is evaluated (Shar et al., 2020). James Ferrier (1854), who coined the term, argued that epistemology—a theory of knowledge—was necessary to answer such questions as "What is knowing and the known? ... What is knowledge?" (p. 46). These are clearly helpful questions when also contemplating the relationships between knowledge, knowing, and assessment. Epistemology sits at the root of all teaching, learning, and assessment as educators communicate stances towards knowledge (i.e., how teachers interpret curriculum, learning, and broader reality; what students are to learn); pedagogy and learning (i.e., the actions that lead to students' construction of knowledge); and assessment (i.e., activities that help make what students know and can do 'visible' and involve the evaluation of students' knowledge, broadly defined). Each of these aspects is important because, as Bernstein (2000) notes, schools distribute access to different knowledge systems and values through the interplay of the message systems of assessment, pedagogy, and curriculum. In our Assessment Capacity Framework, our interest lies in how preservice teachers, and teachers more generally, identify, develop, challenge, and possibly change their epistemological understandings about teaching, learning, and assessment. *How do the various knowledge sources and knowledge systems inform how teachers approach assessment?* Inherent to this process of challenge and change is the necessity to open spaces for epistemic awareness, interrogation, and growth.

It is this interest in the enactment of becoming knowledgeable through assessment that we emphasise the related concept of the epistemic. *Epistemic* refers to how knowers enact, encounter, and elaborate their knowing in diverse contexts (Brownlee et al., 2016; Siegel, 2006). In Australia, Canada, England, and New Zealand, epistemic assumptions that have informed educational assessment have evolved over time as understandings of what it means to learn have shifted. They have shifted as societies have become more diverse, and practices based on assumptions grounded in our shared colonial heritage have been challenged by greater recognition of the sophistication and relevance of Indigenous knowledges and worldviews. The shared colonial history of the four focal countries is further emphasised through Bernstein's concepts of vertical knowledge with an emphasis on formal school curriculum and disciplinary knowledge rooted in university structures and church canonical knowledge. The socially created and collective forms of knowledge that Bernstein recognises as horizontal knowledge are also important assessment orientations, as teachers acknowledge diversity in ways of knowing and coming to know, of demonstrating knowledge, and of being informed by social contexts.

Preservice teachers need opportunities to develop their epistemic awareness as public discourses about 'fake news' and colonisation, issues of equity and sustainability, and debates about truth in science and history are part of everyday life and national curriculum agendas. Researchers have also highlighted that there are different types of epistemologies: one's personal epistemologies—which involve how an individual views their own learning and knowledge construction and professional epistemologies—like relationships between learning theory and assessment, and disciplinary epistemologies that describe how those in a particular profession or field value and practise knowledge acquisition, enactment, and evaluation.

We introduce these complexities because *epistemology* and the *epistemic* are often overlooked in education and teacher preparation (Markauskaite & Goodyear, 2017). Moreover, education itself is not always given much attention in mainstream philosophy (Bakhurst, 2020), just as assessment receives little attention in research on pedagogy (Black & Wiliam, 2018). Yet epistemology, education, and assessment are deeply intertwined. As teachers learn to assess, they move between personal and professional epistemological experiences, negotiating their understandings and applying different epistemic resources in diverse ways (McLaughlan & Lodge, 2019). These experiences underpin teachers' epistemic assessment capacity. Brownlee et al. (2022), in a study with Australian and New Zealand teacher educators, proposed that epistemic reflexivity is essential for teacher educators. Teacher educators discern epistemic aims and ideals and deliberate and decide on epistemic processes and activities that preservice teachers can engage in to develop their awareness. Awareness of ideals, beliefs, and the epistemic agendas and resources within assessment practices becomes an important starting point.

Digging in deeper, a teacher who believes knowledge is constructed, learned, and shaped by feedback might endorse formative assessment and performance-based assessment practices, while a teacher who values knowledge as fact might instead value memorisation activities and paper-and-pencil summative assessments. The situation becomes more complex when layering contextual and systemic assessment priorities onto teachers' assessment practices, as each is imbued with its own epistemology. Take, for instance, a teacher who is personally committed to Assessment as

Learning—the use of assessment to further a student's self-regulation, metacognition, and capacity for self-learning (Andrade & Brookhart, 2016; Edwards, 2020) and put them into a system of education with a high level of accountability and dominant large-scale assessments. The two epistemologies often run counter to one another, stimulating tension for the teacher and potentially their students. Such complexities abound: a teacher's epistemic beliefs may differ from their colleagues,' the school administration may use different justifications for knowledge prioritisation and evidence with parents than with board officials, and systems of education may incorporate multiple, possibly contradictory, epistemological positions.

Fundamental assumptions underpinning the epistemic capacity are:

- Teachers have diverse epistemologies yielding various orientations and practices of assessment;
- Teachers' epistemic assessment capacity depends on their personal epistemologies (i.e., personal epistemic beliefs) as well as the professional epistemologies they develop through their teacher education experiences (i.e., field-accepted epistemologies about disciplinary knowledge, assessment, teaching, and learning);
- Teachers' epistemic assessment capacity is shaped by their context of learning and teaching, including their micro (classroom), meso (school), and macro (system) contexts; and
- Teachers' epistemic assessment capacity is influenced by their other assessment capacities—ethical, embodied, and experiential—as all are interconnected to one's epistemology; and
- Teachers' epistemic assessment capacity is cultivated through *epistemic awareness, epistemic curiosity,* and *epistemic empathy.*

4.2 Preservice Teachers' Epistemic Learning Experiences

> It's a little distressing to be honest. I'm still stuck between what I consider to be a strong assessment, and what works for me. I think this issue stems from my lack of scope and preparation…My most recent [practicum experiences] are not what I would call hallmarks of success in assessment practice, but I know where to go with my assessment skills for the future. I feel like I'm just a step behind where I should be, but I also still feel on track. (Canadian preservice teacher)

Some readers may see parts of themselves reflected in this preservice teacher's response—as educators, we certainly do. When teachers begin to develop their assessment capacity, they must reconcile existing beliefs with what they learn from their initial teacher education programme, from assessment research, and from placement experiences. They may need to resolve tensions between their own epistemic beliefs and those articulated as so-called best practices by mentor teachers, teacher education programme instructors, and student peers (Ricca, 2012; Wood & Butt, 2014). We see this act of weighing assessment practices as epistemologically essential. If teacher educators are to address the longstanding refrain that teachers do not have sufficient *assessment literacy* (Birenbaum et al., 2015; Mandinach & Gummer, 2013; Schneider et al., 2013), assessment education needs to include the origin stories and foundations of assessment practices so teachers can develop their epistemic assessment awareness. Epistemic assessment capacity depends on a teacher's ability to recognise, interpret, and interrogate the understandings of learning, knowledge, and knowing that underpin these insights. We propose three aspects of *epistemic awareness*, each with the ability to provoke *epistemic curiosity* and *epistemic empathy*. These three aspects can inform preservice teachers and teacher educators as they work to cultivate the epistemic capacity: (1) awareness of knowledge, learning, and assessment concepts and how they change over time, (2) awareness of disciplinary orientations as fundamental to epistemic assessment capacity, and (3) exploring epistemic awareness, curiosity, and flexibility.

4.2.1 Awareness of Knowledge, Learning, and Assessment Concepts and How They Change

Concepts of assessment have changed over time as theories of knowledge and learning have developed. Early assessment orientations reflected behaviourist theories of learning and reflected social values associated with the establishment of mass public education. It was efficient to assess students with multiple choice and essay examinations, especially when learning was understood as an acquisition of knowledge that was fixed, objective, and transferable (Gipps, 1994; Sfard, 1998). Later developments in learning theory from the 1960s onwards extended behaviourist views of learning towards more participatory processes of learning, reflecting constructivist and socio-cultural views of knowledge (Sfard, 1998; Shepard, 2000, 2019; Shepard et al., 2016). These changing views of learning and knowledge led to changes in assessment theories and practices. Assessment theories like summative and formative purposes of assessment and the principles of Assessment for Learning have gained traction in policy and practice around the world. Some foundational assessment knowledge has been represented in professional standards and assessment standards, with Pastore and Andrade (2019) finding some high level of agreement in their Delphi survey of international assessment researchers. Yet within each of these orientations towards assessment are assumptions about the roles of students and teachers in interacting with knowledge. It is important for preservice teachers to have this awareness of the epistemic foundations of the practices and assessment approaches, so they are not just following the 'letter' of the assessment practice but can bring the 'spirit' of the assessment approach to life in their teaching (Marshall & Drummond, 2006; Shepard et al., 2016). In considering the epistemic capacity, teachers ask: *What is important for my students to learn, and how will I know when they have learned it? How am I understanding if a student has really grasped a concept? Are there other ways that students are making meaning and other ways I could be assessing their learning?*

4.2 Preservice Teachers' Epistemic Learning Experiences

We found preservice teachers from each of our country contexts engaging in this sort of epistemological questioning:

> I admit, I am feeling really nervous about starting up again. I suppose it will be worse in my NQT (newly qualified teacher) year…I feel like my A-Level subject knowledge is still so lacking, regardless of how many textbooks I've read, and videos I've watched. (English preservice teacher)

> Allocating time to meaningfully unpack knowledge to remain at the forefront of good assessment practices is an issue I believe I will have to contend with. (Canadian preservice teacher)

In their own ways, each of these preservice teachers has engaged in a questioning of assessment by querying the knowledge sources surrounding them. The English preservice teacher has made an assessment of their curriculum knowledge level and concluded it is "lacking." At this early stage of their learning about curriculum, teaching, and assessment, this English preservice teacher is becoming aware of how a wide or deep awareness of the discipline will give them greater confidence and inform their assessment practice. They anticipate this knowledge and awareness will grow as they begin to teach. The Canadian preservice teacher also is aware that they will need to maintain awareness of their knowledge of assessment theory and practice, conscious that the field is evolving. The Canadian preservice teacher is— to an extent—questioning their own epistemological stance. Their experiences thus far have prompted them to wonder: *How do teachers implement idealised practices in actual classroom spaces? Is the 'jargon' of research articles relevant to class-room practice? How do teachers navigate the beliefs and practices of their peers?* In many ways, these kinds of questions reflect important intersections between views of learning and views of assessment. Whether they are questioning their own capacities as teachers, their ability to reconcile conflicting knowledge sources, or the defensibility of classroom assessment decisions, these teachers are grappling with what knowledge means, how it is used, and the justifications that are invoked in making assessment decisions (Kane, 2006). Such considerations are directly relevant to teachers' developing epistemic assessment capacity.

As teachers develop their capacity to interrogate the nature of knowledge, its construction, and its implications for assessment, they encounter critical 'aha moments' that have the potential to shift their epistemic worldview. In this process, simply being aware enough to wonder and articulate one's epistemic beliefs can be a marker of developing epistemological capacity. In the following comment, a New Zealand preservice teacher analyses the different contributions of tests and daily formative assessment:

> I believe that when teachers make overall teacher judgments from assessment practices, you find out other information that may not be in the standard tests taken throughout the school year. Yes, those tests can help guide you into areas that need more work, but I believe the more information about our students we can find through formative assessment, the better, as this can guide us daily on students' needs. (New Zealand preservice teacher)

Being able to critique an assessment practice and make reasonable and defensible decisions about this is a fundamental feature of classroom assessment (Earl, 2007;

Popham, 2009; Xu & Brown, 2016). The defensibility of a decision rests in no small part on a teacher's ability to justify the source of their inferences and to assess students in ways that align with how curriculum knowledge is constructed and evaluated. In short, these are epistemic decisions.

As preservice teachers engage in their career-long assessment learning journey, they will inevitably encounter assessment epistemologies dissimilar to their own. As indicated by the voices of some of the preservice teachers involved in this study, this can be a somewhat jarring experience. A possible reason that epistemic capacity can be jarring is that it underscores that assessment practices vary and can be inconsistent across contexts. In navigating dissimilar assessment epistemologies, beginning teachers are directly or indirectly forced to (re)consider their own. These potentially generative moments of dissonance are often foregrounded when preservice teachers compare and contrast their teacher education assessment experiences, in both coursework and practicum, with the assessment theory and principles being promulgated in their programme. Developing epistemological capacity is a challenging task, especially when preservice teachers encounter a wealth of knowledge sources, not all of which agree with one another, which is why it is framed as an open-ended capacity.

Developing an epistemic capacity within assessment is an iterative process of experience and developing understanding across contexts. It is highly related to the ethical capacity as teachers consider the consequences of their assessment decisions for students and has been widely incorporated into research examining how teachers develop their identity as assessors. Looney and colleagues (2018) noted that *assessment identity* is always in the making, shaped by experiences within and beyond the classroom: assessment identity is "framed and reframed over a career and mediated by context in which teachers work and live" (p. 446). This can be an intimidating prospect for beginning teachers. For example, an Australian preservice teacher reflected on how they had realised how important it was to interconnect different parts of a classroom assessment task design, but making a rubric that aligned with the task was challenging as they did not yet fully understand the nature and role of rubrics. The level of challenge in achieving full alignment between different aspects of an assessment task design may seem equally familiar to readers, so it can be reassuring for preservice teachers to know that developing assessment knowledge and awareness of the epistemic foundations is an always developing process. Teacher educators have an invaluable role to play in supporting teachers to interrogate these sources and to navigate a complex and contested terrain that teachers will travel through across the course of their professional careers (Timperley, 2015).

4.2.2 Awareness of Disciplinary Orientations

Until recently, research and development in assessment have accorded only limited attention to the epistemic dimension of different curriculum learning areas (e.g., Coffey et al., 2011). Now, greater understanding of how the different disciplines generate, legitimate, and communicate knowledge (e.g., science studies), coupled with the inclusion of the competencies for lifelong and lifewide learning as part of a 'knowledge society,' has led to the inclusion of the epistemic dimensions of some learning areas in some national curricula. The expansion of curriculum to include consideration of the epistemic dimensions has simultaneously increased the challenge for teachers in terms of what they need to teach and assess and provided them with a set of tools that can inform their assessment and students' self-assessment. Closer attention to disciplinary practices and ways of thinking and communicating has highlighted how teacher assessment practice can vary according to learning focus. It has focused attention on the distinct affordances different learning areas have in making student learning 'visible' and offering useful feedback (Cowie & Moreland, 2015; Cowie et al., 2013; Heritage & Wylie, 2020). For example, in writing, there may not be as much explicit subject matter to be taught, and so feedback tends to focus on how individual students could improve their writing. The peer assessment process provides students with an interested and critical audience for their work (Cowie & Khoo, 2018; Parr et al., 2021). By way of contrast, in science, there is a body of knowledge that is generally regarded as giving the subject "unique and objectively defined aims" (Black & Wiliam, 2006, p. 85), and so feedback is more directly focused towards helping all students achieve the same conceptual goal. In technology education, as this is conceived in New Zealand (MOE, 2007), product specifications provide authentic 'success criteria' for teachers and students to use to evaluate and enhance student thinking and work (Cowie et al., 2013).

The preservice teachers in our study called on their epistemic understandings of a curriculum learning area when creating an assessment, as is clearly illustrated in the following reflection on the nature of an appropriate focus for assessment in French:

> Who knew creating quizzes were so difficult? Especially in French where you really need to be careful with the verbs that are chosen (regular vs. irregular), it is very difficult to ensure that the tests are appropriate for students. Majority of the questions are grammar-based, but there is no good way around it. I consistently see spelling errors and poor understanding of verbs in general. It is the basis for communicating in the language! (Canadian preservice teacher)

It is interesting to compare this reflection on the assessment tradition of quizzes in French with the very first reflection in the chapter, where the focus was Organic Chemistry. Both of these reflections focus on the language within assessment in these two different disciplines. Language in Organic Chemistry was more about encapsulating discipline-specific concepts, whereas language precision in French was more about clarity of everyday communication, both written and oral. Clarity and precision of communication in Organic Chemistry are reflective of assessment confirming the epistemic priorities of vertical knowledge compared with the quiz in French, which was prioritising the epistemic domains of performance in terms of horizontal knowledge (Bernstein, 2000). Disciplinary epistemic distinctions are also evident in the next reflection, where the preservice teacher describes circling the room to inquire into student learning in an art class and then a maths class:

> My Arts supervisor explained that the room is structured in a semi-circle so she can sit at the front and physically see every student's artwork from where she is - this is her assessment for

> learning. We also walk around the room and ask students 'What are you representing here?' etc. to check for understanding and give direct feedback … I can hear [my uni lecturer's] voice in my head saying 'Show me, don't tell me!' so I have ideas for my AfL. In Maths, we work similarly by walking around the class and assessing students as we pass by asking them questions or checking their working. (Australian preservice teacher)

The epistemic resources (Elby & Hammer, 2010) the preservice teacher draws on seem similar—involving walking interactions and questioning—but also subtly different in teaching their different subjects. In art, they ask a conceptual question about the epistemic process: "What are you representing here?", whereas, in the maths class, the questions seem to be more about checking that expected disciplinary solution processes are being followed. As many teachers teach more than one subject discipline, an awareness of the epistemic traditions within disciplines can help preservice teachers to be flexible as they develop their assessment capacity.

Epistemologies and epistemic beliefs vary by context and individuals, creating epistemological diversity even within sectors (Robertson, 2013). Teachers may or may not be aware they bring their epistemic histories from their communities to their assessment learning and practice. For example, a teacher from a community that prioritises relationships and oral stories may be more attuned to knowledge from these sources as being valuable. A student whose mother is a historian may be sceptical of the notion of history as objective truth. However, they may engage with evidence—its source, quality, and the dynamics of its interpretation—in a manner similar to the way a student of physics might, albeit the nature of the evidence they use is different (Yates et al., 2016). Teachers recognising that students come with different epistemic orientations, which are likely to be context-dependent, is an important element of the epistemic capacity. Shar and colleagues (2020) offer a compelling example of how a student might think differently: "when a student enters a science class learning about electrostatics, she likely thinks very differently about knowledge than when she is in a discussion with her friends about what pizza to order" (p. 3). Put another way, the personal epistemic resources students activate are sensitive to context and include the processes, histories, and ways of knowing associated with that context (Elby & Hammer, 2010).

These reflections highlight some of the dimensions of epistemic capacity and also highlight the interconnections with the other capacities. There is evidence of embodied capacity to engage with struggle and wonder, with the ethical capacity to ask what is best for students and their learning, and with the experiential capacity to try out new practices with students and be guided by mentor teachers. These dimensions are brought together by epistemic awareness, curiosity, and flexibility that enable the preservice teacher to be open to having their beliefs and knowledge extended by their experiences.

4.2.3 Exploring Epistemic Awareness, Curiosity, and Flexibility

As teachers develop their assessment capacity, they will inevitably encounter episte-mological diversity in how learning, knowledge, and knowing are understood by their colleagues and students. As we have described, not all teachers, students, parents, administrators, and policymakers will hold the same epistemic beliefs. Moreover, assessment scholars themselves disagree on critical aspects of assessment and peda-gogy, including how assessment should be conceptualised or what terms most effec-tively convey the state of the field to teachers and teacher educators (Bennett, 2011; Black & Wiliam, 2018; Moss, 2007). Consider the following response to a university assessment discussion between preservice teachers:

> I noticed that everyone had a lot to say...and had reasoning that they felt needed to be explained. Even in similar groups, the opinions were different. (Canadian preservice teacher)

As this quote suggests, there is a great deal of diversity in preservice teachers' beliefs about knowledge and learning. Indeed, as Markauskaite and Goodyear (2017) reflect: "University is an odd space in which to learn professional knowledge. It is a hybrid space where three epistemic cultures of learning, research and the profession come together" (p. 255). Yet as we have seen from our preservice teacher reflec-tions, epistemic foundations for assessment have been evident when there have been opportunities to notice diversity and encouragement to be curious. Teacher educa-tors can draw on the hybrid spaces of teacher education to cue preservice teachers to develop their awareness and then to be curious about differences and flexible in their assessment planning and responses. A persistent research finding is that teachers and teacher educators have significant variability in their knowledge and attitudes towards assessment—its practices, purposes, and relevance (Brown, 2008; Brown et al., 2019; DeLuca & Klinger, 2010; Volante & Fazio, 2007). This diversity can also be seen in the variability of teacher educators' assessment epistemologies (Coombs et al., 2020) and the multiple aims and nature of assessment education within teacher education (Coombs et al., 2020; Hill et al., 2017; Smith et al., 2014).

For these reasons, epistemic openness and flexibility are important elements of the epistemic assessment capacity for preservice teachers who encounter epistemolog-ical diversity in ways that in-service teachers do not. For example, while all teachers must navigate the epistemological uncertainty of what different stakeholders like parents, school leaders, or students believe and value (Bonner, 2013; Looney et al., 2018; Marshall & Drummond, 2006), preservice teachers are uniquely tasked with additionally navigating the epistemological beliefs of their mentor teachers and their teacher education programme teachers. The possibility for tension between preser-vice and mentor teachers is well-documented in the teacher education literature (e.g., see Cochran-Smith et al., 2008; Darling-Hammond & Bransford, 2005; Falkenberg & Smits, 2010; Hobson et al., 2009; Holden, 2015; Hudson, 2013). Multiple preser-vice teachers articulated how such tensions could involve epistemologies of assess-ment, with their awareness of this sparked/activated by their concern with student experience of the assessment process:

> I did not agree with my [mentor teacher's] methods of formatively assessing her [grade] 5/6 students' understanding of the math lesson. During the math talk, students would need to answer 8 questions correctly before being allowed to leave the carpet and return to their seats to work independently. On multiple occasions, 1 student would cry because he did not understand and therefore could not leave the carpet. I feel as though this method of assessment singles out students who may learn at a different speed, or not well under pressure. I am sure he felt very stressed and embarrassed. I know that this is not a method I will be implementing in my future classroom. (Canadian preservice teacher)

> Unfortunately, I don't have much to say about assessment and evaluation in my [mentor teacher's] classroom, and I believe we differ in our opinions on assessment and evaluation in quite a few areas. While we both believe in descriptive feedback, [my mentor teacher] is unable to provide timely assessments for their students. It could be up to two weeks between submission and handing back assignments. … This is a point of frustration for me. Students come up to me and ask about work, but I am unable to provide any useful information as I am completely removed from the assessment part of teaching. (Canadian preservice teacher)

Consistent with the extant literature on initial teacher education, these preservice teachers are grappling with the difference between their mentor teachers' assessment practices and their own epistemic beliefs about assessment and its impact on learning and learners. We do not include these quotations as a critique of mentor teachers; rather, they reflect the reality of learning to assess amid varied epistemological positions towards assessment. This context for learning to assess is further complicated by the power relationships that exist between preservice teachers and mentor teachers, even in highly productive relationships. It is inevitable that preservice teachers will encounter tensions as they navigate their personal epistemologies, their mentors' epistemological stances, and the dominant epistemological stances of their placement schools, teacher education programmes, and broader educational systems. We propose that epistemic awareness, curiosity, and flexibility enable the preservice teacher to wonder what beliefs about assessment, learning, and knowledge are informing different perspectives and that understanding can inform their assessment learning.

Navigating epistemological diversity is, therefore, not a problem to be solved but rather a recognition that this is how learning communities function. Schools, classrooms, universities, and communities represent a great diversity of ways of knowing. In order to develop their epistemic assessment capacity, teachers need to interrogate their own conceptions of knowledge, learning, what it means to know, and assessment. Such interrogations can emerge out of and benefit from encounters with different perspectives. A preservice teacher who reflected on not having experienced peer assessment because it somehow felt "academically dishonest" to read the assessment drafts written by peers was asked by a mentor teacher to plan for students to give one another peer feedback. The successful lesson challenged the epistemic assumptions the preservice teacher had started with. Here, the mentor teacher's epistemic beliefs (that peer review is a valuable source of co-learning) differed from the preservice teacher's initial concern (that peer review may encourage plagiarism). But, with the mentor teacher's encouragement, the preservice teacher was able to experiment with a new assessment practice, and this experience shifted their epistemic view. Rather than worrying about students colluding on their assignments, the

4.2 Preservice Teachers' Epistemic Learning Experiences

preservice teacher instead came to see peer review as a promising pedagogy and assessment process that they might implement in the future.

In another example, a preservice teacher related how she discussed her vision of co-constructing success criteria with her mentor teachers, who were sceptical about students' capacity to engage in this process:

> My [mentor teachers] and I talked about the idea of co-constructing success criteria. Neither of them were a big fan of the idea. They seemed to believe that, realistically, it was a lot to ask of some classrooms and that it would be difficult to mediate – they said that some students would not respond well, and many do respond well to clear instructions and goals. Finally, they said in preparation for postsecondary, in which goals are clearly stated, they believed that providing criteria that was created by the teacher was the best way to prepare them. We had a long conversation about it, and they said they could see where co-constructing success criteria sounds like a good idea, but are unsure if they believe it would work for all classes. It made me wonder what options there are for co-constructing success criteria in different grades and levels. It would be something I am interested in doing more research into. (Canadian preservice teacher)

We can see here that the preservice teacher is curious—"it made me wonder"—and open to other viewpoints. Moreover, the difference in opinions about success criteria led to a generative discussion of reasons and possibilities, with the preservice teacher stating they would investigate co-construction further.

Experiences and conversations like this are the heart of opportunities to develop the epistemic assessment capacity. As preservice teachers are open to and curious about navigating epistemological diversity—as they reconcile their existing conceptions and beliefs with those presented to them by their mentor teachers, their teacher education programme, and other diverse sources—new possibilities emerge. Supporting preservice teachers as they navigate these waters is directly relevant to teacher education because a teacher's epistemic beliefs directly shape the kinds of teaching, learning, and assessment that unfold (Looney et al., 2018; Stobart, 2008). As Susan Brookhart (2003) reminded us two decades ago, "instructional goals are not just pages in the district's curriculum. Instructional goals are heavily influenced by teacher beliefs about the subject matter and about what constituted appropriate instruction" (p. 10). Put simply, how we support teachers in navigating and developing epistemological capacity is critical to the lived curriculum students' encounter in classrooms every day (Aoki, 1993).

As we have illustrated, developing epistemological capacity requires teachers to question their own beliefs about knowledge, how it is constructed, and how it may be assessed. This process occurs amid diverse belief systems, and there is the very real possibility that teachers may simply ignore epistemology or not think deeply about the beliefs that underlie their practice (Looney et al., 2018; Xu & Brown, 2016). To that end, we suggest that to support preservice teachers in developing their epistemological capacity, researchers, teacher educators, and teacher education programmes need to cultivate epistemological awareness and curiosity as a basis for epistemic flexibility—to lay the foundations for an ongoing capacity to consider alternative ways of understanding teaching, learning, knowing, and assessment.

4.3 Developing Epistemic Assessment Capacity in Teacher Education

Teachers who enter the profession with an awareness and curiosity to explore the link between their beliefs about knowledge, learning and what it means to know, and their orientation and practice of assessment will be better suited to innovate and adapt their practice. While the need for innovation and adaptation has been omnipresent in the teaching profession, the recent impact of climate change, pandemics, technology, and mass migration has underscored how difficult it is to prepare teachers for the (un)known challenges of a future classroom. Fundamentally, what a teacher believes about knowledge—its nature, how it is constructed and communicated, and how it should be evaluated—will directly affect the kinds of assessment decisions that teacher makes in their daily practice. Teachers who are actively aware of their own conceptions of knowledge and learning and how these shape their approaches to assessment are better positioned to make assessment decisions that they can coherently explain to students, parents, and administrators.

The possibility for fostering epistemological flexibility does not mean that this is readily achievable in every teacher education programme. The short and fragmented structures of many teacher education programmes and the limited focus on assessment education in many contexts means preservice teachers may have few opportunities for contemplation and curiosity. Put another way, while epistemological curiosity does occur, it may not emerge on its own. Teacher educators can support preservice teachers' epistemological curiosity and meaningfully engage preservice teachers in the philosophically and pedagogically complex work of making assessment decisions through questioning and reflections such as:

- *What makes for effective assessment practice? How do these principles of assessment align with particular views of what knowledge is, how it is created, and how it can be assessed?*
- *What sources of evidence do teachers prioritise in their assessment practices, and how are they reflective of disciplinary expectations of knowledge and learning?*
- *How are different perspectives illuminating my own epistemic commitments, and what can I learn by approaching assessment differently?*

4.4 Conclusion

In this chapter, we have introduced more questions than we have answered. This is intentional. We do not posit a 'correct' or comprehensive epistemic stance for beginning teachers, nor do we suggest there is an ideal path to develop epistemic assessment capacity. In this sense, we reject the notion that there is an objective epistemological stance to be had (Banks, 1993; Knight et al., 2014). At the same time, we also reject the stance of absolute relativism, where anything goes and any epistemic interpretation is immediately a defensible one (Brownlee et al., 2016; Siegel,

2006). Plainly, there are more and less valid sources and uses of assessment data and defensible and indefensible assessment decisions based on context (Earl, 2007; Kane, 2006; Messick, 1989; Pastore & Andrade, 2019). We propose that teacher educators can provide preservice teachers with the capacity to be aware, curious, and empathetic about assessment epistemologies and the decisions they result in. In foregrounding epistemic assessment capacity as one of the critical capacities for teachers as assessors, our goal is to directly engage teachers and teacher educators in questions of what knowledge is, how it is constructed and valued, and how it may be assessed. As evident throughout the remaining capacities, engaging with epistemological and epistemic learning is always interconnected with embodied, ethical, and experiential capacities. All capacities, we contend, are essential for more sound and productive assessment in schools and classrooms.

Michael Holden is a PhD Candidate at Queen's University, Ontario, Canada. His SSHRC-funded doctoral research examines principles of classroom assessment for emergent learning, with a focus on collaborating with teachers to foster learning through formative classroom assessment in complex spaces. ORCID: 0009-0000-0193-6861.

References

Andrade, H., & Brookhart, S. M. (2016). The role of classroom assessment in supporting self-regulated learning. In *Assessment for learning: Meeting the challenge of implementation* (pp. 293–309). Springer.

Aoki, T. T. (1993). Legitimating lived curriculum: Towards a curricular landscape of multiplicity. *Journal of Curriculum and Supervision, 8*(3), 255–268.

Bakhurst, D. (2020). Teaching and learning: Epistemic, metaphysical, and ethical dimensions—Introduction. *Journal of Philosophy of Education, 54*(2), 255–267.

Banks, J. A. (1993). The canon debate, knowledge construction, and multicultural education. *Educational Researcher, 22*(5), 4–14.

Bennett, R. E. (2011). Formative assessment: A critical review. *Assessment in Education: Principles, Policy and Practice, 18*(1), 5–25.

Bernstein, B. (2000). *Pedagogy, symbolic control, and identity: Theory, research, critique* (Vol. 5). Rowman & Littlefield.

Birenbaum, M., DeLuca, C., Earl, L., Heritage, M., Klenowski, V., Looney, A., Smith, K., Timperley, H., Volante, L., & Wyatt-Smith, C. (2015). International trends in the implementation of assessment for learning: Implications for policy and practice. *Policy Futures in Education, 13*(1), 117–140.

Black, P., & Wiliam, D. (2006). Developing a theory of formative assessment. In J. Gardner (Ed.), *Assessment and learning* (pp. 81–100). Sage.

Black, P., & Wiliam, D. (2018). Classroom assessment and pedagogy. *Assessment in Education: Principles, Policy and Practice, 25*(6), 551–575.

Bonner, S. M. (2013). Validity in classroom assessment: Purposes, properties, and principles. In J. H. McMillan (Ed.), *SAGE handbook of research on classroom assessment* (pp. 87–106). Sage.

Brookhart, S. M. (2003). Developing measurement theory for classroom assessment purposes and uses. *Educational Measurement: Issues and Practice, 22*(4), 5–12.

Brown, G. (2008). *Conceptions of assessment: Understanding what assessment means to teachers and students.* Nova Science Publishers.

Brown, G., Gebril, A., & Michaelides, M. (2019). Teachers' conceptions of assessment: A global phenomenon or a global localism. *Frontiers in Education, 4*(16). https://doi.org/10.3389/feduc.2019.00016 (online).

Brownlee, J. L., Schraw, G., Walker, S., & Ryan, M. (2016). Changes in preservice teachers' personal epistemologies. In J. A. Greene, W. A. Sandoval, & I. Bråten (Eds.), *Handbook of epistemic cognition* (pp. 300–317). Routledge.

Brownlee, J. L., Walker, S., L'Estrange, L., Ryan, M., Bourke, T., Rowan, L., & Johansson, E. (2022). Developing a pedagogy of teacher education for teaching for diversity: Exploring teacher educators' epistemic cognition for epistemic agency. In T. Bourke, D. Henderson, R. Spooner-Lane, & S. White (Eds.), *Reconstructing the work of teacher educators: Finding spaces in policy through agentic approaches—Insights from a research collective* (pp. 263–285). Springer Nature Singapore.

Cochran-Smith, M., Feiman-Nemser, S., & McIntyre, D. J. (Eds.). (2008). *Handbook of research on teacher education: Enduring questions in changing contexts* (3rd ed.). Routledge.

Coffey, J. E., Hammer, D., Levin, D. M., & Grant, T. (2011). The missing disciplinary substance of formative assessment. *Journal of Research in Science Teaching, 48*(10), 1109–1136.

Coombs, A. J., Ge, J., & DeLuca, C. (2020). From sea to sea: The Canadian landscape of assessment education. *Educational Research, 63*(1), 9–25.

Cowie, B., & Khoo, E. (2018). An ecological approach to understanding assessment for learning in support of student writing achievement. *Frontiers in Education, 3.* https://doi.org/10.3389/feduc.2018.00011 (online).

Cowie, B., & Moreland, J. (2015). Leveraging disciplinary practices to support students' active participation in formative assessment. *Assessment in Education: Principles, Policy & Practice, 22*(2), 247–264.

Cowie, B., Moreland, J., & Otrell-Cass, K. (2013). *Expanding notions of assessment for learning.* Springer.

Darling-Hammond, L., & Bransford, J. (Eds.). (2005). *Preparing teachers for a changing world: What teachers should learn and be able to do.* Jossey-Bass.

DeLuca, C., & Klinger, D. A. (2010). Assessment literacy development: Identifying gaps in teacher candidates' learning. *Assessment in Education: Principles, Policy & Practice, 17*(4), 419–438.

Earl, L. (2007). Assessment—A powerful lever for learning. *Brock Education Journal, 16*(1), 1–15.

Edwards, F. (2020). The effect of the lens of the teacher on summative assessment decision making: The role of amplifiers and filters. *The Curriculum Journal, 31*(3), 379–397.

Elby, A., & Hammer, D. (2010). Epistemological resources and framing: A cognitive framework for helping teachers interpret and respond to their students' epistemologies. In L. D. Bendixen & F. C. Feucht (Eds.), *Personal epistemology in the classroom: Theory, research, and implications for practice* (pp. 409–434). Cambridge University Press.

Falkenberg, T., & Smits, H. (Eds.). (2010). *Field experiences in the context of reform of Canadian teacher education programs* (Vol. 1). Canadian Association of Teacher Education.

Ferrier, J. F. (1854). *Institutes of metaphysic: The theory of knowing the mind.* W. Blackwood and Sons.

Gipps, C. (1994). Developments in educational assessment: What makes a good test? *Assessment in Education: Principles, Policy & Practice, 1*(3), 283–292.

Heritage, M., & Wylie, E. C. (2020). *Formative assessment in the disciplines: Framing a continuum of professional learning.* Harvard Education Press.

Hill, M. F., Ell, F., Grudnoff, L., Haigh, M., Cochran-Smith, M., Chang, W. C., & Ludlow, L. (2017). Assessment for equity: Learning how to use evidence to scaffold learning and improve teaching. *Assessment in Education: Principles, Policy & Practice, 24*(2), 185–204.

Hobson, A. J., Ashby, P., Malderez, A., & Tomlinson, P. D. (2009). Mentoring beginning teachers: What we know and what we don't. *Teaching and Teacher Education, 25*, 207–216.

References

Holden, M. (2015). *Associate-candidate relationships: A study of teacher education field experiences* (Unpublished master's thesis). Brock University.

Hudson, P. (2013). Desirable attributes and practices for mentees: Mentor teachers' expectations. *European Journal of Educational Research, 2*(3), 107–119.

Kane, M. T. (2006). Validation. In R. L. Brennan (Ed.), *Educational measurement* (4th ed., pp. 17–58). Praeger Publishers and National Council on Measurement in Education and American Council on Education.

Knight, S., Shum, S. B., & Littleton, K. (2014). Epistemology, assessment, pedagogy: Where learning meets analytics in the middle space. *Journal of Learning Analytics, 1*(2), 23–47.

Looney, A., Cumming, J., van Der Kleij, F., & Harris, K. (2018). Reconceptualising the role of teachers as assessors: Teacher assessment identity. *Assessment in Education: Principles, Policy and Practice, 25*(5), 442–467.

Mandinach, E., & Gummer, E. (2013). A systemic view of implementing data literacy in educator preparation. *Educational Researcher, 42*(1), 30–37.

Markauskaite, L., & Goodyear, P. (2017). *Epistemic fluency and professional education: Innovation, knowledgeable action and actionable knowledge.* Springer.

Marshall, B., & Drummond, M. J. (2006). How teachers engage with assessment for learning: Lessons from the classroom. *Research Papers in Education, 21*(2), 133–149.

McLaughlan, R., & Lodge, J. M. (2019). Facilitating epistemic fluency through design thinking: A strategy for the broader application of studio pedagogy within higher education. *Teaching in Higher Education, 24*(1), 81–97.

Messick, S. (1989). Validity. In R. L. Linn (Ed.), *Educational measurement* (3rd ed., pp. 13–103). Macmillan.

Moss, P. A. (2007). Reconstructing validity. *Educational Researcher, 36*(8), 470–476.

New Zealand Ministry of Education (MOE). (2007). *New Zealand curriculum.* Ministry of Education. https://nzcurriculum.tki.org.nz/The-New-Zealand-Curriculum

Parr, J., Jesson, R., Gadd, M., & Si'ilata, R. (2021). *Review of research in teaching and learning of writing.* New Zealand Ministry of Education.

Pastore, S., & Andrade, H. L. (2019). Teacher assessment literacy: A three-dimensional model. *Teaching and Teacher Education, 84*, 128–138.

Popham, W. J. (2009). Assessment literacy for teachers: Faddish or fundamental? *Theory into Practice, 48*(1), 4–11.

Ricca, B. (2012). Beyond teaching methods: A complexity approach. *Complicity: An International Journal of Complexity and Education, 9*(2), 31–51.

Robertson, E. (2013). The epistemic value of diversity. *Journal of Philosophy of Education, 47*(2), 299–310.

Schneider, M. C., Egan, K. L., & Julian, M. W. (2013). Classroom assessment in the context of high-stakes testing. In J. H. McMillan (Ed.), *SAGE handbook of research on classroom assessment* (pp. 55–70). Sage.

Sfard, A. (1998). On two metaphors for learning and the dangers of choosing just one. *Educational Researcher, 27*(2), 4–13.

Shar, K., Russ, R. S., & Laverty, J. T. (2020). Student epistemological framing on paper-based assessments. *Physical Review Physics Education Research, 16*(2), 1–15.

Shepard, L. A. (2000). The role of assessment in a learning culture. *Educational Researcher, 29*(7), 4–14.

Shepard, L. A. (2019). Classroom assessment to support teaching and learning. *Annals of the American Academy of Political and Social Science, 683*(1), 183–200.

Shepard, L. A., Penuel, W. R., & Davidson, K. A. (2016). *Using formative assessment to create coherent and equitable assessment systems.* University of Colorado Boulder.

Siegel, H. (2006). Epistemological diversity and education research: Much ado about nothing much? *Educational Researcher, 35*(2), 3–12.

Smith, L. F., Hill, M. F., Cowie, B., & Gilmore, A. (2014). Preparing teachers to use the enabling power of assessment. In C. Wyatt-Smith, V. Klenowski, & P. Colbert, Peta (Eds.), *Designing assessment for quality learning* (pp. 303–323). Springer.

Stobart, G. (2008). *Testing times: The uses and abuses of assessment*. Routledge.

Timperley, H. S. (2015). Continuing professional development. In W. Darity & E. Mielants (Eds.), *International encyclopedia of the social & behavioral sciences* (2nd ed., pp. 796–802). Elsevier.

Volante, L., & Fazio, X. (2007). Exploring teacher candidates' assessment literacy: Implications for teacher education reform and professional development. *Canadian Journal of Education, 30*(3), 749–770.

Wood, P., & Butt, G. (2014). Exploring the use of complexity theory and action research as frameworks for curriculum change. *Journal of Curriculum Studies, 46*(5), 676–696.

Yates, L., Woelert, P., Millar, V., & O'Connor, K. (2016). *Knowledge at the crossroads?: Physics and history in the changing world of schools and universities*. Springer.

Xu, Y., & Brown, G. T. L. (2016). Teacher assessment literacy in practice: A reconceptualization. *Teaching and Teacher Education, 58*, 149–162.

Chapter 5
Embodied Assessment Capacity

with Frances Edwards and Andrew Gibson

Abstract This book presents a novel framework, *Thinking the Unthinkable*, aimed at cultivating teacher assessment capacity. The framework includes four fundamental capacities: epistemic, embodied, ethical, and experiential. In this chapter, the embodied capacity is explored through literature, preservice teacher reflections and narratives, and interpretive analysis. Centrally, the embodied capacity responds to the physical, emotional, and socio-material experiences of assessment as felt within teachers' bodies as they learn about and implement assessment. The driving reflective question to attend to the embodied capacity is: *What effects does the assessment have on me emotionally and physically, and how do I deal with it?* The chapter concludes with guidance for developing the embodied capacity in initial teacher education.

Keywords Embodied learning · Embodied knowing · Reflexive agency · Teacher action · Assessment · Teacher education · Teacher reflection · Teacher development

Worry, late nights, feeling like everything is piling up—these are familiar feelings for teachers, often associated with assessment. For preservice teachers, these emotions and time pressures are compounded by being assessed themselves in their coursework and in their practical teaching placements, in which they receive ongoing feedback from students, mentor teachers, and teacher educators. In those placement experiences, preservice teachers are also learning to manage the emotions of the students they are assessing and their own emotional responses. Throughout our study of preservice teachers across four countries (Australia, Canada, England, and New Zealand), the range of *embodied* assessment experiences preservice teachers managed for themselves and their students featured in their ongoing reflections, such as in the following reflection:

> During my first few weeks at practicum, I felt very stressed out about teaching. Talking to my mentor teacher just caused me to get even more stressed, especially when it came to getting feedback that was used to improve my teaching strategies to further aid the students. My biggest issue was based on my poor time management skills. I was spending hours and hours on research and creating resources for my classes that were only finished the night

before or the morning before the class started. I have been trying to work to get ahead with my lesson planning and unit planning but I feel that everything was piling up. I find that I will need to get my sleep schedule sorted out because I think that the way that I had gone was very unsustainable and gearing up for a major crash. (Canadian preservice teacher)

I am a bit worried about this coming week back at School 2. I enjoyed teaching the students at School 1, and I think I connected and worked better with my Gr. 8's there. I'm a bit worried about going back to teaching Gr. 9's because the environment in high school is different and my class is bigger (Gr. 8: 22, Gr. 9: 29). I am currently writing a unit test for my Gr. 9 class and I'm not sure how well they will take it. When I gave them a quiz for AaL, they did not take it seriously. It was supposed to be a mock practice for the summative, but some of them treated it as a joke. I hope that they will be more serious on this test as it is an AoL. (Canadian preservice teacher)

These everyday assessment demands on teachers are not new. However, their pervasive regularity makes them influential in guiding teacher actions. Emotional demands and managing time pressures are the two biggest factors influencing teachers' intentions to leave the profession (Heffernan et al., 2022; Stacey et al., 2023). By identifying and naming the *embodied assessment capacity*—the capacity to manage the emotions and physical demands associated with assessment—as a key part of teaching, we acknowledge that teacher preparation includes learning to attend to the whole self of the assessor. The embodied assessment capacity also leads preservice teachers to consider the emotions and physicality of assessment experiences for themselves and their students. This chapter explores the literature about embodied experiences in assessment and learning research and identifies some of the embodied experiences that were evident in the assessment reflections of preservice teachers. The chapter highlights the value of developing awareness of and acknowledging that assessment has emotional and physical aspects, and this awareness can lead to preservice teachers developing their assessment agency.

5.1 What Is Embodied Assessment Capacity?

An *embodied assessment capacity* involves preservice teachers learning to manage the demands of assessment enacted through their bodies and emotions as they learn about, teach for, and lead their students in assessment. Learning to be aware of their own and their students' embodied experiences can enable teachers to navigate and promote sustainable, healthy, and manageable assessment experiences. As highlighted in the core questions at the heart of this book (see Fig. 5.1), an embodied assessment capacity asks: *What effects does assessment have on me, and how do I deal with it?*

The embodied assessment capacity is not about learning to be more embodied in the sense of using more gestures, but rather it is about becoming more aware and able to feel a greater sense of awareness over the personal effects of and materials of assessment. For example, for preservice teachers, this awareness and sense of control over assessment effects might be seen in the way that the preservice

5.1 What Is Embodied Assessment Capacity?

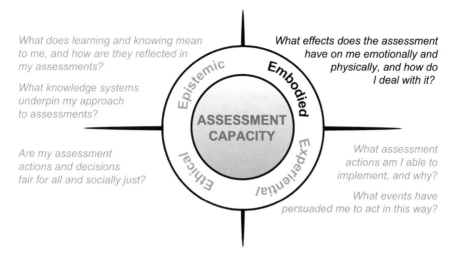

Fig. 5.1 Core questions with focus on the embodied capacity

teacher responds to challenging feedback from a mentor teacher, managing their emotions of defensiveness or uncertainty to make the most out of feedback to learn and improve. Lacking this awareness may mean that a preservice teacher engages in reactive responses to challenging feedback, such as withdrawal from a mentor teacher or a sense of inadequacy and despair. An embodied assessment capacity could help the preservice teacher in the second reflection begin to consider that students may treat a mock test as a joke if they are masking a lack of understanding, unfamiliarity with this form of assessment, or anxiety about their performance. This awareness could help the preservice respond by checking in with individual students rather than responding to students' emotions with an angry lecture about the need to take the assessment seriously and warnings like "if you don't pay attention, you will fail." Teacher educators have opportunities to directly teach that assessment is more than a neutral or objective activity; it is a set of practices that are socially situated and created through language, routines, and interactions. Teacher educators can also raise awareness about the embodied aspects of assessment with preservice teachers through scenarios or debriefing conversations as part of coursework. Exploring the consequences of each course of action with preservice teachers and discussing how to manage the emotions of assessment can lead to insights into how a teacher's actions can either strengthen the social bonds needed for learning (Bellocchi, 2019) or quickly escalate the initial problem.

Embodied assessment capacity acknowledges emotions and also suggests that an agent uses their whole body and environment to think (Gibson & Lang, 2019). Embodied assessment capacity shifts over time as it involves bodies and minds in assessment decision-making in situations that are continually changing (Charteris & Dargusch, 2018). Knowing that this capacity is one that will always be developing as teachers adapt to situations is an important realisation for preservice teachers, to prepare them for assessment and schooling contexts that are still to come. Also, the recognition that expertise in assessment is embodied and will become easier to manage and sustain as rhythms become familiar routines is potentially a helpful new way of thinking about learning to be assessors (Green & Hopwood, 2015). This chapter proposes that there is value for preservice teachers in developing active awareness of embodied aspects of being an assessor and learning to reflexively attend to how they are responding to assessment demands. Reflexivity is an extension of the concept of reflection as it is more than a rational process of deliberately looking back to identify learning that can inform decisions. Reflexive awareness is becoming aware of your own feelings and thoughts as they blend in continuous streams of evaluations and decisions, moving back and forth between past, present, and future (Archer, 2000; Lunn Brownlee et al., 2022). This awareness can support preservice teachers in their assessment development during their initial teacher education, transition into practice, and continued development through practice as teachers. As outlined in Chapter 6 about ethical assessment capacity, joyful teaching and assessment interactions are outcomes worth aiming for.

5.2 Preservice Teachers' Embodied Learning Experiences

Preservice teacher reflections frequently referred to embodied ways of learning and point to three implications for teacher educators. Promoting awareness for preservice teachers is one aspect, as many reflections included strong emotions associated with moments of realisation of what it meant to be an assessor. These realisations often included mixtures of positive and negative phrases and metaphors of physical and metaphysical struggle. Acknowledgement of the way that material and social environments were part of the physicality of learning to be an assessor was an aspect of assessment literacy that is not often identified. The embodied experiences could have been working with assessment tools or within the physical space but learning to manage these physical elements was consistently recognised by preservice teachers as essential to their assessment success. Finally, the role of self-assessment and reflexive awareness was associated with developing greater agency in learning to be an assessor. Thus, the following three themes are elaborated with excerpts from preservice teacher reflections and related to literature to exemplify how learning to be an assessor requires developing an embodied capacity: (a) assessment is an emotional rollercoaster, (b) embodied assessment occurs in situ with materials and spaces, and (c) learning occurs through managing competing demands through reflexive agency. Across these themes, the foundations principles for the embodied assessment capacity are evident:

- Teachers have diverse emotional and physical responses to assessment experiences;
- Awareness that assessment is an embodied act, and that learning to assess occurs through embodied knowing, is foundational to assessment capacity;

5.2 Preservice Teachers' Embodied Learning Experiences

- Acknowledging and naming the emotional and physical demands and dimensions of assessment, both for teachers and students, and considering how these demands and dimensions influence assessment decisions, consequences, outcomes, and learning supports is valuable in cultivating assessment capacity; and
- Teachers can transform their embodied responses to assessment through reflexive agency and action.

5.2.1 Awareness That Assessment Is an Emotional Rollercoaster

If assessment is represented only as a rational and purely cognitive activity, it can come as a shock for preservice teachers when they experience an emotional rollercoaster as described by a Canadian preservice teacher, "It's been a rollercoaster of learning and growing as a teacher." This sense of contending was evident in many of the reflections, such as this from an Australian preservice teacher who stated, "I know it's my juggle and my struggle but I'll get there!" If assessment is not acknowledged as a social and emotional process, the preservice teacher who experiences negative or unexpectedly strong emotions may question if something is wrong with them or if they are doing assessment 'right.' Acknowledging that assessment always involves emotions may help the preservice teacher to recognise, accept, and respond to those emotions as part of their developing professional identity. Steinberg (2015) has argued that assessment is an emotional practice and emphasises that assessment decisions are not neutral and always invoke emotions. He, too, describes teachers as being on an emotional rollercoaster, and the ups and downs were certainly evident in the reflections from preservice teachers.

The preservice teachers often started or ended their reflections by making declarations about their emotional state. These ranged from feeling lost, unsure, uncertain, and nervous to being hopeful, excited, and even angry. Across the reflections, preservice teachers used embodied language like having to "*juggle*" assessment commitments with other responsibilities, "*scrambling* to catch up," "still *struggling to catch up*," "very *behind* in the work due to stopping to do the assignments, and it "*hangs over my head*." Learning to be an assessor was occurring as part of other simultaneous life pressures. Learners were managing their workload as university or preservice teachers, paid employment, and their roles as preservice teachers on school-based placement experience. The metaphorical language that referenced the way the whole body was involved in learning not only communicated a range of emotions but also involved the learners as whole selves.

Embodied language can amplify the intensity of emotions and the active and far-reaching effects of these emotions. Recognising and naming these emotions often preceded some further reasoning that was associated with follow-up insights or actions. Sometimes the action was just to recognise the various life stressors and remind themselves of one next step:

94   5 Embodied Assessment Capacity

Feeling a bit stressed and overwhelmed today, I've just got back from attending my father-in-law's funeral and now trying to catch up on all the assessment readings to start my assignment. I'm confident I will get there, one reading at a time…but it's a slow process. Have to pick the kids up from school soon, this is never-ending. (Australian preservice teacher)

Very poor sleep, very poor diet. I am struggling to prioritise university work alongside all the new tasks arising from living alone, unpacking boxes, looking for furniture, paying bills, etc. I have an extension for SSA [an assessment task] until 14th May but I am worried that I will struggle to do the work once we get back to school. My first week back - I have 9 lessons (which I asked for) - but just trying to stay on track/on top of everything is a lot. Trying to spend this Easter break to relax has been impossible so far! (English preservice teacher)

The growing series of reflections over time helped the preservice teachers develop their awareness of their assessment commitments, and to narrate their changing emotions. Over time they could recognise their progress in learning and identify what was generating the strong emotions:

I'm feeling a bit better today. I've been working on this assignment all weekend and I've got the task sheet, rubric and sample response done. I just need to complete the rationale and the annotations and with 3 weeks to go, I should be okay. It will give me time to concentrate on my new job which has been horrendous so far, so much to learn and juggling uni as well is not a great mix. (Australian preservice teacher)

For these preservice teachers, there was recognition of having to persist through the discomfort of emerging or unclear knowledge as they were learning about assessment theory and practice, as well as juggling the emotions and embodied demands of other life responsibilities.

Teacher educators who work closely with preservice teachers will not be surprised by these ups and downs and may see them as essential perturbations needed to challenge and rebuild everyday prior concepts of learning and teaching. However, there may be new insights into how emotions connect so strongly with learning to be assessors. The emotional highs and lows within a reflection, as well as across a series of reflections, indicate that learning about assessment theory and how to apply it in practice was occurring under demanding conditions. Embodied commitments to people and roles beyond their initial teacher education course blend into their thinking and learning about how to assess. Reflections returned to positive emotions and commitments to persist with the assessment learning when positive emotions and ideals were connected to a future of making a difference for students or when past positive recollections of success were recounted with positive emotions. As evident in Chapter 6 about ethical assessment capacity, strong emotions were also a trigger for considering whether something may or may not be fair.

Learning to attend to emotions as a point of learning is something that all teachers need to learn, as embodied assessment learning is not just for the preservice teacher years. Assessment is a topic that can evoke an array of emotions. Emotions in reflections included wonder, surprise, enjoyment, and pride. Dissonance and conflict, tiredness and confusion were also evident. Tiredness was a frequent topic and raised a question about whether it was an emotion. It provoked emotional responses for us as readers and was certainly an indication that learning is fully embodied. Emotions are notoriously difficult to conceptualise, with terms such as *emotion, affect, mood,*

5.2 Preservice Teachers' Embodied Learning Experiences

and *feelings* often used interchangeably and inconsistently in the literature (Rowe, 2017). Perhaps more important than strictly classifying emotions is noting the intensity. Intense emotions indicate that the situation is of high importance and can guide the inner reflexivity that is associated with making evaluative judgements like what to do next and what is important (Archer, 2000; Steinberg, 2008). In a study that analysed the reflections of beginning teachers across their first year of full-time teaching, assessment was the topic associated with the most emotional intensity (Willis & Gibson, 2020). Where the beginning teachers noticed disjunctures between their ideals of social justice and the assessment and reporting activities they were engaged in, they experienced their strongest emotional responses. When assessment is viewed as a rational and emotionless activity, as it may be by some who maintain an acquisitional epistemic perspective (Sfard, 2008), emotions like frustration may be seen as an impediment or to be avoided or smoothed away. Instead, emotions are important to recognise and acknowledge, to identify critical ideas for practice and as motivators for assessment actions. Emotions are the signposts for what is important (Archer, 2000). For example, when strong emotions like distress are associated with feeling under constant time pressures, teacher educators can help preservice teachers identify and recontextualise the individual's experience within the wider structural realities for teachers in cultures of performativity and neo-liberalism (Stacey et al., 2023). Awareness and recognition that they are not alone is an important aspect of being able to manage their emotions. Issues can be raised for discussion with more experienced colleagues who can provide different perspectives (Willis et al., 2017). Strong emotions might highlight dilemmas to do with ethical decision-making (see Chapter 6) or an experiential problem of practice (see Chapter 7) that needs more development.

Teachers' physiological and emotional reactions to assessing can affect their approaches to using assessment tasks and making judgements (Edwards, 2020, 2021). Several studies have highlighted the emotional work of teachers and the influence that emotions bring to bear on teachers' decisions (Näring et al., 2006; Nias, 1989; Soini et al., 2010; Vogl & Pekrun, 2016). Teachers' beliefs and backgrounds produce emotional responses that act as amplifiers and/or filters that can affect assessment decision-making (Edwards, 2020). For example, at times, teachers may work to reduce negative emotions in their students because they know that students react emotionally to being assessed and receiving feedback (Vogl & Pekrun, 2016). This awareness of students' potential negative reactions to assessment in itself adds an extra emotional burden on the teachers. Teachers' views about protecting and caring for students can also increase emotional labour and influence their assessment actions, especially for teachers who desire to develop a deep bond with students or take a learner-centred approach (Xu, 2013). Brown et al., (2018, p. 207) identify three points of ongoing emotional tension for teachers: "(1) How do I tell my student that this part of their work is not very good and needs to be improved? (2) How do I face my students after I have given them negative feedback (e.g., a low or failing score or comments) about their work? (3) Who is responsible for failure—me or my students?" Teachers express anxiety about creating fair and equitable assessments for all students, including students with disability (Forlin et al., 2008) (see also Chapter 6). Steinberg (2015) noted teachers feel less confident about making fail decisions than pass decisions at times and have also been found to pay more attention to less robust information than to more robust evidence if they can support a student to pass (Brackett et al., 2013; Tweed et al., 2013). Teachers' emotional engagement with students can also cause them to become disappointed or frustrated with student attitudes towards assessment and their assessment results (Graham et al., 2010; Hipkins et al., 2005; Meyer et al., 2009; O'Connor, 2008). Shapiro (2010) argues such feelings are a result of the tension between teachers' concerns that relate to principles of assessment and their emotional responses. This sort of tension adds to teachers' emotional labour (Isenbarger & Zembylas, 2006) and may well be more keenly felt in beginner teachers, given their lack of experience.

Embodied assessment capacity may be seen in the work of teachers who acknowledge that assessment is emotional and so guide their students towards positive assessment emotions, such as those featured in Munns and Woodward's (2006) study of student engagement through self-assessment. Students were able to engage in learning more fully through self-assessment, where they simultaneously found value in the assessment task (high emotion), were reflectively developing deep understanding and expertise (high cognition), and actively participated in school and classroom self-assessment activities (high behaviour). Students may also need support to engage with emotions like being challenged or making mistakes, so they can identify gaps in knowledge and build on them in formative assessment cycles. Experienced assessors also develop reflexive awareness of how assessment practices designed to motivate students, like displaying results on data walls (i.e., bulletin boards of student work and assessments), have emotional impacts on students and teachers. The review by Harris et al. (2020) noted a mix of emotions depending on how the data was used and displayed. Managing the emotions of students in summative or formative assessments can also be an emotional task for teachers. While the research fields of "teachers' emotions and assessment are not yet talking to each other" (Steinberg, 2008, p. 47), there is evidence that more recent conceptions of assessment literacy highlight the importance of teacher emotions. Looney et al. (2018) acknowledge the importance of beliefs and feelings in teacher assessment identities, including "I feel …" in their construct of teacher assessment identity.

In their reflections in our study across Australia, Canada, England, and New Zealand, preservice teachers' emotions highlighted that learning to assess was raising questions about their developing teacher identity. They shared their beliefs and concerns, including details about how they wanted to work and be viewed as teachers. There was a sense of idealism in much of how they projected their teacher selves:

> My love for lifelong learning is what I want to share with my future students and through assessment for learning without a focus on the endgame results of success and fail. (New Zealand preservice teacher)

However, preservice teachers also shared doubts and frustrations as they talked about the highs and lows of their experiences of learning to assess, voicing their uncertainty over whether they were going to end up being the teacher they had envisaged themselves to be:

5.2 Preservice Teachers' Embodied Learning Experiences

.... I am struggling to understand academic principles, coupled with curriculum documents, and the stress of understanding the differences between the year levels has made me question my potential ability as a teacher. (Australian preservice teacher)

Through their school-based placement experiences, preservice teachers described that they often struggled and faltered, including when trying out their emerging formative assessment practices. However, many conveyed hope and anticipation as they saw things in themselves that identified them as a teacher:

Nonetheless I will try because I have been convinced of the benefits to my students and their learning, and my own want to improve and become the most effective educator possible. (Australian preservice teacher)

Early in the week was a real struggle and I had a very difficult moment on Tuesday evening when planning a particular lesson got on top of me. I went in early on Weds morning to talk through my lesson with the class teacher and was reassured by their feedback ahead of the lesson. I also had a very positive discussion with my mentor who reassured me that it was ok not to be feeling ok. Lessons this week have been very positive and I feel that after my Tuesday night struggles I am starting to see the planning process a little more clearly. Confidence in subject knowledge is still a headache for me but I am continuing to work on this and as I teach repeating lessons on topics I am becoming more secure. (English preservice teacher)

I was so proud of them that they were able to make the connections, I was also proud of myself that I was able to effectively teach the lesson. (Canadian preservice teacher)

This socio-emotional dimension was recognised as an important teacher assessment literacy by Pastore and Andrade (2019) in their Delphi survey of 35 international assessment experts. The consensus view of experts noted that assessment is a social practice, and teachers manage social and emotional aspects of assessment, including self-awareness, responding to student anxiety and engagement, attending to issues of fairness, and working with others to generate shared understandings.

Where preservice teachers reflected with positive emotion about their growing confidence or new perspectives as assessors, it was often when they were able to make connections to their personal histories, to their practices in schools, and to their hopes for the future. Whether they had poor or good experiences, they found emotional connections to the type of assessor they would like to be and how they would like their students to feel when engaging in assessment activities. Finding connections to their other professional experiences and social values seemed to reinforce idealistic identities as a teacher. Sometimes these led to excited realisations like, "The social and problem-solving skills I was taught in the last decade of my life in sales, can be transferred to teaching. What an epiphany!!!" (Australian preservice teacher). Connections were also made possible when they saw that their mentor teachers were working through similar issues. Feeling like they were rising to the challenge of teaching also was associated with positive emotions:

It is the challenge I have been needing. Not that Uni life has been challenging - in fact, it has been a great challenge and yet, I thrive. Why? I haven't had a day off in weeks.... I think I've said this so many times over and over. I don't feel like I need a day off, in fact, I push myself to continue through the daily grind of doing every single pre-workshop/workshop and post workshop learning in order to prepare myself for this. (Australian preservice teacher)

Pride and growing confidence in themselves provided an impetus for preservice teachers to push on through the "daily grind" in order to better prepare themselves for the work of teaching. The metaphors of *"pushing on"* and *"experiencing the grind"* reflect the embodied experiences of many teachers. We can acknowledge that embodied language about the demands of teaching is also evident in stories of increasing teacher workloads that are often associated with assessment and increased accountabilities. Discussions with preservice teachers can acknowledge that sometimes the emotional and physical *"push"* is not a sustainable and manageable assessment capacity but a sign to exercise collective agency to *"push back"* towards systemic reform.

5.2.2 Embodied Assessment Occurs In Situ with Materials and Spaces

Assessment, whether it be a summative performance or an everyday discussion about how learning is going, occurs in physical spaces with materials. Students make, say, do, or write their Assessment of Learning performances. Where Assessment as Learning is the focus, learning often involves collaboration around material representations and performances. Assessment for Learning—whether through feedback, questioning, and/or exemplars—depends on interactions where students are expected to manage physical materials like checklists, drafts, worksheets, and rubrics alongside their interpersonal relationships. Students infer meaning from where their teachers stand to survey their work, disliking it when teachers look over their shoulders, as they can't see their faces, and preferring it when teachers sit beside them (Cowie, 2005). Teacher attention and presence are also feedback, indicating whether students may be struggling, in trouble, or are expected to engage in peer feedback (Willis, 2011). The classroom is a public arena, and the embodied decisions that teachers make about how to arrange the room or where to stand are part of their embodied assessment capacity.

Reflections from preservice teachers highlight a connection between physical space and their developing capacity to engage in assessment. The embodied agent's thinking is inseparable from their environment and their experiences associated with their immediate environment: the individual's learning and being assessed on their learning is situated and interdependent with practices of learning. Charteris and Dargusch (2018) highlight that teacher bodies and minds in social situations inform how teachers enact assessment and how teachers are transformed through their experiences in specific contexts. For example, being physically present in the staff room enabled a sense of safety and support, as well as incidental learning through the social engagement of teachers. The following preservice teacher had a desk allocated to them and felt that they were physically positioned as a colleague; this proximity provided emotional and social support, as well as intellectual assessment support as they experienced collaborative discussions:

I also felt safe and supported in the professional learning community at this school. I was fortunate to have a desk in an art office, and have observed a lot of positive interactions between teachers. The art teachers often share ideas for lesson plans and openly discuss what their classes are working on. (Canadian preservice teacher)

The physical layout of the classroom was highlighted as essential for Assessment for Learning practice in another preservice teacher reflection. The classroom was structured to enable the teacher to look up and have easy oversight and readily move around the room to have physical access to student work and to socially engage in questions with students. This has links to epistemic capacity, as studio collaborations and feedback are part of the disciplinary practices of artists:

My Arts supervisor explained that the room is structured in a semi circle so she can sit at the front and physically see every student's artwork from where she is - this is her assessment for learning. We also walk around the room and ask students 'what are you representing here?' etc. to check for understanding and give direct feedback….I can hear my uni lecturer's voice in my head saying 'show me, don't tell me!' so I have ideas for my AfL. In Maths, we work similarly by walking around the class and assessing students as we pass by asking them questions or checking their working. (Australian preservice teacher)

Another preservice teacher reflection focused on learning to manage the physical materials for an Assessment as Learning task as part of an embodied assessment learning experience in a school. The emotional demand and stress of managing the materials prompted a reflection that led to new assessment awareness and how to make use of routines so students could self-advocate and self-organise:

In my grade 10 photography class I observed the importance of multitasking and the teachers need to be flexible, and the ability to plan and keep order in an art room which could quickly become chaos…I found observing this very stressful as I imagine that the stress of handling all this at once alone would be incredibly difficult. From this experience I learned the importance of having students aware of routines and teaching them early on to self advocate and organize when the teacher is busy. (Canadian preservice teacher)

Embodiment in learning is also occurring in schools through the daily use of laptops, mobile phones, and online platforms. Where learning with digital technologies was once an add-on to daily learning, the experiences of 2020 onwards, where students and teachers engaged in learning from home and online in response to the COVID-19 pandemic, rapidly changed where and how teachers could assess learners' progress. As Lindgren and Johnson-Glenberg (2013, p. 450) note, as learning environments become more immersive, teacher and student assessment capabilities will need to evolve, especially as new school designs intentionally disrupt traditional approaches to learning:

Embodied learning environments…may have demonstrable effects on learners' intuitions and understanding, their perceptual acuity, and their willingness to explore the domain, but these important effects may simply not be detected by traditional paper-and-pencil-style assessments. As learning environments become more immersive, embodied, and praxis centred, so too should the instruments that one uses to assess them. (Lindgren & Johnson-Glenberg, 2013, p. 450)

Such an embodied view of assessment can be challenging to enact when traditional assessment instruments and traditional physical school designs often reflect the rational and disembodied industrial age view of cognition.

In traditional school spaces, assessment often occurs in silence, at individual desks, reflecting a shared colonial cultural embodiment that Gleason (2018) describes as:

> industriousness, nationalism, patriotism, and loyalty... Standing up and sitting on demand, lining up, responding to bells and whistles... remaining silent, raising one's hand: the repertoire of school embodiment was intent on compliance. (p. 10)

In contrast, new school designs tend to emphasise interconnected learning spaces, with a focus on collaboration and the learner's physiological wellbeing (Wells et al., 2018). Learning spaces are designed to engage senses and emotions and be manageable, meaningful, and feasible for learners and teachers to make a wide range of flexible learning choices (Franz, 2019). Where assessment in traditional spaces might focus on individual compliance and silent reproduction, new learning spaces point to activity-based, group, and open-ended assessment forms. For some students, the noise or visibility in innovative learning environments may make Assessment for Learning practices like questioning and peer feedback more challenging for some students (Trask et al., 2023). Preservice teachers need to be able to understand the paradigms of traditional and flexible learning environments and move between them (Scarino, 2013). Preparation for more flexible embodied assessment experiences can potentially occur through modelling in university classrooms and by experiences in practical teaching in schools (Wright & McNae, 2019). In their study of preservice teachers doing their practical placements in innovative learning environments (ILE), Nelson and Johnson (2021) identify how innovative learning spaces required different skills in planning collaborative workshops and managing classroom transitions and routines for student agency. Embodied forms of knowing were valued by the preservice teachers, alongside collegiality with their mentor teachers:

> Collegiality as a social force encounter eased the physical tiredness PSTs experienced as part of their practicum teaching. ILEs invoke less formalised feedback to PSTs, and more ongoing collaborative support. This feedback takes the form of daily conversational, reflective and informal collegial interaction. (p. 236)

Awareness of the connections among physical spaces and technologies and assessment can prepare a preservice teacher for assessment that *is*, as well as assessment that *will be*.

Artificial intelligence and virtual reality are beginning to change assessment practices. Already, feedback from social robots helps children to learn and assess their developing social and emotional regulation, motor skills, and language (Fridin & Belokopytov, 2014). Further developments in the field of biometrics—already part of teacher and student lives in the form of smartwatches and wearable devices—will mean that student and teacher bodies will be sites of intense data collection (Gleason, 2018). Intelligent tutoring systems and edu-business platforms gather learning analytics from embodied engagement with formative assessment tasks. These platforms host adaptive assessment in the form of testing with students presented different options depending on what responses have been recorded (Gibson & Lang, 2019). Traces of learning over time might be recorded by small data-gathering wearables or dashboards in place of traditional assessment tasks (Blundell, 2021; Cope & Kalantzis, 2016; Lindgren & Johnson-Glenberg, 2013). While preparing this book, ChatGTP, an artificial intelligence interface that can respond quickly to questions and prompts with outputs such as writing essays, songs, and play scripts has raised many questions about the future form and function of assessment.

Preservice teachers need some awareness of these new frontiers of assessment innovation so that they can be critically aware of creative possibilities and consequences when new technologies are introduced (Willis & Gibson, 2020). Such awareness can come from their preservice coursework grounding in principles of assessment along with some understanding of the wider technology ecosystem and whose interests are represented or considered in new assessment innovations. Emotions towards assessment innovations can range from excitement to suspicion, and recognition that assessment is an embodied capacity can also provide a foundation for feeling secure in emerging assessment practices. Balancing the uncertainty with the possibility of new assessment practices can occur through ongoing reflexive conversations that the teacher has with themselves and with others.

5.2.3 Learning to Manage Competing Demands Through Reflexive Agency

Giving preservice teachers opportunities to be reflexive about their emotions and experiences during their preservice preparation can help them become aware of the emotions and embodied practices involved with assessment. When coupled with opportunities to be reflexive and practice managing their possible responses, they can develop their assessment agency. Reflexive self-assessment enables preservice teachers to make connections between past, present, and future or to work out what will guide their assessment practices. When these temporal chords are in harmony and when routines from the past and practical evaluations of what is possible in the present align with an imagined future, there is a dynamic interplay of action that Emirbayer and Mische (1998) define as *agency*. This situated view of agency recognises that teachers can be collectively and individually enabled to take action within the cultural, structural, relational, and policy environments within which they find themselves (Priestley et al., 2015). For the following preservice teachers, the process of reflecting was a structural condition of their initial teacher education assessment course that supported them in making these connections. The value of reflecting was sometimes explicitly recognised by the preservice teacher:

> One thing that has surprised me this week is how effective reflection and self assessment has been for me so far. (Australian preservice teacher)

> I am grateful for the metacognitive component of the assessment which has allowed me to reflect on previous stigma and the growth away from this, that I felt is a necessary shift

prior to emerging as an educator. Without this reflection, I question how much shift I would have actually felt occurred as it was through deep consideration that these shifts happened. (Australian preservice teacher)

Reflexive connections occurred as students engaged with academic readings, for example, "I had never thought about the influence of culture over assessment and testing" or "To be honest when I first thought this subject was about assessment I was not really that excited…But the Shepard reading sparked some interest for me" (Australian preservice teacher). Assessment readings and theories prompted some new perspectives. Reflexive connections also occurred through considering their own personal experiences with assessment, for example, where they had or had not experienced support for their learning through Assessment for Learning or accommodations in summative assessment as a student. Opportunities to reflect and make connections to their own experiences led to a greater sense of their capacity to make sense of and manage complexity in assessment.

Reflexivity has a long history in teacher education and preparation, but in contexts where high-stakes assessment can dominate the expectations of preservice teacher preparation and teaching in schools, it is in danger of becoming a marginalised focus. Dorman (2020) noted that preservice education students in a USA context were increasingly focused on "chasing assessment grades" and were "emotionally fragile" about assessment. The influence of high-stakes assessment is felt by all teachers, even when teaching in classes without high-stakes assessment (Gonzalez et al., 2017). Well-documented side effects include teachers feeling disempowered with a "narrowed sense of educational purpose, fostering a sense of inadequacy, anxiety, confusion, frustration, mistrust, alienation, fear, shame, and anger and/or apathy" (Segall, 2003, p. 290). We would argue that while performance pressures create conditions where reflexivity is hard to prioritise, it is also an essential approach to managing those same pressures.

Reflexivity about embodied assessment experiences is an essential ballast to the distorting effects of high-stakes assessment pressures. As a beginning teacher noted in the study by Allard et al. (2014), "I know that the only way I will notice that I am 'defaulting' is to take some time off the hamster wheel and examine my practice." In their study of agency and reflexivity with preservice teachers, Jones and Charteris (2017, p. 508) describe how a preservice teacher took agentic action on the basis of her reflection, saying, "we suggest this reflection enabled her to bring her emotions under control so that she could act, rather than react." Through reflexivity, teachers make connections between their situation, their emotions, and their responsibilities to students to manage their embodied cognitive experiences in assessment and learning. Feeling a greater sense of control or self-management is essential in the development of teacher agency.

Preservice teachers need opportunities in their preparation programmes to be able to make sense and learn about assessment by reflexively making connections about their situated experiences, emotions, their past, and their future identities as assessors. Not only is this reflexivity important to help them develop their embodied assessment knowledge, but also as preparation for their roles as teachers. Teachers have to do a lot of emotional work to navigate what to do in various assessment situations. Often it was not only the immediate experience of the assessors and assessed, but also their wider experiences—past and present, their context, and the knowledge and beliefs—that they bring to their assessment identity (Edwards, 2020; Stuart & Thurlow, 2000). Kelchtermans (2005) argues that "emotion and cognition, self and context, ethical judgement and purposeful action: they are all intertwined in the complex reality of teaching" (p. 996). Assessment can be a messy world that is difficult to navigate and has conflicts and incompatibilities. It can be emotional as teachers have to manage expectations that do not always align with their values or skills. Considering assessment from an embodied perspective means that preservice teachers can be made aware of and acknowledge the tensions in assessment emotions and settings that will inevitably be encountered and, through reflexive awareness, be able to recognise the opportunities for agency and action.

An embodied assessment capacity is highly interrelated with the other capacity dimensions highlighted in other chapters. In this chapter, reflexive insights from preservice teachers have been synthesised alongside current literature to propose some helpful dimensions of an embodied assessment capacity and implications for initial teacher education. In the next section, we propose that including an awareness of the embodied aspects of assessment in initial teacher education can support preservice teachers to reflexively consider and recontextualise assessment in the interests of learners and learning.

5.3 Developing Embodied Assessment Capacity in Initial Teacher Education

When asked why they chose to become teachers, preservice teachers often replied that they were motivated to make a difference and to experience the pleasure of helping others learn. An embodied view of assessment capacity allows for holistic consideration and acknowledgement of the people, relationships, decisions, and activities in a classroom that contribute to judgements about student learning and progress, rather than limiting assessment to the cognitive ability to mark an answer right or wrong.

Teacher educators already take notice of the embodied ways that preservice teachers experience their university and school placements. However, embodied experiences are traditionally seen as topics separated from the curriculum or theoretical assessment topics being studied in their teacher preparation coursework. Emotions and embodied responses may be considered as individual reactions that need to be managed by the individual. Recognising that assessment is inherently emotional and embodied brings the topic of management and understanding to the foreground and as a topic of explicit preparation in teacher education coursework as well as school-based placements. This capacity requires awareness, acknowledgement, reflexive agency, and action. It requires reflection and questioning:

- *What are the emotions that are associated with assessment, and what concerns or realisations do they point towards?*
- *How are the physical and digital materials of assessment impacting on the bodies engaged in assessment?*
- *What could make assessment more physically and emotionally authentic and accessible?*
- *What opportunities for reflexivity are there for making connections between situations, emotions, and opportunities for agentic action?*

5.4 Conclusion

To return to the theoretical framing at the beginning of this book, an embodied assessment capacity is a form of *unthinkable* knowledge. It is *unthinkable* in the way that Bernstein (2000) uses the term to refer to new ideas that are not yet part of everyday practice. Connecting assessment with embodiment is not an idea that features often in current assessment research, advice to practitioners, or teacher preparation programmes. Finding purposeful opportunities for regular reflexivity in teacher education courses is a perennial challenge, alongside this additional proposal to spend time with preservice teachers asking them to reflexively evaluate what it is that they have learned from their reflections. Embodied assessment capacities are also *unthinkable* as they challenge assumptions about what is involved in thinking. By emphasising cognition as embodied (i.e., embodied cognition), places new horizons for assessment (and assessment learning) before us, and moves beyond strictly the rational, skill-bound activity of assessment and towards assessment as situated and entwined with emotions. These are horizons that teacher educators can co-develop as part of their role in reshaping educational futures that attend to embodied experiences of assessment.

Frances Edwards is a Senior Lecturer in the Division of Education, University of Waikato (Hamilton, New Zealand). Her research interests include assessment and professional learning and development for teachers. Frances is currently leading a project investigating culturally responsive assessment for Pacific tertiary students. Website: https://profiles.waikato.ac.nz/frances.edwards.

Andrew Gibson is a Senior Lecturer in Information Science at Queensland University of Technology (Brisbane, Australia). Andrew's research includes theoretical inquiry into the relationship between reflexive thinking and learning, as well as applied socio-technical investigations into how people express reflexive thinking.

References

Allard, A. C., Mayer, D., & Moss, J. (2014). Authentically assessing graduate teaching: Outside and beyond neo-liberal constructs. *The Australian Educational Researcher, 41*(4), 425–443.

References

Archer, M. S. (2000). *Being human: The problem of agency*. Cambridge University Press.

Bellocchi, A. (2019). Early career science teacher experiences of social bonds and emotion management. *Journal of Research in Science Teaching, 56*(3), 322–347.

Bernstein, B. (2000). *Pedagogy, symbolic control, and identity: Theory, research, critique* (Vol. 5). Rowman & Littlefield.

Blundell, C. N. (2021). Teacher use of digital technologies for school-based assessment: A scoping review. *Assessment in Education: Principles, Policy & Practice, 28*(3), 279–300.

Brackett, M. A., Floman, J. L., Ashton-James, C., Cherkasskiy, L., & Salovey, P. (2013). The influence of teacher emotion on grading practices: A preliminary look at the evaluation of student writing. *Teachers and Teaching, 19*(6), 634–646.

Brown, G. T., Gebril, A., Michaelides, M. P., & Remesal, A. (2018). Assessment as an emotional practice: Emotional challenges faced by L2 teachers within assessment. In *Emotions in second language teaching* (pp. 205–222). Springer.

Cope, B., & Kalantzis, M. (2016). Big data comes to school: Implications for learning, assessment, and research. *AERA Open, 2*(2). https://doi.org/10.1177/2332858416641907 (online).

Charteris, J., & Dargusch, J. (2018). The tensions of preparing pre-service teachers to be assessment capable and profession-ready. *Asia-Pacific Journal of Teacher Education, 46*(4), 354–368.

Cowie, B. (2005). Student commentary on classroom assessment in science: A sociocultural interpretation. *International Journal of Science Education, 27*(2), 199–214.

Dorman, E. H. (2020). A cycle of fragility: Prospective teachers' emotions and perspectives around being assessed and evaluated. In *Curriculum & teaching dialogue* (Vol. 22, 1 & 2, pp. 265–279). Information Age Publishing.

Edwards, F. (2020). The effect of the lens of the teacher on summative assessment decision making: The role of amplifiers and filters. *The Curriculum Journal, 31*(3), 379–397.

Edwards, F. (2021). The influence of emotion on preservice teachers as they learn to assess student learning. *Australian Journal of Teacher Education, 46*(4).

Emirbayer, M., & Mische, A. (1998). What is agency? *American Journal of Sociology, 103*(4), 962–1023.

Forlin, C., Keen, M., & Barrett, E. (2008). The concerns of mainstream teachers: Coping with inclusivity in an Australian context. *International Journal of Disability, Development and Education, 55*(3), 251–264.

Franz, J. (2019). Towards a spatiality of wellbeing. In *School spaces for student wellbeing and learning* (pp. 3–19). Springer.

Fridin, M., & Belokopytov, M. (2014). Embodied robot versus virtual agent: Involvement of preschool children in motor task performance. *International Journal of Human-Computer Interaction, 30*(6), 459–469.

Gibson, A., & Lang, C. (2019). Quality indicators through learning analytics. In M. A. Peters (Ed.), *Encyclopedia of teacher education* (pp. 1–6). Springer.

Gleason, M. (2018). Metaphor, materiality, and method: The central role of embodiment in the history of education. *Paedagogica Historica, 54*(1–2), 4–19.

Gonzalez, A., Peters, M. L., Orange, A., & Grigsby, B. (2017). The influence of high-stakes testing on teacher self-efficacy and job-related stress. *Cambridge Journal of Education, 47*(4), 513–531.

Graham, J., Meyer, L., McKenzie, L., McClure, J., & Weir, K. F. (2010). Māori and Pacific secondary student and parent perspectives on achievement, motivation and NCEA. *Assessment Matters, 2*, 132–157.

Green, B., & Hopwood, N. (2015). The body in professional practice, learning and education: A question of corporeality. In *The body in professional practice, learning and education* (pp. 15–33). Springer.

Harris, L., Wyatt-Smith, C., & Adie, L. (2020). Using data walls to display assessment results: A review of their affective impacts on teachers and students. *Teachers and Teaching, 26*(1), 50–66.

Heffernan, A., Bright, D., Kim, M., Longmuir, F., & Magyar, B. (2022). 'I cannot sustain the workload and the emotional toll': Reasons behind Australian teachers' intentions to leave the profession. *Australian Journal of Education.* https://doi.org/10.1177/00049441221086654 (online).

Hipkins, R., Vaughan, K., Beals, F., Ferral, H., & Gardiner, B. (2005). *Shaping our futures: Meeting secondary students' learning needs in a time of evolving qualifications.* New Zealand Council for Educational Research.

Isenbarger, L., & Zembylas, M. (2006). The emotional labour of caring in teaching. *Teaching and Teacher Education, 22,* 120–134.

Kelchtermans, G. (2005). Teachers' emotions in educational reforms: Self-understanding, vulnerable commitment and micropolitical literacy. *Teaching and Teacher Education, 21*(8), 995–1006.

Jones, M., & Charteris, J. (2017). Transformative professional learning: An ecological approach to agency through critical reflection. *Reflective Practice, 18*(4), 496–513.

Lindgren, R., & Johnson-Glenberg, M. (2013). Emboldened by embodiment: Six precepts for research on embodied learning and mixed reality. *Educational Researcher, 42*(8), 445–452.

Looney, A., Cumming, J., van Der Kleij, F., & Harris, K. (2018). Reconceptualising the role of teachers as assessors: Teacher assessment identity. *Assessment in Education: Principles, Policy & Practice, 25*(5), 442–467.

Lunn Brownlee, J., Bourke, T., Rowan, L., Ryan, M., Churchward, P., Walker, S., L'Estrange, L., Berge, A., & Johansson, E. (2022). How epistemic reflexivity enables teacher educators' teaching for diversity: Exploring a pedagogical framework for critical thinking. *British Educational Research Journal, 48*(4), 684–703.

Meyer, L. H., McClure, J., Walkey, F., Weir, K. F., & McKenzie, L. (2009). Secondary student motivation orientations and standards-based achievement outcomes. *British Journal of Educational Psychology, 79*(2), 273–293.

Munns, G., & Woodward, H. (2006). Student engagement and student self-assessment: The REAL framework. *Assessment in Education: Principles, Policy & Practice, 13*(2), 193–213.

Näring, G., Briët, M., & Brouwers, A. (2006). Beyond demand–control: Emotional labour and symptoms of burnout in teachers. *Work & Stress, 20*(4), 303–315.

Nelson, E., & Johnson, L. (2021). 'Jump in off the deep end': Learning to teach in innovative learning environments on practicum. In *Pedagogy and partnerships in innovative learning environments: Case studies from New Zealand contexts* (pp. 225–242). Springer..

Nias, J. (1989). *Primary teachers talking: A study of teaching as work.* Routledge.

O'Connor, K. E. (2008). 'You choose to care': Teachers, emotions and professional identity. *Teaching and Teacher Education, 24,* 117–126.

Pastore, S., & Andrade, H. L. (2019). Teacher assessment literacy: A three-dimensional model. *Teaching and Teacher Education, 84,* 128–138.

Priestley, M., Biesta, G., & Robinson, S. (2015). Teacher agency: What is it and why does it matter? In *Flip the system* (pp. 134–148). Routledge.

Rowe, A. D. (2017). Feelings about feedback: The role of emotions in assessment for learning. In *Scaling up assessment for learning in higher education* (pp. 159–172). Springer.

Scarino, A. (2013). Foreword. In L. Harbon & R. Moloney (Eds.), *Language teachers' narratives of practice* (pp. xiii–xviii). Cambridge Scholars Publishing.

Segall, A. (2003). Teachers' perceptions of the impact of state-mandated standardized testing: The Michigan Educational Assessment Program (MEAP) as a case study of consequences. *Theory & Research in Social Education, 31*(3), 287–325.

Sfard, A. (2008). *Thinking as communicating: Human development, the growth of discourses, and mathematizing.* Cambridge University Press.

Shapiro, S. (2010). Revisiting the teachers' lounge: Reflections on emotional experience and teacher identity. *Teaching and Teacher Education, 26*(3), 616–621.

Soini, T., Pyhältö, K., & Pietarinen, J. (2010). Pedagogical well-being: Reflecting learning and well-being in teachers' work. *Teachers and Teaching, 16*(6), 735–751.

Stacey, M., McGrath-Champ, S., & Wilson, R. (2023). Teacher attributions of workload increase in public sector schools: Reflections on change and policy development. *Journal of Educational Change, 1–23.* https://doi.org/10.1007/s10833-022-09476-0

References

Steinberg, C. (2008). Assessment as an "emotional practice." *English Teaching: Practice and Critique, 7*(3), 42–64.

Steinberg, C. (2015). Teachers dealing with learners' achievement–what do their emotions tell us? *Journal of Education, 63*, 9–28.

Stuart, C., & Thurlow, D. (2000). Making it their own: Pre-service teachers' experiences, beliefs and classroom practices. *Journal of Teacher Education, 51*(1), 113–121.

Trask, S., Charteris, J., Edwards, F., Cowie, B., & Anderson, J. (2023). Innovative learning environments and student orientation to learning: a kaleidoscopic framework. *Learning Environments Research*, 1–5. https://doi.org/10.1007/s10984-023-09453-1

Tweed, M. J., Thompson-Fawcett, M., & Wilkinson, T. J. (2013). Decision-making bias in assessment: The effect of aggregating objective information and anecdote. *Medical Teacher, 35*, 832–837.

Vogl, E., & Pekrun, R. (2016). Emotions that matter to achievement. In G. T. L. Brown & L. R. Harris (Eds.), *Handbook of human and social conditions in assessment* (pp. 111–128). Routledge.

Wells, A., Jackson, M., & Benade, L. (2018). Modern learning environments: Embodiment of a disjunctive encounter. In *Transforming education* (pp. 3–17). Springer.

Willis, J. (2011). Affiliation, autonomy, and Assessment for Learning. *Assessment in Education: Principles, Policy and Practice, 18*(4), 399–415.

Willis, J., Crosswell, L., Morrison, C., Gibson, A., & Ryan, M. (2017). Looking for leadership: The potential of dialogic reflexivity with rural early-career teachers. *Teachers and Teaching, 23*(7), 794–809.

Willis, J., & Gibson, A. (2020). The emotional work of being an assessor: A reflective writing analytics inquiry into digital self-assessment. In *Teacher education in globalised times* (pp. 93–113). Springer.

Wright, N., & McNae, R. (2019). *An architecture of ownership.* NZCER.

Xu, Y. (2013). Language teacher emotion in relationships: A multiple case study. In X. Zhu & K. M. Zeichner (Eds.), *Preparing teachers for the 21st century* (pp. 371–393). Springer.

Chapter 6
Ethical Assessment Capacity

with Jeanine Gallagher and Kerry Earl Rinehart

Abstract This book presents a novel framework, *Thinking the Unthinkable*, aimed at cultivating teacher assessment capacity. The framework includes four fundamental capacities: epistemic, embodied, ethical, and experiential. In this chapter, the ethical capacity is explored through literature, preservice teacher reflections and narratives, and interpretive analysis. At the heart of it, the ethical capacity asks teachers to consider how diversity in their classroom shapes their assessment practice. It considers how teachers plan, make decisions about, and create opportunities for and interpret student agency within and through assessment processes. It also involves socio-cultural considerations within assessment practices, fair distribution of resources for learning and assessment, procedural fairness, equity in assessment, and explicit consideration for the consequences of assessment actions on diverse students and the learning collective. Guiding teachers' ethical capacity development is the following reflection question: *Are my assessment actions and decisions fair for all and socially just?* The chapter concludes with guidance for developing ethical capacity in initial teacher education.

Keywords Ethics · Ethical knowing · Social justice · Student agency · Teacher agency · Identity · Diversity · Equity · Assessment · Teacher education · Teacher reflection · Teacher development

In this chapter, we locate concerns with fairness, equity, inclusion, and social justice in the process and consequences of assessment as fundamental to the *ethical* assessment capacity. In so doing, we acknowledge that assessment does not simply measure what is already there; it also constructs and makes visible what is of value. Put another way, it makes visible what and whose knowledge is valued, what counts as evidence of knowing, and shapes the agency and identities of students (Stobart, 2008). The challenge for teacher educators is how to engage the ethical complexities of assessment with their preservice teachers, to explore and understand the possibilities and consequences of assessment for students. The challenge includes ensuring preservice teachers are aware that their assessment practice also constructs them as a teacher who is variously attuned to, interested in, and responsive to their students' needs and strengths—individually and collectively, in the short and longer term. In addition to this awareness and development of identity, there is an outworking of action where assessment contributes to social justice.

Preservice teacher reflections in our study across teacher education programmes in four countries (Australia, Canada, England, and New Zealand) evidenced a growing sense of responsibility for students and an awareness of the ethical capacity of teaching and assessment. The following reflection illustrates how preservice teachers grapple with the ethical aspects of assessment:

> The grade 9 applied science class had a unit test this week as their final summative assessment for their chemistry unit. Given that this class has many exceptional learners (many of whom require accommodations in class and on assessments) my associate teacher (AT) provides all students with accommodation for their test. Students are given a unit review with topics and questions that students are expected to know. Students are able to create memory aid sheets with all the information they want on them to use during their test (this is separate from their notebook). I observed that most students didn't create detailed enough reviews.

> All students were given the opportunity to have more time (beyond one entire period) to complete the test. Again, despite accommodating with memory aids and extended time, students still struggled a lot. After looking at the assessment itself, it appeared to be fairly standard. It contained multiple choice, matching, and short answer. There were no surprises or any material on the test that had not been covered. He had taught his lessons in a way and assigned homework such that he modeled what students would be expected to do on the test.

> There was one student, who is an ESL learner, did particularly poorly on the test. Despite having two periods to work on it, he only answered about half the questions on the test and he essentially got all the answers wrong. This situation made me think about, how are we supposed to assess a student who does not fully understand spoken or written English, and who is in a regular class?. How can they learn science before they learn English? It is not fair to assess this student in their ability to do science when they don't have the English knowledge they need to be able to understand the question asked of them. (Canadian preservice teacher)

As evident in this reflection, the curriculum, pedagogy, and assessment foci were aligned. Moreover, assessment requirements were articulated, and additional time was allowed, indicating the teacher's commitment to procedural fairness. Given the scope of these actions, the preservice teacher's recognition that many students still "struggled," with one student, in particular, standing out as facing challenges, prompted them to ask, "How are we supposed to assess…?"

Teachers are routinely faced with assessment situations like this, where there may be no clear 'best,' 'most appropriate,' or even viably fair course of action. In these deliberations, teachers are faced with the question of what would be the likely consequences of the different approaches they could take, remembering that no action is also an action. In these deliberations, teachers and teacher educators are concerned with the impacts of assessment on students as individuals and as a group. At the same time, they are challenged to consider the implications of their assessment practices, for who they are and who they aspire to be as a teacher themselves. Attending to how the assessment simultaneously constructs teachers' and students' identities as particular kinds of learners, knowers, and teachers is entangled with matters of fairness, where social justice is fundamental to an understanding of ethical assessment capacity.

6.1 What Is Ethical Assessment Capacity?

Ethical assessment capacity is evident as both the recognition of how to design aligned and procedurally fair assessments for students and also how to continually inquire and attend to the consequences of assessment for students, including consequences related to identity, agency, and justice. An ethical assessment capacity involves preservice teachers learning to identify, critique, and move towards addressing factors that might influence their students' opportunities to learn and to demonstrate and progress in their learning. Ethical assessment capacity requires an awareness of the socio-cultural contexts in which assessment takes place—the diversity of students and teachers, the historical oppressions associated with certain curriculum and assessment practices, and imperatives to leverage education and assessment for more socially just ends. Working towards ethical assessment practices means working towards anti-oppressive forms of assessment including anti-racist and decolonised forms of assessment that are barrier free for diverse students, socially just, and agentic. In this chapter, some key themes are raised to guide teachers and teacher educators who are interested in foregrounding ethical assessment capacities within contexts of learning. These themes are an awareness of what is being valued in assessment and anticipates the consequences of assessment actions.

As highlighted in the core questions at the heart of this book (see Fig. 6.1), the ethical assessment capacity asks: *Are my assessment actions and decision fair for all and socially just?*

Ethical concerns relate to the constructs of fairness, equity, inclusion, and social justice—all of which question how and if the education system, and those within it, meet their obligations to support the learning of each and every student. Of these constructs, fairness has gained the most prominence as a consideration in formal summative assessment (Rasooli et al., 2022) and is often positioned alongside validity and reliability as foundational to quality. Teachers and students view fairness as central to equitable classroom assessment (Cowie, 2015; Cowie et al., 2014; Gipps & Murphy, 1994; Gipps & Stobart, 2009; Klenowski, 2014; Rasooli et al., 2022; Scott et al., 2014; Tierney, 2013, 2014, 2016). At one time, being 'fair' in assessment was viewed as ensuring all students had equal or the same opportunities. The focus has shifted to ensure assessments are now 'equitable' (Heritage & Wylie, 2018; Moss et al., 2008); that is, whether the assessment process provides each student with the best possible opportunity to learn and grow as a person based on their learning and assessment needs.

Equitable assessment enables students to translate the opportunity to learn into achievement and to demonstrate what they know and can do in ways that build

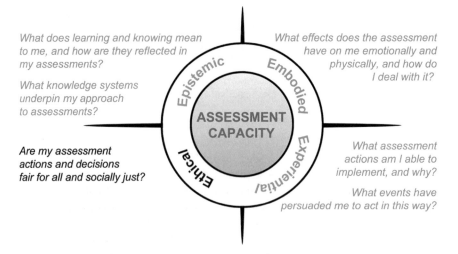

Fig. 6.1 Core questions with focus on the ethical capacity

on the diversity of student backgrounds, goals, and capabilities as key resources for their learning. A number of other fields of research and scholarship focused on student diversity provide insight into the design and enactment of assessment, with possible student responses to assessment highlighting ethical matters. Examples include research into culturally valid/responsible assessment (e.g., in Ireland, Brown et al., 2022; in New Zealand, Civil & Hunter, 2015, Cowie et al., 2011; in Australia, Klenowski, 2009; in the USA Solano-Flores & Nelson-Barber, 2001; Trumbull & Nelson-Barber, 2019), into inclusive assessment (e.g., Ajjawi et al., 2023; Bourke & Mentis, 2013; Gallagher & Spina, 2021; Graham et al., 2018), into decolonising assessment (e.g., Crossouard & Oprandi, 2022; Kerr & Averill, 2023), and research into the assessment experiences of migrant and refugee students (e.g., Heritage & Wylie, 2018; Herzog-Punzenberger et al., 2020; Nortvedt et al., 2020; OECD, 2015). This work recognises that students bring to school their previous knowledge, experience, and cultural/linguistic/gender/religious/and other identities that shape how they approach learning and assessment. It also recognises students come with cultural preferences for ways of engaging and communicating (e.g., Civil & Hunter, 2015; Hang & Bell, 2015; Moschkovich & Nelson-Barber, 2009; Wylie et al., 2018). Adding complexity, scholars are exploring the implications of the intersection of the multiple social groups that individuals embody, such as being a second language speaker or someone from an Indigenous group (e.g., Powers et al., 2018). Across these different fields, the distinction between equality and equity in assessment is foregrounded, as is the distinction between a deficit and accommodation view and a credit/resource or accessibility view (e.g., Johnstone et al., 2022; Nieminen, 2022). The accessible orientation, which considers how an assessment might limit or "disable" students, is currently advocated (Nieminen, 2022, p. 65). The preservice teacher in the reflection from the start of this chapter, like others in the study, was concerned with providing students with a variety of opportunities and means to demonstrate their learning as part of task design. This agenda is discussed in this chapter in terms of fairness and equity.

A social justice perspective of assessment includes the above aspects but goes further. It considers how assessment can and should foster students' agency and sense of collective responsibility for and orientations towards socially just outcomes and social good (Lingard et al., 2006; McArthur, 2016, 2018, 2023). Enabling student agency "allows for the creation and maintenance of students as embodied, knowledge-making persons situated within communities, rather than as abstracted individuals to whom academia imparts knowledge created by others" (Morreira et al., 2020, p. 137). Assessment which informs and affirms individual student development and alerts them to how they might contribute to and even transform society not only supports student learning and wellbeing but also leads to greater teacher satisfaction (McArthur, 2023). In asking how to design and enact assessment that is fair, equitable, and socially just, it is important that preservice teachers have opportunities to develop a positive and agentic sense of themselves as learners, teachers, and assessors.

A teacher's ethical assessment capacity is honed over time and through experience. As O'Neill (2015) put it, "teachers need to learn to be ethical by framing and taking ethically justifiable decisions when they are faced with a professional dilemma. For most teachers, it is not something that will occur naturally just because there is a code of ethics or a code of professional responsibility to require such behavior" (p. 279). However, as Snook (2003) has observed, "ethics is a process of thinking about matters of concern, not about producing neat answers" (p. 18). As with other chapters, this chapter proposes there is value in teacher educators fostering preservice teachers' awareness of the ethical capacity of being an assessor and providing tools or processes to assist them to reflexively and proactively attend to this capacity. Underpinning preservice teachers' wrestling with ethical assessment dilemmas were fundamental principles for supporting and understanding the ethical assessment capacity. These principles were:

- *Awareness*, an awareness of what is being valued in assessment;
- *Identity*, realising that assessment is identity work; and
- *Social justice*, being critically aware of how assessment contributes to broader ideas of social justice.

An awareness that assessment has an ethical dimension can support preservice teachers in their assessment knowledge and practice development (i.e., their assessment capacity) during their initial teacher education and guide them during their transition into the profession. This awareness can also assist in the process of developing a collective, collaborative, and ethical assessment capacity which is grounded in asking: *What do we value here? And, how can my assessment practices better support the identities and agency of my students, individually and collectively?*

6.1.1 What Is Being Valued in Assessment?

As curriculum, pedagogy, and assessment are the three key message systems in education (Bernstein, 2000), how they come together shapes and frames teacher and student experience and *what* and *who* they come to view as valued. More specifically, what assessment makes explicit and what it leaves implicit privileges some knowledge, some ways of representing knowledge, and some ways of knowing and being over others. The power and persuasion of assessment are such that *what* and *who* are the focus of assessment, along with the visible outcomes or consequences of assessment, simultaneously attributes and documents value. Teacher assessment decisions and actions become matters for ethical consideration as whether they recognise it or not; teachers have to create messages of what and who are the focus of assessment. In this way, "Pedagogy [and we suggest assessment] is never innocent. It is a medium that carries its own message" (Bruner, 1996, p. 63). What needs to be included as a focus for assessment is an important question for teachers to ask in their quest for assessment that is ethical and fair. This focus is usefully summed up by the question signalled by Stobart's (2005) analysis of the nature of fairness in multicultural educational systems: "Whose knowledge is taught and assessed and equated with achievement?". This awareness is part of the epistemic assessment capacity introduced in Chapter 4. Considering this question also reminds us to ask what is *not* accorded value through *not* being a focus of teaching and assessment.

In the preservice teachers' reflections, such questioning was evident, prompted by reflection on theoretical readings:

> I am finding these readings incredibly helpful and with each one, I'm gaining more confidence in my ability to successfully complete the assignment. 'Assessment and Learning: differences and relationships between formative and summative assessment' by Wynne Harlen & Mary James This highlights the confusion between formative and summative assessment in that the lines can be blurred between them. I've always thought they were distinct forms of assessment. (Australian preservice teacher).

Preservice teachers also reflected on how assessment had changed since their schooling, commenting that the shift from examination-dominated assessment towards formative assessment meant assessment was more equitable and fairer. Some reflective comments also served to remind us that what counts as fair in assessment can be contested (O'Neill, 2017). Unless students understand the rationale for adjustments to tasks, such as the extra time given to the student in the reflection in this chapter's introduction, they can consider these adjustments to give their peers an unfair advantage (Grimes et al., 2019; Tai et al., 2021). Teacher educators can bring to the surface some of these beliefs in discussions of assessment fairness.

Becoming aware that assessment choices articulate value positions the ethical assessment capacity and leads preservice teachers towards asking and exploring answers to the question: *Are the format and mode of assessment appropriate for different groups of students?* That is, it involves teachers anticipating the conceptual demands and interactional norms inherent in an assessment activity in relation to student backgrounds, the classroom curriculum, and the assessment processes

6.1 What Is Ethical Assessment Capacity?

students might be familiar with. For example, preservice teachers were exploring how they could respond to issues of valued learning:

> Valued learning needs to be acknowledged by a range of assessment rather than just one or even two forms of assessing. Students should be given the option in how they want to show their learning. I would give the option (depending on the subject) of either a discussion between the teacher and the student, a visual representation such as a poster, drawing or anything similar, a piece of writing, or a presentation/group idea. (New Zealand preservice teacher)

Across all four contexts, the preservice teachers in our study recognised that knowing their students well enough so that they could anticipate what their students would experience as engaging and accessible ways to show their learning would take time and experience. Some were aware that students might be too "shy" to share their ideas with their teacher and valued the use of peer assessment as a means of feedback for these students. They were developing an awareness that student perceptions of the classroom social milieu influence students' willingness to participate in assessment interactions that disclose their thinking (Cowie, 2005; Gipps & Murphy, 1994). Some preservice teachers queried if all learning was measurable by assessment. As in the following comment, these reflections were linked with the more expansive goals of curriculum in terms of skills and competencies and also, in this case, with an understanding of the longer term and wider societal agenda of curriculum and assessment:

> An assessment is a good tool to measure learning and success. However, this is not always the case. Not all learning can be measured in the form of assessment. In the 21st century, there are so many valuable skills that need to be learnt that can not be measured in an assessment. Life can take so many different pathways in this day and age, the same skills that were needed 20 years ago may not be as helpful now or may not even be needed to become an effective member of society. (New Zealand preservice teacher)

The preservice teachers were also reflecting on how to respond to multiple student needs through the interplay of formative and summative assessment. Some of them began to plan how they might give students options of assessment, like choosing between a presentation and an essay, recognising that such a plan would depend on the practicality in the context and whether it would be a reliable enough representation. Other preservice teachers recognised that they needed to learn more about how to respond to the ethical tensions involved in differentiation (referred to as accommodation in some contexts) and validity in assessment task design.

Conceptually, the ethical assessment capacity is encapsulated in the question: *Is this fair?* As the reflections and literature in this section outline, this question can include many dimensions. Teachers may consider the scope, focus, and methods of assessment by anticipating the impact of these assessment processes and products and their consequences or outcomes for students. These consequences may be a consideration of to what extent the assessment processes do or do not recognise, affirm, and progress the breadth and depth of students' individual knowledge, skills, and dispositions. As we conceptualise it, the ethical assessment capacity engages directly with how assessment practices shape student identities as learners, knowers, and actors and with teachers' identities as assessors.

6.1.2 Assessment as Identity Work

Developing awareness of fairness and teachers making choices that are more or less likely to lead to socially just outcomes inevitably leads to awareness of the ontological aspect of ethical assessment capacity, or how this capacity is made real within our own identity. The ontological aspect of ethical assessment capacity encompasses student and teacher identity through "how we make sense of potential, capability, and belonging as assessors and assessed" (Burke, 2022, p. 87). It acknowledges that assessment does more than measure what exists, "it makes up people" (Stobart, 2008, p. 171, citing Hacking, 2006). The phrase "making up people" refers to the way assessment can be used to assign labels to people and for learners to see themselves reflected in assessment categories—like "I am an A student" or "I am a failure"—and teachers to construct themselves as "I am just a hard marker" and students as "the Bs" or "the fails." An ethical assessment capacity enables a preservice teacher to question the way these labels are socially constructed through everyday school talk and to question the consequences of these identity labels beyond the moment. Consideration of how assessment 'makes up' people is reflected in the assessment field considering teacher assessment identity in addition to teacher assessment literacy (see Chapter 3 for a discussion of this).

Assessment identity is understood as an amalgam of teacher beliefs, emotions, prior experiences and professional learning, knowledges, sense of self-efficacy, and classroom experiences (Adie, 2013; Cowie et al., 2014; Edwards & Edwards, 2017; Looney et al., 2018; Willis et al., 2013; Xu & Brown, 2016). Teacher assessment identities are understood as "multifaceted and multi-purposed, entailing tensions and contradictions as well as shifts in perspective about the role of assessment" (Leonardsen et al., 2022, p. 1; see also Adie, 2013; Cowie et al., 2014; Scarino, 2013). Crafting an assessment identity is an open-ended process that is particularly relevant to the ethical assessment capacity as it involves teacher reflexivity about what knowledge is valued and how it impacts the lives and learning of students. Burke (2015, 2022) describes *ethical reflexivity* about assessment as an ongoing commitment to critically considering the values, assumptions, and perspectives that shape assessment discourses and practices and teachers' own situatedness in the relations of power involved in assessment practices.

Seen this way, ethical reflexivity supports active awareness and critical consideration of the multiple and flexible identities and responsibilities involved in teachers responding to students in an ethical manner in a variety of assessment situations. It highlights the need for preservice teachers' deliberate consciousness of their relational and pedagogical power because not only can such an awareness "expand what they believe to be possible" (Magill, 2021, p. 103), but it also establishes patterns that persist over time (Darling-Hammond & Bransford, 2007).

6.1.2.1 Developing Awareness Through Reflective Insights and Empathy

Preservice teachers are able to draw on their prior and contemporaneous experiences of assessment to understand and engage with the role of teacher-as-assessor. These experiences include being assessed as students, as part of leisure and sports activities, and assessing others as tutors and coaches. However, research across settings has found that their feelings, beliefs, and thinking about assessment are often dominated by prior experience of formal summative assessment, which can have the 'backwash effect' of limiting practice and identity development (Crossman, 2007; Deneen & Brown, 2016; Hamodi et al., 2016; Hill et al., 2017; Smith et al., 2014). The preservice teachers' awareness of their experiences can assist them in reimagining and negotiating their various assessment responsibilities (Scarino, 2013; Sonu, 2022). In our study, the preservice teachers made links between their own experiences of and orientations towards assessment as siblings, partners, students, and teachers, the ideas they were introduced to in their courses, and what they saw and did during their time in the classroom. For some, these links to prior experience alerted them to the impact of teacher assessment practices on students, leading them to empathise differently with their students (Jaber et al., 2022) and to identify "the type of teacher I wish to be in the future." For example, the following teachers reflected:

> Throughout the year I have learnt a variety of ways to implement assessment as a more equitable and accessible approach in the classroom. Learning that just pen and paper tests are not the only ways to assess students is very eye opening. This is what a final mark meant to me growing up and something I really struggled with. I love the idea of making assessments fun and exciting for the students. The summative component is still the most important part of reflecting students' knowledge, but it needs to be meaningful. It needs to be something all students can complete, and it needs to reflect the learners in the class. I feel more confident in providing assessment that is equitable for each learner. (Canadian preservice teacher)

> One aspect of a peer's ideas that I had not previously considered was the impact that we can have on students. I always considered how teachers could create a positive environment for students. However, I had not given much thought to how teachers can negatively impact upon students (whether it be the learning environment, the emotional or educational state of the student). I will now think carefully about the possible consequences of my actions before enacting them in the classroom. I will also strive to develop into the type of teacher I wish to be in the future; a positive, encouraging and uplifting teacher. (Australian preservice teacher)

We introduced the following reflection in Chapter 4. There we foregrounded the epistemic aspect. Here, we foreground ethical issues, recognising the two capacities as inextricably entangled and proposing the mentor teacher's epistemic understanding of mathematics and of learning was consequential for student identity as capable in mathematics. For one student, we can assume this view had an ongoing negative identity and affective consequences, which led the preservice teacher to the realisation of the kind of assessor she did *not* want to be:

> I did not agree with my [mentor teacher's] methods of formatively assessing her [grade] 5/ 6 students' understanding of the math lesson. During the math talk, students would need

118   6 Ethical Assessment Capacity

to answer 8 questions correctly before being allowed to leave the carpet and return to their seats to work independently. On multiple occasions, 1 student would cry because he did not understand and therefore could not leave the carpet. I feel as though this method of assessment singles out students who may learn at a different speed, or not well under pressure. I am sure he felt very stressed and embarrassed. I know that this is not a method I will be implementing in my future classroom. (Canadian preservice teacher)

Developing a coherent sense of identity as an assessor is a continuous process, full of uncertainty and ambiguity. For these preservice teachers, there was an awareness of the impacts and consequences of assessment, as well as what they valued in assessment. They were articulating ideals of assessment as fun, meaningful, equitable, and encouraging for students. Importantly, those foundations can be shaped by teacher education experiences that enable preservice teachers to develop an awareness of the impact of assessment on their students.

6.1.3 Being Critically Aware of How Assessment Contributes to Broader Ideas of Social Justice

An ethical assessment capacity recognises the ways that the broader education and social landscape might impact students' learning progress and achievement. A New Zealand preservice teacher was beginning to engage with big ideas of social justice and was seeking practical 'how-to' answers regarding eliminating bias in this reflection:

I'm struggling to understand the place of culture, identity and our teaching philosophy in the assessment. How will this influence my assessment and what can I do to eliminate bias? Māori and Pasifika achievement is paramount so why haven't we learned anything regarding this? (New Zealand preservice teacher)

Some preservice teachers were beginning to orient themselves to wider considerations of equity and social justice by grappling with the question of whether their assessment practices were identifying if their students had learned what they intended or what their students actually knew and could do:

I think that it [assessment] shows whose learning we value. But do we assess what we wanted the students to learn, or do we value the knowledge that the student gained? (New Zealand preservice teacher)

Comments such as this echo the distinction Torrance and Pryor (2001) made between convergent and divergent assessment: convergent assessment being a focus on what the teacher intended as learning, and divergent assessment as a focus on what students actually know and can do. Torrance and Pryor argue both are needed. In other reflections, preservice teachers wondered where the balance of responsibilities for learning and task completion might fall between the students and teachers, especially where formative feedback for summative assessment was involved. Observing mentor teachers also raised preservice teachers' awareness that giving feedback in

6.1 What Is Ethical Assessment Capacity?

time for students to make changes or realise that they may have misunderstood what was required is an ethical matter because it impacts student opportunities to succeed. As Simpson et al. (2018) explain, teacher action on behalf of others is always situated and relational, implicated in teachers' personal and professional agency or what they consider possible, if not imaginable and desirable, within a setting.

Teachers make decisions about balancing the assessment purposes as part of their epistemic assessment capacity (see Chapter 4). In our elaboration of the ethical assessment capacity, the balancing out of assessment purposes is also linked to critical consideration of how assessment impacts wider issues of social justice so that epistemic and ethical capacities are always interconnected. Assessment impacts students' sense of themselves as learners and knowers who have knowledge to contribute; that is, it impacts their relationship with curriculum content (Ashwin, 2020). Students are known to disengage when there is no attention accorded or value attributed to the life experiences, worldviews, and languages they have to contribute, often expressed as leaving who they are at the school gate (Macfarlane et al., 2007). The dilemma in this for teachers as they consider ethical assessment choices is about balancing their obligations to system expectations and wider society and to the students they are teaching, with this challenge amplified as the diversity among students increases.

Observing a mentor teacher's practice helped preservice teachers expand their repertoire of practices and how to respond to ethical dilemmas. One preservice teacher observed that extra assistance and differentiated feedback provided by the teacher enabled students to complete the summative task and supported authentic learning. They also observed that the additional time for students put pressure on the teacher to complete their reporting in less time. Mentor teachers can also give access to the ongoing work of responsive, ethical capacities as demonstrated by this preservice teacher reflection:

> I just entered a classroom that my Associate Teacher, who has been teaching in challenging schools for over 20 years, describes as the most difficult class she has ever taught. … Only perhaps 4 of the entire class do not have some kind of significant challenge. There are behavioural, language, and learning difficulties of many kinds, not to mention cultural integration issues that create physical safety issues within the classroom. The children are working from kindergarten to grade 3-4 levels in reading, writing and mathematics, making assessment particularly challenging. … Before any real teaching or assessment of academic learning can happen, these children need to develop a basic sense of respect and self-worth so the class can function without the constant banter, fighting, back-talk and disengagement that is currently present. … My most obvious first assessment of the class as a whole is that most of them really need work on self-regulation … Several children reported to me during the first few days of practicum that they get headaches every day at school from the noise and stress in the class. … I am totally overwhelmed with what I am seeing and experiencing so far, and the ways we are being taught to teach and assess seem totally removed from what is possible in this scenario. (Canadian preservice teacher)

This reflection illustrates the preservice teacher's awareness of how the diversity of students is informing their discernment of the most appropriate focus for teaching and assessment. As this preservice teacher states starkly, "Before any real teaching or assessment of academic learning can happen, these children need to develop a basic sense of respect and self-worth, so the class can function without the constant banter, fighting, back-talk and disengagement that is currently present." It is evident that the preservice teacher is developing an ethical capacity in considering the diversity of students and the link to student wellbeing. While we tend to focus on assessment's impact on student achievement, here, assessment is being put to the service of student wellbeing in a manner consistent with Jones et al. (2021), who argue there is "a bidirectional relationship between wellbeing and assessment experiences" (p. 439). It is also clear that the language and expectations for "these children" needing to develop self-worth reflect some assumptions about students not having self-worth or respect, which would be cues for teacher educators to explore further. An ethical assessment capacity encourages preservice teachers to focus on respecting the dignity of students while also addressing the safety and inclusiveness of classroom cultures.

As scholars and teacher educators focus their attention on decolonising education and enacting Indigenous perspectives towards assessment, there is greater attention being drawn to matters such as racism, the politics of power, language revitalisation, and the ongoing impact of colonisation on equity. Indigenous ways of knowing, which hold different values than Western ways of knowing, can bring the interconnectivity of relationships, reciprocity, and ecology and place them into positions of importance (Eizadirad, 2019; Penetito, 2009). Research and practice associated with decolonising assessment are only now emerging in response to a focus on decolonising the curriculum (Bodkin-Andrews et al., 2019; Te Maro & Averill, 2023; Walker, 2022).

Likewise, there is a need to further examine the ways in which assessment practices have systemically marginalised cultural groups, and work towards anti-racist and anti-oppressive forms of classroom assessment, ones that create new opportunities for students to identify with and through assessment processes. Developing an awareness that assessment practices can be rewritten from new cultural narratives invites preservice teachers to interrogate Western paradigms and places emphasis on the social justice imperative embedded within the ethical capacity, the valuing of diversity, relationships, and agency that can stem from reformed assessments. Rethinking assessment from different cultural grounds is part of that important work teachers, teacher educators, and others need to do that may feel as yet *unthinkable* to some.

6.1.3.1 Joy as an Aspect of Assessment That Is Socially Just

Chapter 5 explored the emotional assessment capacity in-depth and is revisited here as emotions raise the prospect of joyful, positive outcomes (Griffiths, 2013) and where conflicting emotions can raise awareness for a teacher that they are experiencing an ethical dilemma. We concur with McArthur et al.'s (2022) proposal that, from an assessment for social justice perspective, assessment that is 'fair' should not cause injustice or misrecognition of students *or* teachers. She notes that assessment impacts the life of a teacher in two ways: (1) it can be a "joyous event when we see some of the outcomes of our students' learning" and (2) it can signify where and how our students need help. McArthur asserts, "If assessment processes are so stressful and

6.1 What Is Ethical Assessment Capacity?

overwhelming that staff never get to feel recognition for their professional expertise, the same issue of misrecognition, and hence injustice, occurs [as does for students - comment added for clarification]" (p. 22). Joy was seen in preservice teachers' reflections when they prepared students for success in a summative task through carefully crafted formative assessment. Another example was when preservice teachers were experiencing group activities and success in their university class activities:

> Our English workshop this week was about marking and moderation for student summative assessment. It was interesting the process of creating rubrics to match assessments in English. The class group activity of adjusting the rubric from the QCAA standard elaborations was interesting and introduced us to moderation and teachers working together to mark student work. I found this class very enjoyable and am finally starting to feel like I understand assessment in English. (Australian preservice teacher)

Appreciation of ethical implications of assessment and how to manage these is an ongoing challenge and collective responsibility. Preservice teacher reflections indicated that, for some, assessment learning experiences had left them confident in their capacity to undertake fair and equitable assessments. In contrast, other reflections indicated preservice teachers had concerns about whether they would be able to act in line with their ideals (DeLuca et al., 2021). This latter group presents something of an ethical conundrum for the teacher educators who are responsible for preservice teachers' learning and wellbeing. As the following two quotes suggest, many preservice teachers were very aware of the complexity of teacher assessment design decisions:

> There is a time and place for assessment. Assessment caters for a particular group of students but I am unsure how to design assessment activities that ensure fairness for all students regardless of gender, cultural background and learning ability. (New Zealand preservice teacher)

> I am understanding the importance of assessment and the various methods, however I am unsure on how to make assessment fair for everyone with such diversity in the classroom. (New Zealand preservice teacher)

Often, such comments indicated a resolution to keep working to develop their assessment practice. Teacher educators and mentor teachers can propose next steps and offer insights that can inform preservice teachers who are struggling with the challenges inherent in ethical assessment practice. Social justice pedagogy advocates the introduction of tools for social action and change on the basis that only through integrating socially just pedagogic approaches—for example, in Assessment for Learning practices—will teachers provide opportunities for students to move from cynicism and despair to hope and possibility (Chawla, 2020). The proposition is that these tools act as sources of creative energy and empowerment or agency. For assessment educators, a possibility for such a socially just pedagogic tool or practice can be linked with ideas of effective feedback, which ideally assists students in identifying new sources for learning and reflection and seeking out options for next steps in their assessment learning and practice.

This chapter has included many examples of preservice teachers identifying positive changes in practice and future actions to better meet the needs of their students.

Others felt the weight of responsibility for differentiated assessment practice. A challenge for teacher educators in assessment is to position the development of an ethical assessment capacity within collective opportunities to work with and learn from peers and mentor teachers, where this includes learning new classroom strategies and learning about the affordances of wider policy, societal, and professional contexts in which they work (Livingston & Hutchinson, 2017; Looney et al., 2018; Xu & Brown, 2016). An ethical assessment capacity can be a source of joy and hope for teachers as well as students.

6.2 Developing Ethical Assessment Capacity in Initial Teacher Education

In considering the ethical capacity of preservice teachers, we have been guided by the following quote (OECD, 2022):

> Success in education today is about identity, it is about agency and it is about purpose. It is about building curiosity – opening minds; it is about compassion – opening hearts, and it is about courage – mobilising our cognitive, social and emotional resources to take action. (p. 6)

We have outlined some of the ethical dilemmas and challenges preservice teachers reported and experienced, given their desire and professional responsibility to assess and support the learning of all of their students. We described the ways that preservice teachers' attunement to matters of fairness, equity, inclusion, and social justice was grounded in their own experiences of being assessed and informed by readings, lectures, and their classroom learning. We have sought to highlight the range of strategies they discussed and their consideration of actions they could or would take in the future to ameliorate issues and or enhance students' ethical experience of assessment. We have proposed that a focus on identity, which is often a focus for teacher education, should be included as a key principle and foundation for developing an ethical assessment capacity. Teacher assessment identity is more than a personal set of beliefs; as an assessment capacity, it acknowledges that a teacher's agency is both distributed and situated in their context of practice, and in relation to assessment, is enabled and shaped by assessment decisions. Understanding an ethical assessment capacity as situated and filled with potential for changing the situation could provide a means for understanding how preservice teachers might be empowered to consider and take action on what *might be*.

The book *Ethics for Evaluation: Beyond "Doing No Harm" to "Tackling Bad" and "Doing Good"* (van den Berg et al., 2021) encapsulates a vision that is appropriate for the ethical assessment capacity going forward. Across the book, the authors argue the need to go beyond 'what works' to what needs to be done and what would help. They highlight the importance of trust and respect in classrooms, of maintaining the dignity of students, and of empowering students to be agentic in curriculum- and assessment-making (i.e., to shape the lived and enacted curriculum and assessment in classrooms) through their diverse backgrounds and perspectives. Yet, it is teachers that need to provide permission and a platform for such student agency to become reality in classroom assessment practice. Preservice teachers' awareness of the ethical assessment capacity, as encompassing these attributes, and their expressed desire to engage in more ethical assessment practices, has important implications for teacher educators.

We have highlighted some of the factors that are foundational to advancing an ethical assessment capacity in preservice teachers: (a) *awareness*, an awareness of what is being valued in assessment; (b) *identity*, realising that assessment is identity work; and (c) *social justice*, being critically aware of how assessment contributes to broader ideas of social justice. These factors stemmed from our data, yet other factors may be equally important because influences on ethics are necessarily situated, dynamic, and emergent. We have sought to highlight those that are foundational and also aspirational. As highlighted in the questions at the heart of this book, guiding teacher education, the ethical assessment capacity preservice teachers, and teacher educators to reflect on the following questions:

- *Is this assessment decision fair, equitable, and socially just? What are individual and collective consequences for students resulting from this decision?*
- *Who am I as assessor, and who do I want to be?*
- *What is my positionality in relation to curriculum, teaching, assessment, and my students?*
- *How are all my students empowered and agentic in my assessment processes?*
- *How can I develop my capacity for social justice and the experience of joy in assessment?*

6.3 Conclusion

Decisions about when, how, and why a teacher might adjust assessments are everyday decisions, but, as with many ethical dilemmas, the answer often begins with 'it depends.' Furthermore, what it depends on is situated in past experiences, the current situation, and future possibilities. It also depends on teachers' views of learning and *when* and *how* students can and should take responsibility for their own learning. Preservice teachers' personal histories and initial experiences of the power and persuasion of assessment influence their reflections on practice and reflexivity about the role(s) involved in teacher-as-assessor. These various identities and ontological orientations as assessor unfold across lessons and interactions, sometimes activated through questions of what would be fair and just, and sometimes through a sense that their practice is not aligned with the teacher they aspire to be. Preservice teachers, as all teachers, can experience tensions and contradictions across their identities as facilitators of learning (via formative assessment/assessment for learning) and their identities as evaluators (via summative assessment/assessment of learning). They can experience dilemmas around the need for their assessment practices to engage students and maintain their interest and motivation, affirm effort and achievement, and enact assessment that is valid, fair, accessible, and agentic for all students.

Teacher educators can support preservice teachers in forming valuable networks (Révai, 2020) and assist them in developing the confidence and capacity to seek out advice and share their ethical challenges with others, which Edwards (2005) describes as *relational agency*. They need opportunities for developing relationships of professional trust so that they are comfortable and feel safe to raise questions, critique, and suggest different and new assessment practices that challenge historical assessment practices and that truly confront the ethics of assessment. They need opportunities for reflection and reflexivity based on observing the practice of others and exploring different ideas themselves. We propose preservice teachers need opportunities to develop the knowledge, capacity, commitment, and confidence to pursue a vision of ethical and socially just assessment, one based in an understanding of assessment as linked to identity and agency of themselves and their students.

Jeanine Gallagher is an education researcher at the Queensland University of Technology (Brisbane, Australia). Her research interests include educational policy for students with disability, teacher work, inclusive practices and learning spaces, and the use of data to inform learning, teaching, and assessment.

Kerry Earl Rinehart is a Senior Lecturer in Te Kura Toi Tangata, Division of Education, University of Waikato (Hamilton, New Zealand). Her key research interest is in how people's learning and work are judged through assessment, evaluation, and appraisal, particularly for students, teachers, and school principals. ORCID: 0000-0003-0618-8617

References

Adie, L. (2013). The development of teacher assessment identity through participation in online moderation. *Assessment in Education: Principles, Policy & Practice, 20*(1), 91–106.

Ajjawi, R., Tai, J., Boud, D., & Jorre de St Jorre, T. (2023). *Assessment for inclusion in higher education: Promoting equity and social justice in assessment.* Routledge.

Ashwin, P. (2020). *Transforming university education. A manifesto.* Bloomsbury.

Bernstein, B. (2000). *Pedagogy, symbolic control, and identity: Theory, research, critique* (Vol. 5). Rowman & Littlefield.

Bodkin-Andrews, G., Clark, T., & Foster, S. (2019). Aboriginal and Torres Strait Islander secondary students' experiences of racism. In S. Ratuva (Ed.), *The Palgrave handbook of ethnicity* (pp. 1383–1401). Springer.

Bourke, R., & Mentis, M. (2013). Self-assessment as a process for inclusion. *International Journal of Inclusive Education, 17*(8), 854–867.

Brown, M., Burns, D., McNamara, G., & O'Hara, J. (2022). Culturally responsive classroom-based assessment: A case study of secondary schools in Ireland. *Revista de Investigación Educativa, 40*(1), 15–32.

Bruner, J. (1996). *The culture of education.* Harvard University Press.

Burke, P. J. (2015). Re/imagining higher education pedagogies: Gender, emotion and difference. *Teaching in Higher Education, 20*(4), 388–401.

References

Burke, P. J. (2022). Inclusive assessment: Recognising difference through communities of praxis. In *Assessment for inclusion in higher education* (pp. 87–97). Routledge.

Chawla, L. (2020). Childhood nature connection and constructive hope: A review of research on connecting with nature and coping with environmental loss. *People and Nature, 2*(3), 619–642.

Civil, M., & Hunter, R. (2015). Participation of non-dominant students in argumentation in the mathematics classroom. *Intercultural Education, 26*(4), 296–312.

Cowie, B. (2005). Pupil commentary on assessment for learning. *The Curriculum Journal, 16*(2), 137–151.

Cowie, B. (2015). Equity, ethics and engagement: Principles for quality formative assessment in primary science classrooms. In C. Milne, K. Tobin, & D. DeGennaro (Eds.), *Sociocultural studies and implications for science education, cultural studies of science education* (pp. 117–133). Springer.

Cowie, B., Cooper, B., & Ussher, B. (2014). Developing an identity as a teacher-assessor: Three student teacher case studies. *Assessment Matters, 7*(6), 64–89.

Cowie, B., Otrel-Cass, K., Glynn, T., Kara, H., Anderson, M., et al. (2011). *Culturally responsive pedagogy and assessment in primary science classrooms: Whakamana tamariki.* Teaching & Learning Research Initiative Nāu i Whatu Te Kākahu, He Tāniko Taku.

Crossman, J. (2007). The role of relationships and emotions in student perceptions of learning and assessment. *Higher Education Research & Development, 26*(3), 313–327.

Crossouard, B., & Oprandi, P. (2022). Decolonising formative assessment. In *Theory and method in higher education research* (Vol. 8, pp. 181–196). Emerald Publishing Limited.

Darling-Hammond, L., & Bransford, J. (Eds.). (2007). *Preparing teachers for a changing world: What teachers should learn and be able to do.* Wiley.

DeLuca, C., Ge, J., Searle, M., Carbone, K., & LaPointe-McEwan, D. (2021). Toward a pedagogy for slow and significant learning about assessment in teacher education. *Teaching and Teacher Education, 101.* https://doi.org/10.1016/j.tate.2021.103316 (online).

Deneen, C. C., & Brown, G. T. (2016). The impact of conceptions of assessment on assessment literacy in a teacher education program. *Cogent Education, 3*(1). https://doi.org/10.1080/2331186X.2016.1225380 (online).

Edwards, A. (2005). Relational agency: Learning to be a resourceful practitioner. *International Journal of Educational Research, 43*(3), 168–182.

Edwards, F., & Edwards, R. (2017). A story of culture and teaching: The complexity of teacher identity formation. *The Curriculum Journal, 28*(2), 190–211.

Eizadirad, A. (2019). *Decolonizing educational assessment: Ontario elementary students and the EQAO.* Palgrave Macmillan.

Gallagher, J., & Spina, N. (2021). Caught in the frontline: Examining the introduction of a new national data collection system for students with disability in Australia. *International Journal of Inclusive Education, 25*(12), 1410–1424.

Graham, L. J., Tancredi, H., Willis, J., & McGraw, K. (2018). Designing out barriers to student access and participation in secondary school assessment. *The Australian Educational Researcher, 45,* 103–124.

Gipps, C., & Murphy, P. (1994). *A fair test? Assessment, achievement and equity.* Open University Press.

Gipps, C., & Stobart, G. (2009). Fairness in assessment. In C. Wyatt-Smith & J. Joy Cumming (Eds.), *Educational assessment in the 21st century* (pp. 105–118). Springer.

Griffiths, M. (2013). Social justice in education: Joy in education and education for joy. In *International handbook of educational leadership and social (in)justice* (pp. 233–251). Springer Netherlands.

Grimes, S., Southgate, E., Scevak, J., & Buchanan, R. (2019). University student perspectives on institutional non-disclosure of disability and learning challenges: Reasons for staying invisible. *International Journal of Inclusive Education, 23*(6), 639–655.

Hamodi, C., López-Pastor, V., & López-Pastor, A. (2016). If I experience formative assessment whilst studying at university, will I put it into practice later as a teacher? Formative and shared assessment in Initial Teacher Education (ITE). *European Journal of Teacher Education, 40*, 171–190.

Hang, D., & Bell, B. (2015). Written formative assessment and silence in the classroom. *Cultural Studies of Science Education, 10*(3), 763–775.

Heritage, M., & Wylie, C. (2018). Reaping the benefits of assessment for learning: Achievement, identity, and equity. *ZDM Mathematics Education, 50*, 729–741.

Herzog-Punzenberger, B., Altrichter, H., Brown, M., Burns, D., Nortvedt, G. A., Skedsmo, G., Wiese, E., Nayir, F., Fellner, M., McNamara, G., & O'Hara, J. (2020). Teachers responding to cultural diversity: Case studies on assessment practices, challenges and experiences in secondary schools in Austria, Ireland, Norway and Turkey. *Educational Assessment, Evaluation and Accountability, 32*, 395–424.

Hill, M. F., Ell, F., Grudnoff, L., Haigh, M., Cochran-Smith, M., Chang, W. C., & Ludlow, L. (2017). Assessment for equity: Learning how to use evidence to scaffold learning and improve teaching. *Assessment in Education: Principles, Policy & Practice, 24*(2), 185–204.

Jaber, L. Z., Dini, V., & Hammer, D. (2022). "Well that's how the kids feel!"—Epistemic empathy as a driver of responsive teaching. *Journal of Research in Science Teaching, 59*(2), 223–251.

Johnstone, C., Geller, L. R. K., & Thurlow, M. (2022). Opportunities and limitations of accommodations and accessibility in higher education assessment. In *Assessment for inclusion in higher education* (pp. 131–141). Routledge.

Jones, E., Priestley, M., Brewster, L., Wilbraham, S. J., Hughes, G., & Spanner, L. (2021). Student wellbeing and assessment in higher education: The balancing act. *Assessment & Evaluation in Higher Education, 46*(3), 438–450.

Kerr, B., & Averill, R. (2023). Arotakehia te rerenga—Assessment as a powerful instrument of navigation: Knowing how well we are doing. In P. Te Maro & R. Averill (Eds.), *Ki te hoe! Education for Aotearoa*. NZCER Press.

Klenowski, V. (2009). Australian Indigenous students: Addressing equity issues in assessment. *Teaching Education, 20*(1), 77–93.

Klenowski, V. (2014). Towards fairer assessment. *The Australian Educational Researcher, 41*, 445–470.

Leonardsen, J. K., Støen Utvær, B. K., & Fjørtoft, H. (2022) The five faces of an assessor: Conceptualizing the enactment of teacher assessment identity in vocational education and training. *Educational Assessment, 27*(4), 339–355. https://doi.org/10.1080/10627197.2022.2106967

Lingard, B., Mills, M., & Hayes, D. (2006). Enabling and aligning assessment for learning: Some research and policy lessons from Queensland. *International Studies in Sociology of Education, 16*(2), 83–103.

Livingston, K., & Hutchinson, C. (2017). Developing teachers' capacities in assessment through career-long professional learning. *Assessment in Education: Principles, Policy & Practice, 24*(2), 290–307.

Looney, A., Cumming, J., van Der Kleij, F., & Harris, K. (2018). Reconceptualising the role of teachers as assessors: Teacher assessment identity. *Assessment in Education: Principles, Policy & Practice, 25*(5), 442–467.

Macfarlane, A., Glynn, T., Cavanagh, T., & Bateman, S. (2007). Creating culturally-safe schools for Māori students. *The Australian Journal of Indigenous Education, 36*(1), 65–76.

Magill, K. R. (2021). Identity, consciousness, and agency: Critically reflexive social studies praxis and the social relations of teaching. *Teaching and Teacher Education, 104*. https://doi.org/10.1016/j.tate.2021.103382 (online).

McArthur, J. (2016). Assessment for social justice: The role of assessment in achieving social justice. *Assessment & Evaluation in Higher Education, 41*(7), 967–981.

McArthur, J. (2018). *Assessment for social justice: Perspectives and practices within higher education*. Bloomsbury.

McArthur, J. (2023). Rethinking authentic assessment: Work, well-being, and society. *Higher Education, 85*(1), 85–101.

References

McArthur, J., Blackie, M., Pitterson, N., & Rosewell, K. (2022). Student perspectives on assessment: Connections between self and society. *Assessment & Evaluation in Higher Education, 47*(5), 698–711.

Morreira, S., Taru, J., & Truyts, C. (2020). Place and pedagogy: Using space and materiality in teaching social science in Southern Africa. *Third World Thematics: A TWQ Journal, 5*(1–2), 137–153.

Moschkovich, J. N., & Nelson-Barber, S. (2009). What mathematics teachers need to know about culture and language. In B. Greer, S. Mukhopadhyay, A. Powell, & S. Nelson-Barber (Eds.), *Culturally responsive mathematics education* (pp. 111–136). Routledge.

Moss, P. A., Pullin, D. C., Gee, J. P., Haertel, E. H., & Young, L. J. (Eds.). (2008). *Assessment, equity, and opportunity to learn*. Cambridge University Press.

Nieminen, J. H. (2022). Inclusive assessment, exclusive academy. In *Assessment for inclusion in higher education* (pp. 63–73). Routledge.

Nortvedt, G. A., Wiese, E., Brown, M., Burns, D., McNamara, G., O'Hara, J., Altrichter, H., Fellner, M., Herzog-Punzenberger, B., Nayir, F., & Taneri, P. O. (2020). Aiding culturally responsive assessment in schools in a globalising world. *Educational Assessment, Evaluation and Accountability, 32*(1), 5–27.

OECD. (2015). *Helping migrant students to succeed at school and beyond*. OECD.

OECD. (2022). *Building a future in education*. OECD.

O'Neill, G. (2017). It's not fair! Students and staff views on the equity of the procedures and outcomes of students' choice of assessment methods. *Irish Educational Studies, 36*(2), 221–236.

O'Neill, J. (2015). Teachers and ethics. In *The professional practice of teaching in New Zealand* (pp. 261–278). Cengage Learning.

Penetito, W. (2009). Place-based education: Catering for curriculum, culture and community. *New Zealand Annual Review of Education, 18*(2008), 5–29.

Powers, J. M., Fischman, G., & tefera, A. A. (Eds.). (2018). *Review of research in education: The challenges and possibilities of intersectionality in education research*. Sage.

Rasooli, A., Rasegh, A., Zandi, H., & Firoozi, T. (2022). Teachers' conceptions of fairness in classroom assessment: An empirical study. *Journal of Teacher Education*. https://doi.org/10.1177/00224871221130742 (online).

Révai, N. (2020). *What difference do networks make to teachers' knowledge?: Literature review and case descriptions* (OECD education working papers, No. 215). OECD Publishing.

Scarino, A. (2013). Language assessment literacy as self awareness: Understanding the role of interpretation in assessment and in teacher learning. *Australia Language Testing, 30*(3), 309–327.

Scott, S., Webber, C. F., Lupart, J. L., Aitken, N., & Scott, D. E. (2014). Fair and equitable assessment practices for all students. *Assessment in Education: Principles, Policy & Practice, 21*, 52–70.

Simpson, A., Sang, G., Wood, J., Wang, Y., & Ye, B. (2018). A dialogue about teacher agency: Australian and Chinese perspectives. *Teaching and Teacher Education, 75*, 316–326.

Smith, L. F., Hill, M. F., Cowie, B., & Gilmore, A. (2014). Preparing teachers to use the enabling power of assessment. In C. Wyatt-Smith, V. Klenowski, & P. Colbert (Eds.), *Designing assessment for quality learning* (pp. 303–323). Springer.

Snook, I. (2003). *The ethical teacher*. Dunmore Press.

Solano-Flores, G., & Nelson-Barber, S. (2001). On the cultural validity of science assessments. *Journal of Research in Science Teaching: The Official Journal of the National Association for Research in Science Teaching, 38*(5), 553–573.

Sonu, D. (2022). Possibilities for using visual drawing with student-teachers: Linking childhood memories to future teaching selves. *Teaching and Teacher Education, 110*. https://doi.org/10.1016/j.tate.2021.103599 (online).

Stobart, G. (2005). Fairness in multicultural assessment systems. *Assessment in Education, 12*(3), 275–287.

Stobart, G. (2008). *Testing times: The uses and abuses of assessment*. Routledge.

Tai, J., Ajjawi, R., & Umarova, A. (2021). How do students experience inclusive assessment? A critical review of contemporary literature. *International Journal of Inclusive Education*, 1–18. https://doi.org/10.1080/13603116.2021.2011441

Te Maro, P., & Averill, R. (2023). *Ki te hoe! Education for Aotearoa*. NZCER.

Tierney, R. (2013). Fairness in classroom assessment. In J. H. McMillan (Ed.), *Sage handbook of research on classroom assessment* (pp. 125–144). Sage.

Tierney, R. (2014). Fairness as a multifaceted quality in classroom assessment. *Studies in Educational Evaluation, 43*, 55–69.

Tierney, R. (2016). Fairness in educational assessment. In M. A. Peters (Ed.), *Encyclopedia of educational philosophy and theory* (pp. 1–6). Springer Singapore.

Torrance, H., & Pryor, J. (2001). Developing formative assessment in the classroom: Using action research to explore and modify theory. *British Educational Research Journal, 27*(5), 615–631.

Trumbull, E., & Nelson-Barber, S. (2019). The ongoing quest for culturally-responsive assessment for Indigenous students in the US. *Frontiers in Education, 4*. https://doi.org/10.3389/feduc.2019.00040 (online).

Van den Berg, R. D., Hawkins, P., & Stame, N. (Eds.). (2021). *Ethics for evaluation: Beyond "doing no harm" to "tackling bad" and "doing good"*. Routledge.

Walker, M. (2022). A capabilitarian approach to decolonising curriculum. *Education, Citizenship and Social Justice*. https://doi.org/10.1177/17461979221123011 (online).

Willis, J., Adie, L., & Klenowski, V. (2013). Conceptualising teachers' assessment literacies in an era of curriculum and assessment reform. *The Australian Educational Researcher, 40*, 241–256.

Wylie, C., Bauer, M., Bailey, A. L., & Heritage, M. (2018). Formative assessment of mathematics and language: Applying companion learning progressions to reveal greater insights to teachers. In *Language, literacy, and learning in the STEM disciplines* (pp. 143–168). Routledge.

Xu, Y., & Brown, G. T. (2016). Teacher assessment literacy in practice: A reconceptualization. *Teaching and Teacher Education, 58*, 149–162.

Chapter 7
Experiential Assessment Capacity

Abstract This book presents a novel framework, *Thinking the Unthinkable,* aimed at cultivating teacher assessment capacity. The framework includes four fundamental capacities: epistemic, embodied, ethical, and experiential. In this chapter, the experiential capacity is explored through literature, preservice teacher reflections and narratives, and interpretive analysis. The experiential capacity is purposefully presented last in the framework, as it is the culmination of the previous three capacities in action. Experiential capacity involves constructing knowledge about assessment through first-hand experiences across contexts of practice. Fundamentally, teachers develop this capacity by reflecting on the questions: *What assessment actions am I able to implement, and why? What events have persuaded me to act in this way?* The chapter concludes with guidance for developing experiential capacity in initial teacher education.

Keywords Experiential learning · Know-how · Teacher action · Co-agency · Assessment practice · Classroom assessment · Teacher education · Teacher reflection · Teacher development

The learning trajectory of preservice teachers is steep; they quickly need to gain a strong knowledge of assessment, curriculum, and pedagogy and an awareness of how their students learn and then how to translate that knowledge into practice. They also need to build confidence in their professional self and how to integrate their new assessment knowledge into their previous and ongoing experiences. For this learning to happen in the tight timeframes of teacher education programmes, preservice teachers need to understand and engage with the new community of practice that they are placed in very quickly to make sense of both their role and that of others within the community. This community includes both the university-taught part of the programme and school-based practicum experiences (i.e., classroom placements with mentor teachers, also called host or associate teachers). For preservice teachers in our study across four countries (Australia, Canada, England, and New Zealand), these life experiences can often be unsettling and hectic for preservice teachers as they try to integrate the aspirations, expectations, and demands of their participation

© The Author(s), under exclusive license to Springer Nature Singapore Pte Ltd. 2023
C. DeLuca et al., *Learning to Assess*, Teacher Education, Learning Innovation and Accountability, https://doi.org/10.1007/978-981-99-6199-3_7

in multiple communities within their everyday lives, as shared by participants in our study:

> My first week back - I have 9 lessons (which I asked for) - but just trying to stay on track/on top of everything is a lot. (English preservice teacher)

> I am struggling to prioritise university work alongside all the new tasks arising from living alone, unpacking boxes, looking for furniture, paying bills, etc. I have extension for SSA (assignment) until 14th May but I am worried that I will struggle to do the work once we get back to school. (English preservice teacher)

An *experiential* assessment capacity involves focusing on how the events, contexts, and first-hand experiences of learning to teach and assess can be integrated into a fluent set of practices. Integrating theory and practice through experience is demanding, and because of that demand, it is closely associated with the embodied assessment capacity. This chapter explores some of the literature about experiential learning in teacher education, how experiential learning features in preservice teacher reflections, and what that might mean for designing and supporting educative preservice teacher assessment learning experiences.

7.1 What Is Experiential Assessment Capacity?

The *experiential assessment capacity* involves preservice teachers building their knowledge through multiple first-hand experiences in contexts where they can make connections between theory and practice via reflection on their growing understanding. It is an ongoing capacity throughout teachers' professional lives as teachers continually encounter new events, contexts, and assessment ideas, requiring the teacher to continually reflect on the implications of their assessment actions. The teacher learns to ask: *What events have persuaded me to think this way? What am I able to do?* (Fig. 7.1)

Experiential learning theory defines learning as "the process whereby knowledge is created through the transformation of experience. Knowledge results from the combination of grasping and transforming experience" (Kolb, 1984, p. 41). Kolb builds from Dewey's philosophical concepts of pragmatism, Lewin's theories of social psychology, and Piaget's cognitive developmental approaches to propose four aspects of experiential learning: concrete experience, abstract conceptualisation, reflective observation, and active experimentation (Kolb, 1984; Kolb & Kolb, 2017). Initial teacher education programmes help novice teachers learn to assess by providing them with knowledge and skills along with opportunities in classrooms where they can experience teaching-in-action. As preservice teachers interact with their students in new topic areas, they begin to build up a nuanced understanding of how their students are likely to respond to different activities and each other. Experiential learning emphasises the role of first-hand experiences that can enable the preservice teacher's layers of knowledge to be integrated over time (Rone, 2010). It is more than 'craft knowledge' (Winch et al., 2015) because it values educational

7.1 What Is Experiential Assessment Capacity?

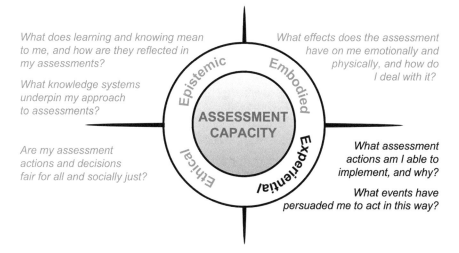

Fig. 7.1 Core questions with focus on the experiential capacity

knowledge as well as the disciplinary knowledge and accepts that knowledge gets reshaped and re-prioritised through experience.

This focus on assessment action in context is similar to the praxeological dimension of assessment literacy proposed by Pastore and Andrade (2019), which includes "the main actions in which a teacher is involved when navigating multiple, and sometimes competing, assessment demands" (p. 135). Experiential capacity is a focus on the teacher as an assessment learner, broadening beyond Pastore and Andrade's articulation of practical assessment strategies, such as learning to "define learning targets and assessment criteria and align them with the assessment aims" and "collect and interpret evidence of student learning." These actions are an essential set of practices for preservice teachers to develop in their repertoire and often involve the translation between theory and practice. An experiential assessment capacity includes these actions as well as the awareness of why these actions are of value and how they are relevant to the context. As with the other assessment capacities that are proposed in this book, principles were drawn for preservice teachers' reflections and narratives of learning that are foundational for the experiential assessment capacity:

- Cultivating *awareness* through reflection in- and on-practice is essential to cultivating assessment capacity; and
- Assessment *know-how* is fostered through assessments experiences and events as students, within preservice teacher programmes, and within practicum schools, all are key sites for experiential learning; and
- Experiential learning is predicated on *co-agency*, the boundaries and possibilities for assessment practice in preservice programmes and schools for preservice teachers, mentor teachers, and teacher educators.

From our study, cultivating experiential awareness, assessment know-how, and co-agency in assessment were a foundation to assessment learning, and to advancing the experiential assessment capacity. Promoting these foundations were evident across assessment learning experiences and events: (a) assessment experiences and events as a student, (b) assessment experiences and events within preservice teacher education programmes, and (c) assessment experiences and events within schools. In this chapter, we propose that experiential assessment capacity develops as preservice teachers are supported to translate their assessment experiences into action by reflecting on the events they have experienced as students being assessed (memory events), their events and interactions in preservice teacher programmes, and classroom events witnessed and carried out first-hand within school-based practicum placements.

7.1.1 Assessment Experiences and Events as a Student

Previous experiences affect how preservice teachers attend to instruction, influencing how and what teachers teach and their planning and decision-making (Fives & Buehl, 2012). Beliefs about teaching and learning are thought to be initially formed from preservice teachers' episodes in their own schooling and the many experiences that make up their life histories (Calderhead & Robson, 1991; Eick & Reed, 2002; Furlong, 2013). For example, teachers entering the teaching profession often give rich descriptions of their favourite teacher and how they want to develop similar skills or attributes. Preservice teachers also bring memories of how they were assessed during their school and university years that tend to focus on what helped them be successful in the contexts they studied. Their reflections on assessment events and how these events were valued and presented by their teachers, and responded to by others in their community, build a conceptual image of assessment purposes and uses that they carry forward as they begin to teach. Ideas about the role of assessment in various scenarios shape how they teach. Unfortunately, memories and reflections on assessment experiences as students often focus on negative experiences. For example, DeLuca et al. (2019) found that over half of the preservice teachers at the start of an initial teacher education programme recounted negative assessment episodes, including failing tests, teachers misjudging their capabilities, or unfairness and bias in assessment results and reporting. Other studies report similar findings with assessment, often being associated with anxiety and stress (Flores et al., 2015), as acknowledged in the embodied assessment capacity.

Preservice teachers may be influenced by these prior experiences and avoid or resist learning about and using some types of assessment when they begin to teach. For example, summative assessment has traditionally been associated with testing where students work as individuals. Preservice teachers may assume all assessment needs to be individual and performance-based. Similarly, any teacher feedback on traditional tests—marks and comments—tends to be private, communicated to the individual, and learners can choose to reveal this information or not to their peers.

7.1 What Is Experiential Assessment Capacity?

Conversely, whole-class dialogue as a teaching and formative assessment strategy is a very public activity where individual performance is viewed and considered by both the teacher and peers. In the context of classrooms, assessment experiences and conversations are open to being overheard by others. The public and private aspects of assessment experiences come with implications for student identity—their sense of self and their reputations within a class as knowers and learners (Cowie, 2005; Crooks, 1988; Gipps, 1999; Stobart, 2008). These assessment identities may continue into their preservice teacher assessment learning experiences, possibly not at a level of cognitive awareness, but informing how readily they approach assessment ideas that are not as familiar or associated with prior experiences that were uncomfortable or presented as incorrect. This preservice teacher has made connections between their experiences as a student, their experiences within their teacher education course, and their future experiences with students. One preservice teacher in our study reflected:

> My initial thoughts on summative assessment as a student raises feelings of anxiety and to resolve these feelings will require a lot of hard work, i.e. study. As a pre-service teacher, setting assessment enables creativity to develop an engaging, challenging and focused task for my students that will increase their zone of proximal development. The challenge will be to align my assessment task to the curriculum and the expectations of my peers, parents, and HoD. (Australian preservice teacher)

In this reflection, experiences in the initial teacher education programme helped this preservice teacher make connections between previous and future assessment experiences.

Research on teacher thinking has raised important issues about initial teacher education programmes and how they support novice teachers in replacing simplistic notions about teaching with more informed understandings of how students learn (Putnam & Borko, 2000) and how assessment might inform their teaching. It is generally accepted that preservice teachers come to teacher education programmes with already well-grounded beliefs about teaching that are resistant to change (Pajares, 1992; Richardson, 1996) through personal experience, schooling and instruction, and formal knowledge. Britzman (1986) describes these beliefs in terms of "implicit institutional biographies-the cumulative experience of school lives.... All this contributes to well-worn and commonsense images of the teacher's work" (1986, p. 443). Bolin (1990) contends that approaching teaching from a craft viewpoint may be a barrier to future development in that the preservice teachers believe they know how to teach and that all they require are a few strategies to get them started. A craft approach reduces education to processes of observation of more experienced teachers and immersion in teaching practice; systematic educational knowledge and research is disregarded (Hordern & Tatto, 2018), resulting in a "horizontal discourse" that is valued, in the shape of the "local, context dependent and specific" (Bernstein, 2000, p. 159). This approach may make preservice teachers reticent to change, using their prior beliefs as filters that prevent them from seeing or exploring beyond experiences that fit with their preconceived notions of teaching (Stofflett & Stoddart, 1994; Weinstein, 1990). Borko et al. (2010) and Desimone (2009) report a consensus around the important features of successful professional learning programmes that involve teacher education; these are content focus, active learning, coherence, duration, and collective participation. While this provides insights into what is considered important, it was Guskey (1986) who suggested that teachers' beliefs were shaped by successful teaching and learning outcomes, such that a change in beliefs was only possible when teachers tried out new classroom approaches and perceived there to be an improvement in student achievement or performance. However, this improvement would be especially difficult for preservice teachers to notice and acknowledge as their classroom practices and understanding of student progress would be at an early stage of development.

7.1.2 Assessment Experiences and Events Within Preservice Teacher Programmes

The role of teacher educators is essential in enabling preservice teachers to recognise how their past experience informs their assessment learning and creating experiences that build their capacity to expand their assessment repertoire. Part of this is driven by the pedagogic discourses and what skills and competencies are legitimised in and through the teaching sessions and assessment tasks. Preservice teachers' practices are also influenced by their interactions with preservice teacher peers and those supporting their initial teacher education programme, such as university course instructors and mentor teachers (Kagan, 1992; van Velzen et al., 2012). Cabaroglu and Roberts (2000, p. 392) tested this assumption with twenty students at the University of Reading in the UK. Their findings revealed that all except one student during the teacher education course changed how they perceived what went on in classrooms. The teacher education programme enabled the majority of participants to reinterpret their ideas about teaching and learning gained from their own education and to understand classrooms from a new perspective. Similarly, in New Zealand, Hill and Eyers (2016) were able to see changes in preservice teachers' assessment conceptions through their teacher education course experiences. Mansour (2009) suggested that "as a teacher's experience in classrooms grows, knowledge grows richer and more coherent and thus forms a highly personalised pedagogy" (p. 27). This perspective of experience being layered over time can be visualised through Goodman's (1988) conceptualisation of guiding images from the past, creating 'intuitive screens' that act as filters when new experiences occur.

The effect of previous experience on practice can be seen in this reflection from our study:

> I am finding these readings incredibly helpful and with each one, I'm gaining more confidence in my ability ….'Assessment for learning? Thinking outside the (black) box' by Eleanore Hargreaves writes about 'turning assessment into a learning event'. This statement is succinct in the years of assessment that I have endured. I must say that motivation levels in reflecting on how hard I have worked and my ultimate result certainly directly relates to my motivation in regards to the next challenge I encounter. If the result is bad, this increases my level of resilience, in that, if I have not achieved it doesn't stop me trying…Assessment cannot define a pupil's capabilities and talents. These capabilities and talents need to be harnessed, nurtured

7.1 What Is Experiential Assessment Capacity?

and encouraged. As teachers, our responsibility is to create several light bulb moments for our pupil's that will permanently commit to their long term memories. (Australian preservice teacher)

This reflection also points to the important role that theory in teacher education courses plays in developing preservice teachers' assessment thinking to focus beyond grades on national and summative assessments, mainly in the form of written examinations, and usually closely bound to a system of reporting and certification (Klenowski & Wyatt-Smith, 2012). Teacher educators who model Assessment for Learning practices as well as teach about them can help preservice teachers to develop their assessment experiences. This formative use of assessment evidence functions differently than the summative approach, since it is an ongoing process that involves classroom interactions and outcomes from activities to inform and improve future teaching and learning. Using classroom assessment to improve student learning is not a new idea. Bloom (1968) showed how to conduct this process in his ideas on mastery learning. Later, Crooke's 1988 review of the effects of evaluation on learners found that the summative function of assessment emphasising grading has been too dominant and that greater emphasis on using assessment to support learning was required. This notion was further developed by Black and Wiliam (1998), whose review drew attention to a number of studies where feedback during the learning process subsequently raised attainment; this led to a number of studies that explored how formative feedback could be fruitful in classrooms. An Assessment for Learning perspective allows teachers to revisualise assessment from a diagnostic and guidance perspective, encouraging the teacher and their students to be more collaborative and active (Black et al., 2003) in both recognising qualities and shortfalls in student work and encouraging agency and improvement through formative action (Black & Wiliam, 2009). In this New Zealand preservice teacher reflection from our study, there is evidence of how Assessment for Learning or formative assessment theory is informing the expectations that the teacher has about taking action for students:

By gathering formative information it helps the teacher assess where the student is at in their learning journey and what will need to be done for further learning and overall teacher judgements. I believe using the right type of assessment for the right students is important but also students need to be able to complete a range of assessments preparing themselves for future study and becoming either qualified in university study or school studies. I think that by providing an adequate assessment practice for students it will further their developing understanding of learning and be able to provide a support base for students to strive and really excel in work as if you know your students you can cater for their needs. (New Zealand preservice teacher).

The preservice teacher is recognising that the layers of assessment actions that may occur in the classroom will also have consequences for their future, reflecting a developing experiential assessment coherence that incorporates the epistemic and ethical dimensions of assessment capacity. Engaging in experiential reflecting that connects across capacities is important as it prevents conservatism in assessment practice, disabling the change process when contexts change and teachers are faced with new ways of assessing. Such an event happened in 2020 when, in many countries, normal assessment arrangements, such as final examinations at the end of courses, could not run because of the disruption of the COVID-19 pandemic. Teachers had to swiftly find new ways of amassing and judging evidence of achievement in order that their students could receive the qualifications they needed for further study or employment.

Problem-based tasks and observational activities are two of the ways that experiential assessment learning can be embedded in teacher education courses, alongside internships, practicums, field trips, and service learning (Radović et al., 2021). A scenario-based activity was helpful for this preservice teacher to bring together their layers of experience in addressing an issue of assessment equity and anticipate what assessment actions would be needed:

> I have seen, both in my own schooling and even on recent professional experience in school, many experiments in classrooms that haven't worked out and there is never time to repeat them in order to achieve better or more usable results. While I have not experienced directly this scenario where a student's anxiety has caused this difficulty to be heightened to the point where it has caused all of their other work (even in other subjects) to be negatively effected in this way, I can see this happening in many different schools, especially as rates of anxiety and depression seem to keep increasing. As I've seen this situation (to a much lower extent and with low impact) before, this seemed like the natural choice for me to use to respond to the task, focusing on what might be done to help the student, while keeping their assessment task authentic and fair. Also, as a potential science teacher, there is a very real chance that this could arise in my future classroom so thinking about it now is certainly beneficial to my budding teaching career. (Australian preservice teacher).

In teacher education programmes in the four country contexts of Australia, Canada, England, and New Zealand, preservice teachers are most frequently expected to learn to assess by translating university preparation courses into action in their practicum placements in schools to make connections between theory and practice of assessment (Hill & Eyers, 2016). While practicum provides the means through which assessment knowledge can be applied, bringing together the theoretical and practical aspects of a course, it also adds considerable complexity where expectations may differ from the realities they encounter. Therefore, practicum places greater demands on the preservice teacher to be reflective, flexible, and agentic in their assessment approaches as they translate their experiences of events within schools.

7.1.3 Assessment Experiences and Events Within Schools

What is seen to be important for assessment is informed by the preservice teachers' experiences within schooling systems. Across many parts of the world, with increasing accountability in many school systems and the rising importance of Assessment for Learning across school levels and contexts, there has been a proliferation of assessment practices and uses within schools (Bennett & Gitomer, 2009; Brookhart, 2011; Herman, 2008; Mansell & James, 2009). Assessment continues to occupy an ever-expanding role in classrooms, from providing initial diagnostic information to guide instruction to dominant traditional summative purposes of assessment for grading student work or testing. This proliferation increases the knowledge

7.1 What Is Experiential Assessment Capacity?

base that teachers need to be introduced to and has contributed to greater complexity in the variety of assessment practices and routines teachers are expected to know and use. Unsurprisingly, many teachers report feeling underprepared for these many assessment demands, particularly as they enter the teaching profession (Herppich et al., 2018; MacLellan, 2004; Volante & Fazio, 2007).

Preservice teachers' developing assessment capacity is also greatly influenced by their supervising mentor teachers during practicum placements (Oo et al., 2021). Preservice teachers witness how teachers in their practicum school approach assessment in their classrooms and recognise that some assessment practices can motivate while others demotivate students (Cauley & McMillan, 2010; Harlen, 2006; Hattie, 2008). Preservice teachers witness how assessment can engage or disengage students in learning (Brookhart, 2008; Gilboy et al., 2015) and promote or hinder student growth (Black & Wiliam, 1998; Garner, 2006). Problems can arise when the mentoring approach overemphasises practice teaching instead of the creation of a context to facilitate preservice teachers' learning and consideration of possibilities and alternatives rather than simple correction of practice. Importantly, preservice teachers need to come to the realisation that teachers' classroom assessment actions powerfully affect learning and progress, ultimately exposing and challenging preservice teachers' fundamental beliefs about teaching and learning (Herppich et al., 2018; Looney et al., 2017; Xu & Brown, 2016). How the knowledge, skills, and experiences are interpreted will depend on what preservice teachers recognise and notice as being important in their development as teachers.

Most initial teacher education programmes consist of periods of time in university with school-based placements of several weeks interspersed. This schedule requires preservice teachers to transition smoothly between these different communities, finding their place in each and drawing ideas and knowledge from each experience to make sense of what they encounter. While a mentor teacher within the practicum school will support the transition to the school environment, the first few weeks of a practicum often present preservice teachers with a range of new experiences they had not envisaged as they prepared for this profession. As a result, this transition can be an anxious time for new teachers as it can challenge their conceptions of what is involved in teaching and undermine their confidence as gaps in knowledge or paucity of resourcing become evident suddenly after being hidden previously:

> I am feeling pretty overwhelmed with lesson planning at the moment. Although, talking to my colleagues, this seems to be a common theme. At this point in my placement I have been spending most of my time learning the content for grade 12 chemistry and following lesson plans from my associate's previous years of teaching chemistry. I feel half guilty about this and half thankful because I don't think I would have time to make all of my own lessons and learn all of this content at the same time. But, the same goes for assessment tools - I have mostly been using what my associate has been providing me with. (Canadian preservice teacher)

As well as the knowledge demands evident within teacher education programmes, assessment ideas and principles are often presented in abstract or decontextualised terms. Preservice teachers need to then translate the principles into the contexts in which they find themselves during their school placements. The resourcing and realities of the classroom may not fit with the ways the preservice teacher has envisaged assessment practices would run and function in their classrooms, as can be seen in the reflection below:

> I am totally overwhelmed with what I am seeing and experiencing so far, and the ways we are being taught to teach and assess seem totally removed from what is possible in this scenario. Very curious how the next 5 weeks will unfold. (Canadian preservice teacher)

Dilemmas of practice engage other aspects of assessment capacity as well, with the emotions of struggling, being overwhelmed, and curious pointing towards some important ethical and epistemic dimensions raised for more thought and action. The experiential capacity enables the preservice teacher to contemplate actions and what they can do, sometimes by interacting with or observing their mentor teachers. This observation helps preservice teachers realise the potential of specific practices within their current context and may allow for a diversity of practices to be considered through the experiences of others.

Preservice teachers learn from observing experienced teachers carrying out assessments in their classrooms, realising what routines they need to establish and how to make the assessment process more effective for learners. In addition, knowledge gained from classroom observations or team teaching with a more experienced teacher can help a novice teacher envision how assessment practices may be incorporated with other classroom routines. Importantly, classroom observations and team teaching help preservice teachers tease out how assessment supports teaching and learning and evaluate the usefulness and effectiveness of various assessment approaches:

> Now that I have completed my winter placement and am one week into my alternative placement, I feel more confident about assessment than I have throughout the entire program. I have had the experience of working in a junior classroom for my winter placement, and I think that this gave me a better understanding of formative assessment (which I think can be a little bit difficult to fully understand at a primary level alone). I also got to give lots of summative assessments and use tools like Plickers to make it more enjoyable for the students. My alternative placement has been amazing. I am working in an ISA (Intensive Support Assessment) classroom and in just one week, I feel that I have gained such a strong understanding of how assessment practices are used and the different cases in which they are used to help students who benefit from extra support. The classroom I am working in offers an ISA program to junior students who have an identified learning disability. They have their own classrooms, but for Language and Math periods, they come to this classroom for the extra support they need. When a student first enters the program, they are assessed on their literacy and math skills. The duration of the program (max. 2 years) is then geared towards supporting each individual student in a way that works for them. At the end of the program, another assessment is done to represent the progress made since the beginning of the program, and to discuss next steps for transitioning into full-day classrooms with their peers. Though I have only been observing in the ISA room for one week so far, I have seen so much growth in each student. My AT has told me that a couple of students entered the program at a level 3 reading level (in grade 5), and over the course of the year have gotten to a level 13. I have really enjoyed watching students grow and learning about all of the amazing assessment practices used in this classroom. If it were possible for all classrooms to work the way ISA works (with the amount of support and individualisation), so many more students would have the opportunity to grow and succeed. (Canadian preservice teacher)

7.1 What Is Experiential Assessment Capacity? 139

As preservice teachers gain experience through planning and delivering part or whole lessons, they become more aware of how theoretical ideas can be translated into practice through both their critical reflection (Farrell, 2007) and their engagement in lesson planning activities (Stuart & Thurlow, 2000). Sometimes there is a perceived tension between what is encouraged as good assessment practice during the university part of the programme and what preservice teachers experience in their practice schools. This tension can lead the preservice teacher to feel they need to seek the permission of their mentor teacher to try alternative assessment practices to those that seem dominant in the school, as teaching within schools is wrapped up within power relations across relationships of university instructors, mentor teachers, and preservice teacher:

> As well, as a personal goal, I want to improve my feedback skills and try and incorporate more peer-feedback for students because that is an important skill they should build on. Obviously, it will depend on my associate teacher, and her expectations. (Canadian preservice teacher)

Sometimes a request to try new assessment practices may result in mentor teachers dissuading preservice teachers from developing new approaches:

> My associate teachers and I talked about the idea of co-constructing success criteria. Neither of them were a big fan of the idea. They seemed to believe that, realistically, it was a lot to ask of some classrooms and that it would be difficult to mediate – they said that some students would not respond well and many do respond well to clear instructions and goals. Finally, they said in preparation for post-secondary, in which the goals are clearly stated, they believed that providing criteria that was created by the teacher was the best way to prepare them. We had a long conversation about it, and they said they could see where co-constructing success criteria sounds like a good idea, but are unsure if they believe it would work for all classes. (Canadian preservice teacher)

In cases where the mentor teacher responds critically to such practices, possibly viewing them as a criticism of the school's current practices or less important for preservice teacher development, it can create a barrier to trying new assessment approaches, limiting the preservice teacher's agency in assessment:

> I am worried about my AT's receptivity to me implementing these methods in the classroom. As well, I sometimes even lack the confidence to ask for what I really want to do in the classroom on prac because I doubt myself and my abilities as a teacher, or I think that my AT may think my methods are too forward thinking to compared to what they do. (Canadian preservice teacher)

Preservice teachers recognise that they learn from applying assessment ideas presented in courses during practicum. Often it is the evaluation and refinement of the process in response to classroom contexts and situations that provide the impetus for this learning. Specific classroom events or professional conversations may be recognised and highlighted as key in helping preservice teachers make sense of how theoretical ideas play out in practice, providing them with ways of articulating their developing assessment capabilities. In some cases, preservice teachers are able to take a more metacognitive approach and gauge their progress in developing assessment concepts over time:

> I feel that my professional judgment has developed in the sense that I am much better at making sensible decisions for each student when it comes to assessment. I have had the chance to put a few assessment and evaluation techniques into practice. Some have worked really well, and I learned from the ones that did not work as well. (Canadian preservice teacher)

> I feel so much more confident in my assessment process after being in 3 very different school the last two months. I have been provided with strategies and techniques that I want to use, but also have realized that final exams are not the end all and be all. Students need a variety of opportunities to display their learning and learn to feel confident in their own capabilities. (Canadian preservice teacher)

7.2 Preservice Teachers' Experiential Assessment Capacity

While the experiential assessment capacity focuses on how ideas are formed and reshaped by the events that preservice teachers encounter, it is also evident that preservice teachers make progress and gain confidence in assessment practices as they move through their initial teacher education programme. Taking stock of progress can provide useful information for the preservice teacher and for university instructors, mentors, and future employers. In this study, we used the Approaches to Classroom Assessment Inventory (ACAI), developed by DeLuca and colleagues (2016), at specific points in preservice teachers' learning trajectories. The ACAI uses a scenario item format that encourages participants to engage with five different assessment scenarios and give their interpretations and reactions to the scenarios. In so doing, it gives an insight into teachers' approaches to assessment, their perceived skills with assessment tasks and responsibilities, and their assessment priorities and preferences. The ACAI is focused on teachers' approaches to assessment and is therefore linked directly to the experiential capacity.

The ACAI was developed from an analysis of 15 contemporary assessment standards (i.e., 1990–2016) across five geographic regions (USA, Canada, UK, Europe, Australia, and New Zealand) (DeLuca et al., 2016). A total of 12 assessment dimensions, evenly divided across four domains (assessment purpose, process, fairness, theory), were identified. In terms of assessment purpose, Assessment of Learning (AoL) refers to assessment activities designed to dependably measure student learning and achievement. Conversely, Assessment for Learning (AfL) and Assessment as Learning (AaL) approaches focus on using evidence to guide teaching and learning and improving students' metacognition, respectively. Three approaches to assessment process—design, use and scoring, and communication—reflect the phases of the assessment process that teachers believe they should dedicate time and effort towards. Regarding assessment fairness, teachers could adopt a standardised approach which values equal treatment of all students in assessment situations, an equitable approach which recognises and supports students formally identified learning needs, or a differentiated approach which tailors assessments to each student's individual needs. Last, three approaches to assessment theory were consistent, contextual, and balanced, which, respectively, prioritise assessment reliability, validity, or strives to optimise both.

Approximately 500 preservice teachers across the four countries in our study completed the ACAI. Within Part A of the ACAI, preservice teachers are presented

7.2 Preservice Teachers' Experiential Assessment Capacity

with five assessment scenarios, each with 12 actions aligned with the 12 assessment dimensions identified from contemporary assessment standards. For example, Scenario 4 presents preservice teachers with the following situation: You are planning a unit for your class. For Scenario 4, actions that preservice teachers would determine their endorsement of included start by designing a summative assessment based upon curriculum standards, then use backward planning to create your lesson plans (Assessment of Learning), co-construct learning goals and discuss assignments and grading criteria for the unit with your students (communication of assessment processes), and plan class lessons and assessments that are the same for all students (a standard approach to fairness). All possible actions are defensible ones that can be taken by a reasonable teacher; therefore, the ACAI taps into how teachers interpret and navigate socio-cultural and policy contexts to use assessment.

As with previous ACAI studies that have examined preservice teachers (e.g., Coombs et al., 2020; DeLuca et al., 2019), our preservice teachers strongly endorsed all assessment dimensions (see Table 7.1). This finding is somewhat unsurprising as many of these preservice teachers were actively engaged in assessment learning at the time in which they completed the ACAI and, as such, were positively disposed to all aspects of assessment practice. Interestingly though, the four dimensions that were the least strongly supported were: Assessment of Learning (AoL), use and scoring of assessments, standard approach to fairness, and valuing consistent assessment information. Importantly, these dimensions are also those most closely associated with teacher-focused assessment practice. It appears that while being enthusiastic

Table 7.1 Endorsement of Approaches to Classroom Assessment (ACAI) dimensions

Dimension	Mean (SD)
Assessment purpose	
AoL	4.20 (0.78)
AfL	4.74 (0.65)
AaL	4.65 (68)
Assessment process	
Design	4.69 (0.67)
Use/Scoring	3.93 (0.72)
Communication	4.91 (0.67)
Assessment fairness	
Standard	3.94 (0.78)
Equitable	4.64 (0.65)
Differentiated	4.64 (0.72)
Assessment theory	
Consistent	4.02 (0.77)
Contextual	4.24 (0.67)
Balanced	4.44 (0.68)

Scale: 1 = highly unlikely, 6 = highly likely

142   7   Experiential Assessment Capacity

Table 7.2 Descriptive statistics (mean, standard deviation) for assessment practices (Part B) of ACAI

Assessment practices	Mean (SD)
I use student assessment data to inform instructional planning and next steps for individual students and the class as a whole	5.16 (0.89)
I monitor and revise my assessment practices regularly	5.14 (0.82)
I use a variety of formative assessment techniques (e.g., structured Q&A, quick-writes) and instruments (e.g., paper–pencil quizzes, personal-response systems) to check for understanding during instruction	5.25 (0.82)
My summative course grades are based on a sufficient body of evidence to provide a dependable and meaningful representation of individual student learning as related to curriculum expectations	5.04 (0.90)
I use a variety of summative assessment types, such as multiple choice type tests, essays, and performance-based assessments	5.13 (0.87)
I engage students in monitoring their own learning and using assessment information to develop their learning skills	5.25 (0.82)
I spend adequate time ensuring that my assessments are responsive to and respectful of the cultural and linguistic diversity of my students	5.29 (0.82)
I regularly engage students in assessment practices during teaching	4.91 (0.95)
I explicitly communicate the purposes and uses of assessment to students	5.13 (0.90)
I provide timely feedback to students to improve their learning	5.43 (0.72)
My determination of students' grades is primarily influenced by factors related to the intended purposes of the assessment or the curriculum expectation being measured	4.59 (0.99)
I am confident in my ability to analyse and make instructional decisions based upon my students' performance on external standardised assessments (e.g., AP tests, state accountability tests, district benchmark tests)	4.19 (1.12)
I monitor and revise my assessment practices to improve the quality of my instructional practices	5.22 (0.81)
My methods of assessing and the types of assessments I use allow students to demonstrate their learning in individualised ways	5.10 (0.83)
I spend adequate time individualising my assessment practices to meet the specific educational needs of each of my students	4.81 (1.03)
I provide adequate resources, time, and accommodations to prepare students with special needs/exceptionalities for assessment	5.20 (0.82)
In my class, all students complete the same assignments, quizzes, and tests	3.73 (1.35)
When grading student work, I use the same rubric or scoring guide for all my students	4.10 (1.22)
I map my assessment tasks/questions to learning objectives	5.08 (0.85)
I am confident that students' performance on my assessments is the best representation of what I really want them to learn	4.41 (1.07)
I can select assessments from test banks, textbook series, and/or online teacher sharing sites that align with my learning objectives and dependably represent my students' learning	4.12 (1.20)

(continued)

7.2 Preservice Teachers' Experiential Assessment Capacity

Table 7.2 (continued)

Assessment practices	Mean (SD)
I use multiple assessments to measure each learning objective so that I am confident in the grades I assign	5.01 (0.91)
My grades and feedback are grounded in the evidence I have collected about student achievement of learning expectations	5.11 (0.81)
I am confident that I apply my scoring guides/rubrics consistently	4.85 (0.89)

Scale: 1 = strongly do not value; 6 = strongly value

practitioners of assessment; our preservice teachers were drawn to more student-focused assessment practices.

Part B of the ACAI examines the same 12 dimensions but by asking our preservice teachers to what degree they value specific assessment practices (Table 7.2). Preservice teachers' endorsement of assessment practices echoed trends from the scenario-based section of the ACAI in that most majority of practices were highly valued. Additionally, the items that were most strongly valued were those associated with student-focused assessment practice (e.g., I provide timely feedback to students to improve their learning; I spend adequate time ensuring that my assessments are responsive to and respectful of the cultural and linguistic diversity of my students; and I engage students in monitoring their own learning and using assessment information to develop their learning skills) while those that were valued the least are associated with teacher-driven assessment practice (e.g., I can select assessments from test banks, textbook series, and/or online teacher sharing sites that align with my learning objectives and dependably represent my students' learning; When grading student work, I use the same rubric or scoring guide for all my students; In my class, all students complete the same assignments, quizzes, and tests).

The ACAI data show that preservice teachers in our study value student-driven and learning-focused assessment practices. While their intentions may be to use these practices, in reality, the complexities of classrooms and schools, including the layering of horizontal and vertical knowledges within contexts, may limit the extent to which these intentions are realised.

7.3 Developing Experiential Assessment Capacity in Initial Teacher Education

Classroom experience is often touted in preservice teacher policy as the most important experience for preparing teachers to become teachers, especially in England and Australia. What this chapter demonstrates is that experience within schools is important for developing preservice teacher assessment capacity when it is interwoven with experiences led by teacher educators. Experience in schools is not enough. As Kolb (1984) and Kolb and Kolb (2017) highlighted, alongside the concrete experience, there needs to be active reflection that can enable experience to be recognised in abstract concepts and opportunities to reflect, observe, and experiment. These opportunities for reflection are most effective when they are structured and guided by action and when they feature opportunities for individual as well as interactive social aspects of learning, a process of co-agentic learning (Radović et al., 2021). More positive outcomes for preservice teachers have been noted in teacher education research studies where there was a balance between autonomous learning and peer collaboration as preservice teachers put theory into action (Williams & Sembiante, 2022). Teacher educators are able to structure and guide assessment learning experiences to enable reflection, collaboration, and translation. The process of reflection on experience can bring the preservice teacher's previous assessment experiences as a student into dialogue with assessment theory and practice to raise the novice teachers' self-awareness. Demonstration, modelling, problematising, and problem-solving are all experiential opportunities to learn to be an assessor that are within reach of teacher educators. Through this co-reflection process, teacher agency is valued, and know-how is cultivated.

Preparing teachers to learn to be assessors also means preparing teachers to be ready to engage with the challenges of assessment that *was*, assessment that *is*, and assessment that *might be*. In their study with preservice teachers in Hong Kong, Harfitt and Chow (2018) looked outside of school experiences to consider how service learning might prepare teachers towards uncertain and exciting futures. They found that preservice teachers became more learner-centred and were able to extend their critical and creative thinking and reflection capacity. However, they also recognised that not all of their faculty colleagues or preservice teachers saw the value in learning in a context not directly related to classroom contexts. Teacher educators play an important role in narrating and creating connections between the layers of experiences that make up a preservice teacher's development over time as an assessor. Experiential assessment capacity requires reflection and questioning:

- *What are my own assessment experiences (as a student and teacher), and how do they inform my assessment knowledge and preferences?*
- *What experiential assessment activities have I engaged in throughout preservice education, and how have they shifted my assessment approach?*
- *What are the constraints on my assessment practice as an educator? How can I overcome these constraints?*

7.4 Conclusion

The experiential assessment capacity helps preservice teachers build their knowledge through multiple first-hand experiences in contexts where they can make sense of learning to teach, assess, and develop a fluent set of practices. Crossing boundaries from university to practicum school during initial teacher education programmes provides the settings for experiential assessment capacity to receive attention and develop. The traditional way to consider practicum is to frame it as a means for implementing theoretical learning in a practical way (Lawson et al., 2015), but this notion is far too simplistic. Preservice teachers may be introduced to theories and ideas about assessment in their teacher education programme, and this gets translated into possibilities of practice; yet these ideas are susceptible to change as they meet the realities, challenges, and social, power, and cultural dynamics of classrooms and schools.

It is through the experiences of witnessing experienced teachers' practices and beginning to develop their own ways of working with their classes that preservice teachers perceive, interpret, and construct an integration between theory and practice. This workplace-based professional learning is key to sense-making, allowing epistemic, embodied, and ethical ideas to both instigate and inform one another through preservice teachers' experiences while on school-based practicum placements. As such, preservice teachers need to be open to reflect on, rethink, and reposition the initial notions of assessment they may have formed during the university contribution to their programme and equally reframe and establish new ways of working in assessment that are underpinned by theory. This reframing requires an assessment capacity that allows teachers to think differently about what *is* and *might be* possible within their current and future contexts. Experiential assessment capacity is enabled through progressive and reflective interactions with instructors, mentors, and peers as preservice teachers build their own classroom assessment practices. Providing opportunities for the articulation and the bringing together of theory, events, and interpretations are key in both the university and practicum parts of teacher education programmes in order for preservice teachers to have sufficient agency and confidence to experiment and learn from classroom experiences.

References

Bennett, R. E., & Gitomer, D. H. (2009). Transforming K-12 assessment: Integrating accountability testing, formative assessment and professional support. In *Educational assessment in the 21st century: Connecting theory and practice* (pp. 43–61). Springer.

Bernstein, B. (2000). *Pedagogy, symbolic control, and identity: Theory, research, critique* (Vol. 5). Rowman & Littlefield.

Black, P., Harrison, C., Lee, C., Marshall, B., & Wiliam, D. (2003). *Assessment for learning—Putting it into practice.* Open University Press.

Black, P., & Wiliam, D. (1998). Assessment and classroom learning. *Assessment in Education, 5*(1), 7–74.

Black, P., & Wiliam, D. (2009). Developing the theory of formative assessment. *Educational Assessment, Evaluation and Accountability, 21*(1), 5–31.

Bloom, B. S. (1968). Learning for mastery. Instruction and curriculum. Regional education laboratory for the Carolinas and Virginia, topical papers and reprints, Number 1. *Evaluation Comment, 1*(2), n2.

Bolin, F. S. (1990). Theme: Teachers' beliefs: Helping student teachers think about teaching: Another look at Lou. *Journal of Teacher Education, 41*(1), 10–19.

Borko, H., Jacobs, J., & Koellner, K. (2010). Contemporary approaches to teacher professional development. In P. Peterson, E. Baker, & B. McGaw (Eds.), *International encyclopedia of education* (Vol. 7, pp. 548–556). Elsevier.

Britzman, D. (1986). Cultural myths in the making of a teacher: Biography and social structure in teacher education. *Harvard Educational Review, 56*(4), 442–457.

Brookhart, S. M. (2008). *How to give effective feedback to your students.* Association for Supervision and Curriculum Development.

Brookhart, S. M. (2011). Educational assessment knowledge and skills for teachers. *Educational Measurement: Issues and Practice, 30*, 3–12.

Cabaroglu, N., & Roberts, J. (2000). Development in student teachers' pre-existing beliefs during a 1-year PGCE programme. *System, 28*(3), 387–402.

Calderhead, J., & Robson, M. (1991). Images of teaching: Student teachers' early conceptions of classroom practice. *Teaching and Teacher Education, 7*(1), 1–8.

Cauley, K. M., & McMillan, J. H. (2010). Formative assessment techniques to support student motivation and achievement. *The Clearing House: A Journal of Educational Strategies, Issues and Ideas, 83*(1), 1–6.

Coombs, A., DeLuca, C., & MacGregor, S. (2020). A person-centred analysis of teacher candidates' approaches to assessment. *Teaching and Teacher Education, 87.* https://doi.org/10.1016/j.tate. 2019.102952 (online).

Cowie, B. (2005). Student commentary on classroom assessment in science: A sociocultural interpretation. *International Journal of Science Education, 27*(2), 199–214.

Crooks, T. J. (1988). The impact of classroom evaluation practices on students. *Review of Educational Research, 58*(4), 438–481.

DeLuca, C., Coombs, A., MacGregor, S., & Rasooli, A. (2019). Toward a differential and situated view of assessment literacy: Studying teachers' responses to classroom assessment scenarios. *Frontiers in Education, 4.* https://doi.org/10.3389/feduc.2019.00094 (online).

DeLuca, C., LaPointe-McEwan, D., & Luhanga, U. (2016). Approaches to classroom assessment inventory: A new instrument to support teacher assessment literacy. *Educational Assessment, 21*(4), 248–266.

Desimone, L. M. (2009). Improving impact studies of teachers' professional development: Toward better conceptualisations and measures. *Educational Researcher, 38*(3), 181–199.

Eick, C. J., & Reed, C. J. (2002). What makes an inquiry-oriented science teacher? The influence of learning histories on student teacher role identity and practice. *Science Education, 86*(3), 401–416.

Farrell, T. S. C. (2007). *Reflective language teaching: From research to practice.* Continuum.

Fives, H., & Buehl, M. M. (2012). Spring cleaning for the "messy" construct of teachers' beliefs: What are they? Which have been examined? What can they tell us? In K. R. Harris, S. Graham, T. Urdan, S. Graham, J. M. Royer, & M. Zeidner (Eds.), *APA educational psychology handbook, Vol. 2. Individual differences and cultural and contextual factors* (pp. 471–499). American Psychological Association.

Flores, M. A., Veiga Simão, A. M., Barros, A., & Pereira, D. (2015). Perceptions of effectiveness, fairness and feedback of assessment methods: A study in higher education. *Studies in Higher Education, 40*(9), 1523–1534.

Furlong, J. (2013, January). Globalisation, neoliberalism, and the reform of teacher education in England. In *The educational forum* (Vol. 77, No. 1, pp. 28–50). Taylor & Francis Group.

References

Garner, R. L. (2006). Humor in pedagogy: How ha-ha can lead to aha! *College Teaching, 54*(1), 177–180.

Gilboy, M. B., Heinerichs, S., & Pazzaglia, G. (2015). Enhancing student engagement using the flipped classroom. *Journal of Nutrition Education and Behavior, 47*(1), 109–114.

Gipps, C. (1999). Chapter 10: Socio-cultural aspects of assessment. *Review of Research in Education, 24*(1), 355–392.

Goodman, J. (1988). Constructing a practical philosophy of teaching: A study of preservice teachers' professional perspectives. *Teaching and Teacher Education, 4*(2), 121–137.

Guskey, T. R. (1986). Staff development and the process of teacher change. *Educational Researcher, 15*(5), 5–12.

Harfitt, G. J., & Chow, J. M. L. (2018). Transforming traditional models of initial teacher education through a mandatory experiential learning programme. *Teaching and Teacher Education, 73*, 120–129.

Harlen, W. (2006). The role of assessment in developing motivation for learning. In *Assessment and learning* (pp. 61–80). Sage.

Hattie, J. (2008). *Visible learning: A synthesis of over 800 meta-analyses relating to achievement.* Routledge.

Herman, J. L. (2008). Accountability and assessment in the service of learning: Is public interest in K-12 education being served? In L. Shepard & K. Ryan (Eds.), *The future of test-based educational accountability* (pp. 211–232). Taylor and Francis.

Herppich, S., Praetorius, A. K., Förster, N., Glogger-Frey, I., Karst, K., Leutner, D., Behrmann, L., Böhmer, M., Ufer, S., Klug, J., Hetmanek, A., Ohle, A., Böhmer, I., Karing, C., Kaiser, J., & Südkamp, A. (2018). Teachers' assessment competence: Integrating knowledge-, process-, and product-oriented approaches into a competence-oriented conceptual model. *Teaching and Teacher Education, 76*, 181–193.

Hill, M. F., & Eyers, G. E. (2016). Moving from student to teacher: Changing perspectives about assessment through teacher education. In *Handbook of human and social conditions in assessment* (pp. 57–76). Routledge.

Hordern, J., & Tatto, M. (2018). Conceptions of teaching and educational knowledge requirements. *Oxford Review of Education, 44*(6), 686–701.

Kagan, D. M. (1992). Implication of research on teacher belief. *Educational Psychologist, 27*(1), 65–90.

Klenowski, V., & Wyatt-Smith, C. (2012). The impact of high stakes testing: The Australian story. *Assessment in Education: Principles, Policy & Practice, 19*(1), 65–79.

Kolb, D. A. (1984). *Experiential learning: Experience as the source of learning and development.* Prentice Hall.

Kolb, A. Y., & Kolb, D. A. (2017). Experiential learning theory as a guide for experiential educators in higher education. *Experiential Learning & Teaching in Higher Education, 1*(1), 7–44.

Lawson, T., Çakmak, M., Gündüz, M., & Busher, H. (2015). Research on teaching practicum—A systematic review. *European Journal of Teacher Education, 38*(3), 392–407.

MacLellan, E. (2004). Initial knowledge states about assessment: Novice teachers' conceptualisations. *Teaching and Teacher Education, 20*(5), 523–535.

Mansell, W., & James, M. (2009). *Assessment in schools—Fit for purpose.* Assessment Reform Group.

Mansour, N. (2009). Science teachers' beliefs and practices: Issues, implications and research agenda. *International Journal of Environmental and Science Education, 4*(1), 25–48.

Oo, C. Z., Alonzo, D., & Davison, C. (2021, April). Pre-service teachers' decision-making and classroom assessment practices. *Frontiers in Education, 6*. https://doi.org/10.3389/feduc.2021.628100 (online).

Pajares, F. (1992). Teachers' beliefs and educational research: Cleaning up a messy construct. *Review of Educational Research, 62*, 307–332.

Pastore, S., & Andrade, H. L. (2019). Teacher assessment literacy: A three-dimensional model. *Teaching and Teacher Education, 84*, 128–138.

Putnam, R. T., & Borko, H. (2000). What do new views of knowledge and thinking have to say about research on teacher learning? *Educational Researcher, 29*(1), 4–15.

Radović, S., Hummel, H. G., & Vermeulen, M. (2021). The challenge of designing 'more' experiential learning in higher education programs in the field of teacher education: A systematic review study. *International Journal of Lifelong Education, 40*(5–6), 545–560.

Richardson, V. (1996). The role of attitudes and beliefs in learning to teach. *Handbook of Research on Teacher Education, 2*(102–119), 273–290.

Rone, T. R. (2010). Engaged education: Experiential learning, intensive field experiences, and social change. In P. Peterson, B. McGaw, & E. Baker (Eds.), *International encyclopedia of education* (3rd ed.). Elsevier.

Stobart, G. (2008). *Testing times: The uses and abuses of assessment.* Routledge.

Stofflett, R. T., & Stoddart, T. (1994). The ability to understand and use conceptual change pedagogy as a function of prior content learning experience. *Journal of Research in Science Teaching, 31*(1), 31–51.

Stuart, C., & Thurlow, D. (2000). Making it their own: Preservice teachers' experiences, beliefs, and classroom practices. *Journal of Teacher Education, 51*(2), 113–121.

van Velzen, C., Volman, M., Brekelmans, M., & White, S. (2012). Guided work-based learning: Sharing practical teaching knowledge with student teachers. *Teaching and Teacher Education, 28*(2), 229–239.

Volante, L., & Fazio, X. (2007). Exploring teacher candidates' assessment literacy: Implications for teacher education reform and professional development. *Canadian Journal of Education, 30*, 749–770.

Weinstein, C. S. (1990). Prospective elementary teachers' beliefs about teaching: Implications for teacher education. *Teaching and Teacher Education, 6*(3), 279–290.

Williams, L., & Sembiante, S. F. (2022). Experiential learning in US undergraduate teacher preparation programs: A review of the literature. *Teaching and Teacher Education, 112.* https://doi.org/10.1016/j.tate.2022.103630 (online).

Winch, C., Oancea, A., & Orchard, J. (2015). The contribution of educational research to teachers' professional learning—Philosophical understandings. *Oxford Review of Education, 41*, 202–216.

Xu, Y., & Brown, G. T. L. (2016). Teacher assessment literacy in practice: A reconceptualization. *Teaching and Teacher Education, 58*, 149–162.

Chapter 8
Learning to Assess

with Andrew Gibson

Abstract In the final chapter of this book, the *Thinking the Unthinkable Assessment Capacity Framework* is revisited and expanded with consideration for how it directs teacher learning and teacher education. The framework invites teachers to question: *What am I thinking, feeling, and doing in assessment now? How did I get here? And what else is possible?* Leveraging the framework across preservice and in-service teacher learning spaces encourages teachers to be active agents in the (re)construction and transformation of the social order that assessment reifies in schools and society, advancing new possibilities for assessment in classrooms. In this chapter, the framework is first presented, followed by a description of the interconnections between the foundational capacities—epistemic, embodied, ethical, and experiential. The chapter concludes with five essential ideas for making use of the framework within teacher education programmes, by individuals or groups of teachers and teacher educators, to envision new assessment futures that support the learning of *all* students in our schools.

Keywords Classroom assessment · Assessment capacity · Epistemic · Embodied knowing · Ethical practice · Experiential learning · Teacher education · Preservice teachers · Teachers · Teacher development

Too often, assessment is (dis)regarded as a simple act in classrooms—the generation and scoring of a test, the giving of feedback, and the writing of report cards. In reality, assessment is perhaps one of the most complex classroom activities, wrapped up in all manners of social, historical, relational, pedagogical, emotional, motivational, and cognitive dimensions. Moreover, students' and teachers' often negative past experiences with classroom assessment make it something feared not favoured, and a topic in teacher education that most would prefer to avoid.

Such a response is unsurprising. Preservice teachers are confronted—through theory, policy, assessments 'done' to them, and assessments they conduct during practical—with a multitude of assessment discourses in their short time in teacher education. These discourses, in many cases, are misaligned in purpose, epistemology, and practice. Learning to assess also involves untangling previous memories of assessment, challenging firmly held assumptions and testing new assumptions and

© The Author(s), under exclusive license to Springer Nature Singapore Pte Ltd. 2023
C. DeLuca et al., *Learning to Assess*, Teacher Education, Learning Innovation and Accountability, https://doi.org/10.1007/978-981-99-6199-3_8

practices—a process which, for many, is uncomfortable and difficult. As recognised by Elbra-Ramsay (2023, p. 2), "when it comes to assessment, student teachers on an ITE [initial teacher education] programme may face something of an identity crisis." It involves walking a path that is both reflective and progressive that climbs vertical knowledge systems while simultaneously exploring horizontal ones (Bernstein, 2000). All this is part of a larger identity-forming arc; one that sees the progression from student to teacher (Lee & Schallert, 2016).

Learning to assess over the past five years—amid a global pandemic—has been particularly challenging as assessment practices in schools have changed faster than a balloon hitting a pin. All at once, new technologies and new assessment priorities were ushered into schools in an effort to support students and teachers as they worked to keep pace with changing regulations, while working to ensure student wellbeing and learning at a time when few certainties were assured. It was, in many contexts, a time of 'emergency teaching' and 'emergency assessment' (Cooper et al., 2022). In addition to the proliferation of technologies to support assessment in classrooms, this period brought forward critical questions on the sustainability of previous assessment practices and policies (IEAN, 2021). Specifically, over the past five years, the pandemic and other social events have intensified essential questions facing assessment in schools, including questioning (a) the adequacy of assessment processes to effectively support the learning and wellbeing of socio-culturally, neurologically, and economically diverse students; and (b) the equity and colonial roots of many assessment practices and priorities, which can limit the demonstration of learning, students' ways of knowing, and the fostering of collaborative learning communities.

Perhaps more than ever, we see teachers as critically important in responding to these and other assessment questions. Teachers are the primary agents of change in education systems in influencing student learning. When equipped with the capacity to think differently about assessment practices, problems, and innovations, they can transform how assessment functions in schools to support *all* students' learning and wellbeing. This book has been an exploration into the foundational capacities teachers need in order to think differently, dare we say radically, about their assessment practices; to challenge assessment that *is*, and transform it into assessment that *will be*, by envisioning assessment from more inclusive grounds.

Born out of challenge presented to us, the lead authors of this book, at an assessment summit in 2016, where we were asked to identify a pressing area of research for the field of assessment, we envisioned a cross-cultural exploration into initial teacher education and an excavation of the foundational principles to support teacher agency and innovation in assessment. This book, including our resulting framework, is the outcome of that investigation. Through a cross-national study involving teacher candidates and teacher education programmes in Australia, Canada, England, and New Zealand, we followed 374 teacher candidates as they learned to assess throughout their preservice programmes, including on-campus and school-based practicum experiences. We used a digital reflection application to invite candidates to share their learning with us (http://goingok.org; Willis et al., 2017). Through analysis of 1630 reflections, we developed key thinking about assessment learning. We employed an abductive reasoning approach, drawing concurrently on data and literature to collectively make meaning of the phenomenon—learning to assess. Abductive reasoning is a systematic process for constructing theories built on new perspectives by exploring empirical findings in light of existing literature (Timmermans & Tavory, 2012). Our process involved repeated conversations, following hunches, analysing data in multiple ways, and going back and forth between literature, contexts, and data to support arguments. The result of this process was the development of our *Assessment Capacity Framework* for supporting teacher learning in assessment. This framework can be used by teacher candidates, teachers, and teacher educators to reflect on their thinking and practices of assessment, as well as their assessment learning experiences, in the hopes of provoking new assessment horizons.

8.1 Thinking the Unthinkable: The Assessment Capacity Framework

> The fundamental aim of our Assessment Capacity Framework—and indeed this book—is to advocate for, promote, and advance a theory for cultivating teacher assessment capacity across time and contexts, one that encourages teachers to challenge and change existing assessment practices to work in service of all students' learning.

In Chapter 1, we drew on Basil Bernstein's (2000, 2003) ideas that there is both *thinkable* and *unthinkable* knowledge in education and that assessment, curriculum, and pedagogy communicate what is thinkable within classrooms, schools, and societies. Our project seeks to challenge what is currently thinkable in school assessment to push beyond its historical colonial architecture, which reproduces and perpetuates an inequitable social order across Western education systems. To *think the unthinkable* requires fostering teacher agency and capacity to think differently about assessment, a process which begins in teacher education programmes. It is through the exploration of past, current, and everyday classroom practices that a new consciousness of assessment can be established in schools; one where learners and their differences are prioritised within learning communities. The Assessment Capacity Framework presented throughout this book (see Fig. 8.1) provides a guide to help teachers reflect on their assessment practices, supporting and provoking new ways to thinking and doing assessment in schools. This framework is also for teacher educators as a heuristic to guide instruction within and across preservice teaching and learning experiences.

At the centre of our framework is *assessment capacity*. Drawn from Doll's (2005, p. 21) poetic notion of capacity, we view assessment capacity as involving "wideness, not narrowness; openness; space for possibilities not yet even imagined, or if imagined, done so with a tremble." Assessment capacity runs on a different path than previous assessment discourses that focus on literacy, competency, capability, and

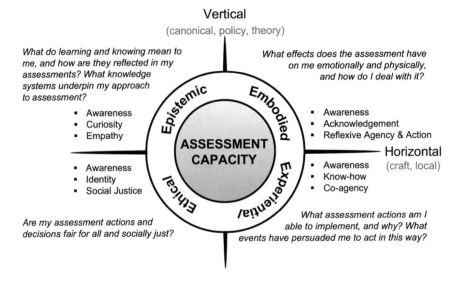

Fig. 8.1 Assessment capacity framework

identity, all of which fundamentally seek to define the scope of teachers' assessment work, roles, and responsibilities (Brookhart, 2011; Herppich et al., 2018; Looney et al., 2018; Pastore & Andrade, 2019; Popham, 2004; Wyatt-Smith et al., 2010; Xu & Brown, 2016). Instead, assessment capacity is about teacher learning, reframing teachers' assessment work and practice as a project always in the making—a space for continual professional reflection and growth.

This move towards professional learning is essential, in our view, for two reasons. First, assessment theory, jurisdictional practices, and assessment policy directives change, and teachers need to keep pace with an evolving assessment landscape. Positioning teachers' assessment work from a professional learning mindset right from their teacher education programmes (i.e., understanding that assessment is a space for continuous learning and development, an open-ended process and practice of teacher work) encourages critique of existing assessment practices, critical interrogation of new assessment agendas and reforms, and a spirit of assessment innovation, adaptation, and creativity. Teachers are more likely to be responsive to and critically reflect on the congruence and appropriateness of new practices to support their students' learning when they engage in ongoing professional learning around assessment.

Second, engaging an open-ended learning orientation towards assessment contributes towards the growth of teachers' professional identities, which are never static or fixed. Identity is understood here as socially and contextually referenced, constantly in flux, comprised of multiple sub-identities, and shaped by professional learning and development throughout a teacher's career (Akkerman & Meijer, 2011). Research shows that when teachers focus on their professional identity; they have greater capacity for decision-making and a stronger understanding of their role, of professional expectations, and of educational reforms, as well as a greater sense of fulfilment and confidence (Alsup, 2006, 2019; Canrinus et al., 2012; Hong et al., 2017; Kelchtermans, 2005). Teachers are also more efficacious in their classroom practices when they prioritise professional identity development over solely pedagogical skill acquisition (Moslemi & Habibi, 2019). Stenberg et al. (2014) note that for preservice teachers, their developing teacher identities shape what practices they choose to learn and retain from their teacher education coursework and practicum experiences. This, in turn, shapes how they view and approach their future classroom practice. By emphasising and focussing on professional learning, assessment capacity is always and inextricably linked to teachers' professional identity, serving to continuously enhance and deepen teachers' classroom practice.

Assessment capacity is defined as a teacher's capacity to continually learn about their assessment practice—through relationships, reflection, reflexivity, collaboration, inquiry, and inventiveness—to imagine and explore new possibilities for assessment in schools.

Our Assessment Capacity Framework articulates four core capacities that we propose can be employed to provoke new possibilities for assessment in teachers' classrooms. Drawing on Bernstein (2000, 2003), these four capacities are situated upon two knowledge axes: vertical assessment knowledge system and horizontal assessment knowledge system. The vertical knowledge system reflects strongly classified knowledge that shapes teachers' assessment work and involves canonical, codified, theoretical, and policy-based knowledge systems associated with what it means to assess and to be an assessor. In contrast, horizontal knowledge involves assessment work in context, craft knowledge, connoisseurship, and know-how cultivated through experience within schools, classrooms, and teacher professional communities. As teachers learn to assess, they are always referencing, balancing, and negotiating knowledge across these axes, even as these knowledge systems conflict, contradict, and counteract one another. Reflecting on how knowledge is culturally valued and expressed, where assessment practices are weakly or strongly classified and by whom, supports critical questioning of the historical ordering of assessment thinking and practices in schools. Through such a process, teachers gain greater awareness of the assessment landscape they are teaching within and can then better navigate their practice, advocacy, and innovations.

Imposed on the two knowledge axes are four capacities: *epistemic capacity, embodied capacity, ethical capacity,* and *experiential capacity.* Each of these capacities enables contextualised reflection and decision-making about assessment thinking and practice through reflection on the past, analysis of the present, and imagining of the yet-to-come. Each capacity is guided by a central reflective question and supported by foundational themes. The first theme for each capacity is 'awareness,' as it was evident in our data that activating an awareness of each capacity (in relation to moments of reflection and reflexivity about experiences of assessment learning and practice) was essential to leveraging the potential of the framework. While each capacity is unique in its contribution to teacher learning, the four capacities are highly connected and interdependent. The four capacities are as follows.

Epistemic capacity: The epistemic capacity connects theories of knowing and learning to assessment actions and decisions, asking teacher candidates to explore and interrogate the underpinning assumptions of their assessment approaches. While there is a tendency to reduce the epistemic to the theories that undergird assessments, what we seek to invoke here are the larger knowledge systems and ways of knowing that diverse students and teachers bring to learning and teaching. *Epistemic* specifically denotes how learners enact, encounter, and elaborate their knowing in diverse contexts (Brownlee et al., 2016; Siegel, 2006). Understanding an educator's epistemic orientation is central to understanding the act of assessment in classrooms. Accordingly, guiding this capacity are the reflective questions: *What do learning and knowing mean to me, and how are they reflected in my assessments? What knowledge systems underpin my approach to assessment?* While there is an acknowledgement that teachers have diverse epistemologies yielding various orientations and practices towards assessment and that teachers' epistemic assessment capacity depends on their personal epistemologies (i.e., personal epistemic beliefs) as well as the professional epistemologies they develop through their teacher education experiences, epistemic capacity can be cultivated and developed over time and experience. Teachers' epistemic assessment capacity is shaped by their context of learning and teaching, including preservice teacher education coursework, practical, and critical reflections. Central to this capacity is the cultivation of *epistemic awareness, curiosity,* and *empathy*—all attributes that attune educators to making sense of learning and knowing in new, different, and more responsive ways.

Embodied capacity: The embodied capacity attends to the physical, emotional, and social-material experiences of assessment as felt within teachers' bodies as they learn about assessment, teach, and lead their students in assessment. The embodied assessment capacity not only acknowledges that emotions are part of assessment processes but also suggests that educators use their whole body and environment to think and learn (Gibson & Lang, 2019). It is through embodied experiences with assessment—and by attending to them—that teachers learn about assessment. Yet, acknowledging that assessment is an embodied act, with emotional and physical components both planned and consequential, is often overlooked in literature and practice despite being a primary motivator for assessment practice (i.e., either encouraging repeated practice or avoiding practice). This capacity calls teacher educators and preservice teachers to attend to the embodied dimensions of assessment, drawing explicit awareness to them and learning to navigate them to promote sustainable, healthy, and manageable assessment experiences. The driving reflective question to attend to the embodied capacity is: *What effects does the assessment have on me emotionally and physically, and how do I deal with it?*

Embodied responses to assessment, and educators' embodied assessment capacity, evolve over time as they engage bodies and minds in assessment decision-making in situations that are continually changing (Charteris & Dargusch, 2018). Building awareness in preservice education programmes that assessment is an 'emotional rollercoaster' is the first key learning in this capacity. Recognising that teachers have agency through reflexive practice and can take proactive actions to manage the embodiment of assessment is the second key learning.

Ethical capacity: Ethics is regarded as a professional standard across jurisdictions, with teachers required to 'do no harm' and accommodate the diverse learning needs of students to enable equitable learning and assessment opportunities for all students. However, the ethical assessment capacity goes further. It asks teachers to consider the difference that difference makes to teaching and assessment practice that would be of benefit to students and their learning. The ethical capacity is wide-reaching, implicating how teachers plan, make decisions about, and create opportunities for and interpret student agency within and through assessment processes. It involves considering and leveraging the socio-cultural diverse backgrounds (as broadly defined) and experiences of students within assessment processes, the fair distribution of resources for learning and assessment, procedural fairness, equity in assessment, and explicit consideration for the consequences of assessment actions on diverse students and the learning collective. Teachers face dilemmas across these ethical spaces, requiring ethical awareness, reflexivity, and empathy. At its core, ethical assessment capacity necessitates not only understanding but also negotiating and rationalising assessment decisions in light of the socio-cultural contexts in which assessment takes place—the diversity of students and teachers, the historical and current oppressions associated with different curriculum and assessment practices, and imperatives to leverage education and assessment for more socially just ends. Guiding teachers' ethical capacity development is the following reflection question: *Are my assessment actions and decisions fair for all and socially just?*

The ethical capacity is about continuously expanding educator awareness on the linkage between assessment and social justice, recognising that assessments shape identity (Stobart, 2008) and therefore are powerfully influential forces in the lives and outcomes of students in both the short and long term. Wrapped within such power structures, the ethically-minded teacher considers how assessment functions in their classroom to affirm and enable the identity, knowing, and agency of students. They are also aware of the impact of assessment on their own identity as a teacher and, consequently, their own sense of wellbeing and agency.

Experiential capacity: The experiential capacity is purposefully presented last, as it is the culmination of the previous three capacities in action. Experiential capacity involves constructing knowledge about assessment through first-hand experiences across contexts of practice. This capacity is premised on the fact that learning is a "process whereby knowledge is created through the transformation of experience. Knowledge results from the combination of grasping and transforming experience" (Kolb, 1984, p. 41). The experiential capacity develops over time through continuous encounters with assessment events, requiring teachers to reflect on their practice, their outcomes, and the alignment between practice and intention. Fundamentally, preservice teachers develop this capacity by reflecting on the questions: *What assessment actions am I able to implement, and why? What events have persuaded me to act in this way?*

The experiential capacity recognises that learning from experience occurs from past events (as memory events), as current events (as learning and reflections in situ), and as future events (as planned activities) related to being assessed and to assessing others and that these experiences occur across preservice coursework and practicum spaces. Across these experiences, cultivating this capacity involves acknowledging the important role experience plays in shaping assessment beliefs, approaches, and practice and how all assessment experiences and assessment learning experiences shape teacher know-how. Like the ethical capacity, however, the experiential capacity—and an educator's ability to enact their assessment intentions—is always imbued within power relations, limiting and enabling an educator's agency for practice.

Engaging the critical questions related to each of the four capacities and honouring the foundational dimensions of each capacity opens up opportunities for teachers to engage in deep reflection about their assessment understandings and practices, provoking them to challenge and change the status quo in their classrooms. Holistically, the framework invites teachers to question: *What am I thinking, feeling, and doing in assessment now? How did I get here? And what else is possible?* Engaging the framework encourages teachers to be active agents in the (re)construction and transformation of the social order that assessment reifies in schools and society (Bernstein, 2000, p. xxi).

8.1.1 Interconnections

Each of the four assessment capacities—epistemic, embodied, ethical, and experiential—was readily recognised in our preservice teachers' reflections as core areas for their overall professional assessment capacity development. Also, one of the most concrete findings from our study was the linkage between the capacities—the ways in which assessment scenarios could not be easily parsed into one capacity or another, but rather how assessment contexts held dynamic and generative potential for learning across the four capacities. The four capacities are interconnected and interdependent, as evident in the qualitative analysis in earlier chapters. For example, strong emotions might highlight dilemmas pertaining to ethical decision-making or an experiential problem of practice that needs more development. This interconnection was also evident in the computational analysis represented in Figs. 8.2, 8.3, 8.4, 8.5, and 8.6.

8.1 Thinking the Unthinkable: The Assessment Capacity Framework 157

Fig. 8.2 Interconnection between capacities

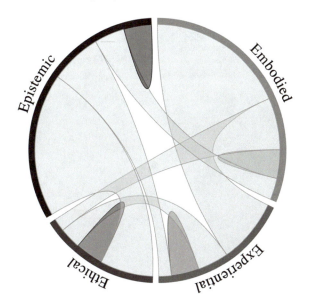

Fig. 8.3 Connections between epistemic capacity and three other capacities

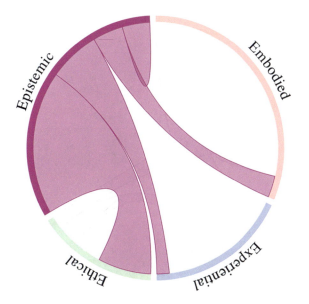

The circle figures (Figs. 8.2–8.6) represent a computational analysis of all the reflections collected in this study. Individual reflections were analysed for their relationship to each capacity. This analysis was based on the occurrence of reflexive expressions associated with each capacity as selected by the research team. The full range of reflective expressions and their derivation process is available from Gibson et al. (2023). Consultation occurred within and across the team about which reflexive

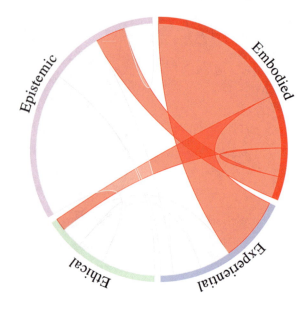

Fig. 8.4 Connections between embodied capacity and three other capacities

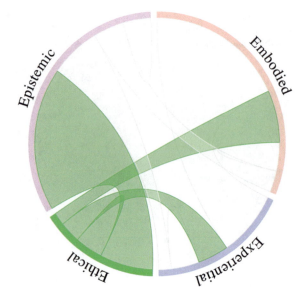

Fig. 8.5 Connections between ethical capacity and three other capacities

expressions were most likely to represent each capacity. For example, the embodied capacity was associated with reflective expressions to do with feelings, reactions, and emotional responses like "i_feel_a_sense_of" or "happy_with_what." The epistemic capacity was associated with reflective expressions to do with knowing, thinking, believing, ideas, and thoughts like "I_was_thinking_about" or "it_seems_to_me_ that." The computational analysis then enabled a purposeful selection from the large

8.1 Thinking the Unthinkable: The Assessment Capacity Framework

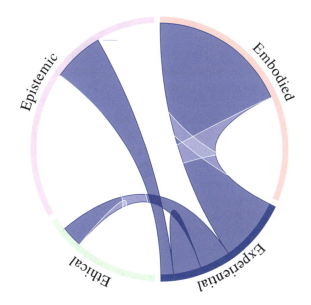

Fig. 8.6 Connections between experiential capacity and three other capacities

volume of reflections that were likely to be highly associated with each capacity. From this selection, the researchers were able to engage in an in-depth qualitative analysis and thinking with the data about the aspects of each capacity.

Figure 8.2 presents the complexity of overlap between the four capacities, with Figs. 8.3–8.6 isolating the proportion and interconnection of each capacity. The chords are not directional but represent proportions of the total number of reflections: the wider the chord, the more reflections associated with its tag. For example, the largest connection in the embodied capacity is with the experiential capacity indicating that almost half of the embodied tagged reflections co-occurred with an experiential tag. The darkly shaded bumps within each capacity in Fig. 8.2 represent reflections that were only associated with that capacity. As evident from these figures, based on our data, not only is there shared terrain, but there is evidence that some capacities were more closely connected, at least in how easily those capabilities were computationally identified within the reflections. For example, epistemic and ethical capacities share strong affinity, as do embodied and experiential capacities.

The computational analysis helped to identify that the capacities were evident across a large group of reflections from preservice teachers in different contexts and highlighted some of the different connections. It was a distinctive and rigorous socio-technical process. It is also innovative. In educational research, reflections and self-report are often used to study teacher learning. The digital reflective tool GoingOK (http://goingok.org/) allowed for a large volume of preservice teacher reflective entries over time and across four country contexts to be collected easily for analysis. Computational representations are a novel way to represent concepts; however, this computational visualisation does not represent the fullness of each reflection, and more relationships may be found. Importantly, the socio-technical approach enabled the combination of qualitative and computational perspectives to inform one another.

It is unsurprising that the capacities overlap as teachers wrestle to make sense of and learn from their assessment encounters. Preservice teachers' reflections often addressed multiple capacities within assessment learning experiences. As McArthur et al. (2022) identify, for example, when teachers pursue more socially relevant and just perspectives in their assessment practices, this can lead to greater outcomes for students and more joyful embodied experiences of assessment for students and teachers. Likewise, when preservice teachers are challenged with the implementation of formative assessment practice and its productive uptake by students due to the presence and prominence of summative assessments (or district assessments), it presses them to (re)consider the epistemological underpinnings guiding assessment policies and practices, systemically and locally. As preservice teachers focus on developing their assessment capacity, we see evidence in both focusing on individual capacities but also on their interconnections. Interconnections and incongruences across capacity experiences provide opportunities to construct deeper understandings about assessment. Naming and acknowledging each capacity is powerful in honouring the complexity of teacher learning in assessment, as well as supporting, in a more specific and targeted way, teacher development.

8.2 Developing Assessment Capacity: Direction for Teacher Education

Our framework offers guidance for teacher educators, both in how to engage preservice teachers in learning about assessment but also potentially how to prioritise, sequence, and plan for effective assessment learning in teacher education programmes. Here, we itemise and articulate some directions to support a reframing of assessment education, which has historically been marginal in teacher education programmes (Coombs et al., 2021; Greenberg & Walsh, 2012). Increasingly, teacher education programmes are acknowledging the importance of learning about assessment and are adding discrete and focal courses in this area within their programmes (DeLuca et al., 2019; Gareis et al., 2020). As demonstrated in Chapter 2, there are differences in the ways assessment is understood, addressed, and valued in national contexts, as well as across teacher education components, including practicum experiences (Charteris & Dargusch, 2018; Richmond et al., 2019). In some instances, assessment is undervalued and underexplored, leaving teacher candidates feeling ill-prepared for practice, while in other cases, teacher candidates receive highly oppositional views towards assessment and the role of assessment in teaching, learning, and schooling (DeLuca et al., 2019). We argue that teacher education programmes can draw on the four capacities to build a concerted and common understanding of assessment across programme components. Our framework can help provide clarity

8.2 Developing Assessment Capacity: Direction for Teacher Education 161

to teacher educators and preservice teachers as they work to identify assessment priorities, values, and practices as a focus for productive and generative learning.

We acknowledge the important role of teacher educators as agentic assessment curriculum makers, and we invite teacher educators to test out and use the framework. The various chapters in this book explicate each capacity and conclude with suggestions for ways to cultivate assessment capacity within initial teacher education programmes. There are questions at the end of each chapter to help teacher educators and preservice teachers reflect on their assessment practices. In addition, we offer the following five ideas for making use of the *Assessment Capacity Framework* within teacher education programmes and by individual or groups of teacher educators.

1. **Change assessment learning discourses**. Teacher educator awareness of the framing of assessment learning is one way to bring the ideas in this book to fruition in teacher education programmes. Framing assessment knowledge as a 'fait au complet,' as a set of practices to be mastered and perfected, rooted solely in strongly classified vertical knowledge, diminishes an orientation towards continuous assessment learning and teacher agency in assessment processes. Drawing on the spirit of assessment capacity means inspiring preservice teachers to be agentic in their assessment decisions by encouraging them to use the framework to think constructively, productively, and progressively about assessment. When students move beyond solely experiencing strongly classified knowledge and beyond the strict practices of assessment to engage the complexities of assessment and the multiple capacities associated with assessment learning, they gain access to the mystery of developing new assessment knowledge, explore the contestability of disciplinary knowledge, and make visible diverse cultural and community knowledges (Bernstein, 2000; Kerr, 2014; Kerr & Averill, 2023). Framing assessment learning as part of a career-long professional learning commitment that engages epistemic, embodied, ethical, and experiential ways of learning and knowing is an alternative discourse to many current assessment and accountability discourses that characterise teachers' assessment work.

2. **Use the capacities explicitly to cultivate a shared language for assessment learning**. Most teacher educators have encountered situations where preservice teachers lament about receiving mixed messages related to assessment (and other topics) within and across their programme. Essential to supporting preservice teachers is providing them with a framework to negotiate and make sense of their varied learning experiences across programme components (i.e., courses and practicum). Explicitly leveraging the *Assessment Capacity Framework* to support preservice teachers throughout their programme can be a useful heuristic to organise experiences, provoke reflections and deep learning, plan assessments, and set goals for continuous professional growth. Talking directly with preservice teachers about the four capacities—what they mean, how to use them, and when and why they might surface in practice—will optimise preservice teachers' learning in assessment throughout their programme and beyond. Doing so also holds the potential for validating and authenticating their learning experiences as

the framework was generated from the lived learning experiences of preservice teachers.

3. **Plan for learning with the capacities and make the capacities visible**. The four capacities are drawn from practice that will be part of everyday work. Making them visible, whether in assessment-specific or other preservice courses, using the capacities' guiding questions and foundational themes to plan pedagogical experiences, reflection activities, and assignments for preservice teachers can help build a coherent and consistent approach to assessment learning. Specifically, consistently using the guiding questions affiliated with each capacity can help develop a reflexive habit that works to expand assessment capacity over time. This practice can be achieved through self-assessment tasks and assignments, collaborative discussions, or peer and/or mentor debriefs. As teacher educators, using the questions to model reflection helps demonstrate the value of the framework to guide learning towards deeper ends. Figure 8.7 provides the guiding question plus sub-questions for each capacity to support preservice teaching and reflection activities.

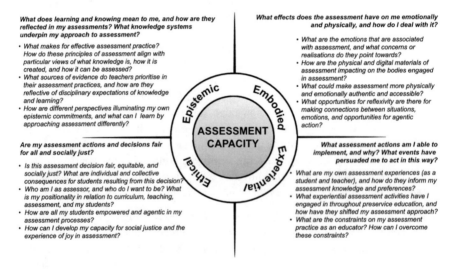

Fig. 8.7 Reflective questions to guide teacher education for each assessment capacity

Digging into the themes associated with each capacity can also be valuable to interrogating the capacities in relation to case studies, practicum experiences, or planned assessment activities. Inviting preservice teachers to articulate past, present, and future stances towards each capacity—setting in motion learning goals and intentions—may also leverage the framework to support a continuous learning orientation towards assessment. Important to planning teaching and learning with the four capacities in mind is 'walking the talk' by engaging in co-learning about assessment alongside preservice teachers.

4. **Use the framework across programme courses and components**. While the framework articulated in this book has been designed specifically for assessment learning, underpinning it are four broad capacities for teacher professional learning. In addition to informing assessment courses and assessment learning across preservice programmes, the four capacities can apply more generally across a teacher education programme. Leveraging a consistent heuristic across programme components and areas for professional development (e.g., inclusive pedagogy, curriculum, and technology integration) can be effective in promoting a signature framework for preservice teacher reflection and learning. Inviting preservice teachers to critically reflect on the *epistemic, embodied, ethical*, and *experiential* components of their learning across professional development areas can bring into focus core values and align those values with practices. Such a framework can be used to guide the development of programme-wide learning objectives, assessment guides and rubrics, and anchor assignments.

5. **Empower teachers to *think the unthinkable***. Teacher candidates can often feel like they have limited agency to make changes within classrooms, schools, and systems, given the power structures and relationships within teacher education programmes and schools. At the heart of this framework is recognising the immense power teachers have to critique and transform the learning experiences of students in their classrooms through the assessment practices they put in motion, knowing that some changes, even quite small ones, can create significant impact. The *Assessment Capacity Framework* can be a resource to grant permission, encourage, and empower preservice teachers to think differently, to challenge convention, and to test the waters of the radical. Teacher educators, including host teachers, have a pivotal role to play here. They can prepare newly qualified teachers to engage with emerging trends early in their careers, even if only by articulating how, as teachers, they are always learning and can be actively part of reframing assessment within their own classrooms, let alone the profession.

> Empowering preservice teachers to *think the unthinkable* is a driving force behind the framework and the impetus for transformative assessment education.

8.3 Assessment That *Will Be*

Our interest throughout this project has been to support teacher learning in assessment, to provoke new possibilities for classroom assessment that challenge and change 'assessment that *is*' and to point towards 'assessment that *will be*.' Our framework lays the groundwork for *thinking the unthinkable* in assessment, a radical reimaging, for in order "to move forward in our assessment systems, we must give teachers both the opportunity to experiment with assessment and equip them with a set of capacities to *think radically* about assessment in schools" (DeLuca, 2021, p. 170). Our framework was born out of one study and a dialogue across scholars and literature. The study was situated across four contexts of practice, four national arenas, and four teacher education programmes. It is a contribution towards efforts to support teachers in understanding and changing assessment practice in schools, which is part of a much larger educational vision. Hence, we look to others—teacher educators, researchers, school and system administrators, and educators—to play with these ideas, to challenge them, and to extend them. Specifically, we see value in pursuing the ideas presented in this book across contexts of classroom practice and teacher education sites, as well as through extension into in-service teacher education contexts.

Our primary goal in writing this book was to inspire teachers' assessment work as a space for their continuous imagining and action. This goal is premised on the fact that teachers are in the best position to change how assessment is experienced and felt in classrooms (Stobart, 2008). This goal is also supported by ample research that shows systemic change is most effectively achieved and sustained through teacher-led reforms and innovations—through grassroots and classroom-based initiatives and through the sharing of initiatives among teacher learning communities (Hargreaves, 2004; McNamara & O'Hara, 2004; Tschannen-Moran, 2009). Teachers are key agents for assessment change. We hope that by empowering teachers to critically understand the landscape that has historically (and currently) shaped assessment in schools and by inspiring teachers to *think the unthinkable* in assessment; they will cultivate new inclusive, authentic, and authenticating possibilities for classroom assessment that truly support the learning of all our diverse students, now and in the future.

Andrew Gibson is a Senior Lecturer in Information Science at Queensland University of Technology (Brisbane, Australia). Andrew's research includes theoretical inquiry into the relationship between reflexive thinking and learning, as well as applied socio-technical investigations into how people express reflexive thinking.

References

Akkerman, S. F., & Meijer, P. C. (2011). A dialogical approach to conceptualizing teacher identity. *Teaching and Teacher Education, 27*(2), 308–319.

Alsup, J. (2006). *Teacher identity discourses: Negotiating personal and professional spaces.* Routledge.

Alsup, J. (2019). *Millennial teacher identity discourses: Balancing self and other.* Routledge.

Bernstein, B. (2000). *Pedagogy, symbolic control, and identity: Theory, research, critique* (Vol. 5). Rowman & Littlefield.

References

165

Bernstein, B. (2003). *Class, codes and control: Applied studies towards a sociology of language* (Vol. 2). Psychology Press.

Brookhart, S. M. (2011). Educational assessment knowledge and skills for teachers. *Educational Measurement: Issues and Practice, 30*, 3–12.

Brownlee, J. L., Schraw, G., Walker, S., & Ryan, M. (2016). Changes in preservice teachers' personal epistemologies. In J. A. Greene, W. A. Sandoval, & I. Bråten (Eds.), *Handbook of epistemic cognition* (pp. 300–317). Routledge.

Canrinus, E. T., Helms-Lorenz, M., Beijaard, D., Buitink, J., & Hofman, A. (2012). Self-efficacy, job satisfaction, motivation and commitment: Exploring the relationships between indicators of teachers' professional identity. *European Journal of Psychology of Education, 27*(1), 115–132.

Charteris, J., & Dargusch, J. (2018). The tensions of preparing pre-service teachers to be assessment capable and profession-ready. *Asia-Pacific Journal of Teacher Education, 46*(4), 354–368.

Coombs, A. J., Ge, J., & DeLuca, C. (2021). From sea to sea: The Canadian landscape of assessment education. *Educational Research, 63*(1), 9–25.

Cooper, A., DeLuca, C., Holden, M., & MacGregor, S. (2022). Emergency assessment: Rethinking classroom practices and priorities amid remote teaching. *Assessment in Education: Principles, Policy & Practice, 29*, 534–554.

DeLuca C. (2021). Provocation 1: Towards more radical assessment systems. In C. Wyatt-Smith, L. Adie, & J. Nuttall (Eds.), *Teaching performance assessments as a cultural disruptor in initial teacher education. Teacher Education, learning innovation and accountability* (pp. 167–170). Springer.

DeLuca, C., Willis, J., Cowie, B., Harrison, C., Coombs, A., Gibson, A., & Trask, S. (2019). Policies, programs, and practices: Exploring the complex dynamics of assessment education in teacher education across four countries. *Frontiers in Education, 4.* https://doi.org/10.3389/feduc.2019.00132 (online).

Doll, M. A. (2005). Capacity and currere. Journal of Curriculum Theorizing, 21(3), 21–28.

Elbra-Ramsay, C. (2023). Assessment in HE initial teacher education: Competing contexts discourses and the unobtainable pursuit for fidelity. In I. Menter (Ed.), *The Palgrave handbook of teacher education research* (1st ed., pp. 341–365). Palgrave Macmillan.

Gareis, C., Barnes, N., Coombs, A. J., DeLuca, C., & Uchiyama, K. (2020). Exploring the influence of assessment courses and student teaching on beginning teachers' approaches to classroom assessment. *Assessment Matters, 14*, 5–41.

Gibson, A., DeVine, L., Canizares, M., & Willis, J. (2023). Reflexive expressions: Towards the analysis of reflexive capability from reflective text. In *The 24th International Conference on Artificial Intelligence in Education (AIED 2023).* Springer Verlag.

Gibson, A., & Lang, C. (2019). Quality indicators through learning analytics. In M. A. Peters (Ed.), *Encyclopedia of teacher education* (pp. 1–6). Springer.

Greenberg, J., & Walsh, K. (2012). *What teacher preparation programs teach about K-12 assessment: A review.* National Council on Teacher Quality.

Hargreaves, A. (2004). Inclusive and exclusive educational change: Emotional responses of teachers and implications for leadership. *School Leadership & Management, 24*(3), 287–309.

Herppich, S., Praetorius, A. K., Förster, N., Glogger-Frey, I., Karst, K., Leutner, D., Behrmann, L., Böhmer, M., Ufer, S., Klug, J., Hetmanek, A., Ohle, A., Böhmer, I., Karing, C., Kaiser, J., & Südkamp, A. (2018). Teachers' assessment competence: Integrating knowledge-, process-, and product-oriented approaches into a competence-oriented conceptual model. *Teaching and Teacher Education, 76*, 181–193.

Hong, J. Y., Greene, B., & Lowery, J. (2017). Multiple dimensions of teacher identity development from pre-service to early years of teaching: A longitudinal study. *Journal of Education for Teaching, 43*(1), 84–98.

International Educational Assessment Network (IEAN) [DeLuca, C., Donaldson, G., Hayward, L., Tan, K., & Wyatt-Smith, C.]. (2021). *Imperatives for a better assessment future during and post Covid.* International Educational Assessment Network.

Kelchtermans, G. (2005). Teachers' emotions in educational reforms: Self-understanding, vulnerable commitment and micropolitical literacy. *Teaching and Teacher Education, 21*(8), 995–1006.

Kerr, B., & Averill, R. (2023). Arotakehia te rerenga—Assessment as a powerful instrument of navigation: Knowing how well we are doing. In P. Te Maro & R. Averill (Eds.), *Ki te hoe! Education for Aotearoa.* NZCER Press

Kerr, J. (2014). Western epistemic dominance and colonial structures: Considerations for thought and practice in programs of teacher education. *Decolonization: Indigeneity, Education & Society, 3*(2), 83–104.

Kolb, D. A. (1984). *Experiential learning: Experience as the source of learning and development.* Prentice Hall.

Lee, S., & Schallert, D. L. (2016). Becoming a teacher: Coordinating past, present, and future selves with perspectival understandings about teaching. *Teaching and Teacher Education, 56,* 72–83.

Looney, A., Cumming, J., van Der Kleij, F., & Harris, K. (2018). Reconceptualising the role of teachers as assessors: Teacher assessment identity. *Assessment in Education: Principles, Policy & Practice, 25*(5), 442–467.

McArthur, J., Blackie, M., Pitterson, N., & Rosewell, K. (2022). Student perspectives on assessment: Connections between self and society. *Assessment & Evaluation in Higher Education, 47*(5), 1–14.

McNamara, G., & O'Hara, J. (2004). Trusting the teacher: Evaluating educational innovation. *Evaluation, 10*(4), 463–474.

Moslemi, N., & Habibi, P. (2019). The relationship among Iranian EFL teachers' professional identity, self-efficacy and critical thinking skills. *How, 26*(1), 107–128.

Pastore, S., & Andrade, H. L. (2019). Teacher assessment literacy: A three-dimensional model. *Teaching and Teacher Education, 84,* 128–138.

Popham, W. J. (2004). Why assessment illiteracy is professional suicide. *Educational Leadership, 62*(1), 82–83.

Richmond, G., Salazar, M. D. C., & Jones, N. (2019). Assessment and the future of teacher education. *Journal of Teacher Education, 70*(2), 86–89.

Siegel, H. (2006). Epistemological diversity and education research: Much ado about nothing much? *Educational Researcher, 35*(2), 3–12.

Stenberg, K., Karlsson, L., Pitkaniemi, H., & Maaranen, K. (2014). Beginning student teachers' teacher identities based on their practical theories. *European Journal of Teacher Education, 37*(2), 204–219.

Stobart, G. (2008). *Testing times: The uses and abuses of assessment.* Routledge.

Timmermans, S., & Tavory, I. (2012). Theory construction in qualitative research: From grounded theory to abductive analysis. *Sociological Theory, 30*(3), 167–186.

Tschannen-Moran, M. (2009). Fostering teacher professionalism in schools: The role of leadership orientation and trust. *Educational Administration Quarterly, 45*(2), 217–247.

Willis, J., Crosswell, L., Morrison, C., Gibson, A., & Ryan, M. (2017). Looking for leadership: The potential of dialogic reflexivity with rural early-career teachers. *Teachers and Teaching, 23*(7), 794–809.

Wyatt-Smith, C., Klenowski, V., & Gunn, S. (2010). The centrality of teachers' judgement practice in assessment: A study of standards in moderation. *Assessment in Education: Principles, Policy, & Practice, 17*(1), 59–75.

Xu, Y., & Brown, G. T. (2016). Teacher assessment literacy in practice: A reconceptualization. *Teaching and Teacher Education, 58,* 149–162.